A Woldsman's Diary

by

Stephen G Prescott

Published by Stephen & Yvonne Prescott

Published in Great Britain in 2016 by Stephen & Yvonne Prescott
Lickham Hall, Scorborough, Driffield, YO25 9BB

Copyright © 2016 Stephen G Prescott
First published December 2016

ISBN 978-0-9955743-0-4

Printed and bound in Great Britain by York Publishing Services Ltd
64 Hallfield Road, Layerthorpe, York, YO31 7QZ

Edited, proofread and typeset in Times New Roman and Calibri by Jill Pick.

Volume 1
Early 1800s to 1982

INDEX

PREFACE

My thanks must go to many people and organisations, family and friends...

Firstly I must thank Yvonne for the use of her diaries, without which I might have struggled, for her unfailing patience and tolerance, typing this story and for other secretarial tasks, and for her love and support over the last 58 years.

Thanks to all our children and grandchildren for their help and support through good times and bad, and for all the ribbing they give me, including going to school in shorts with blue knees during the 1947 winter!

Thanks to Jill Pick for her professionalism, help, guidance, patience, cheerful encouragement and most of all for her friendship. She put this story together in a way I should never have thought possible.

Thanks to the NFU for providing some of the statistics and to the many friends who have helped us in so many ways, sharing our pleasures, and sometimes our sorrows. We have shared many experiences, many through the Red Poll Cattle Society, and the international breeders, which not only gave us friends worldwide but also started us on our travels, with Yvonne and I organising our many coach trips and holidays all over the world: there are so many experiences we have shared.

Lastly, this story would not have been told had it not been for our marvellous National Health Service, and all the medical staff who have kept me alive for the last 80 years, coupled with our great Creator.

The next 35 years to follow...

Stephen G Prescott
December 2016

List of illustrations

List of illustrations cont'd

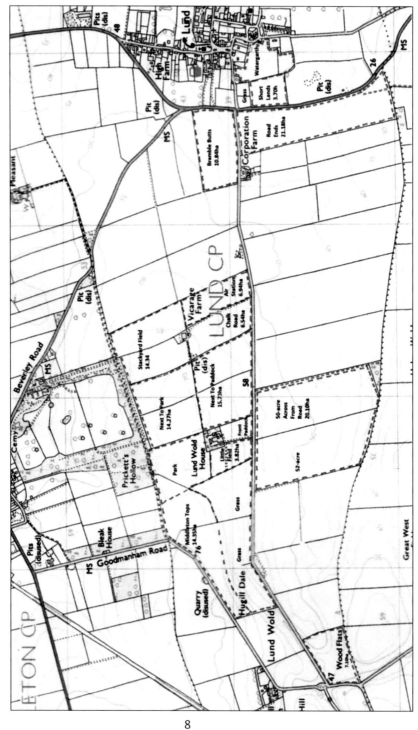

Land at Lund, below, and Scorborough, bottom, farmed by Stephen Prescott in 1982

Boundary lines indicated by a dashed red line.

© Crown copyright 2016 OS 100058214

Spr

Railway Side
24.53ha

Lickham
Hall

Scorborough Gate
House

Grass

Grass

Parkhouse Farm

Lane

Above Dykes
19.16ha

Scorborough

Scorborough Beck

Moat Field
10ha

Moat

Scorborough
Hall

Spr

Bryan
Mills

Mills Beck Spr

ge Pasture

Mills Beck

White House
Farm

rborough
Bridge

9

M y great-grandfather, Robert Prescott, born November 20 1810, and his wife, Elizabeth, left Sproatley in Holderness with four boys in the butcher's cart: a daughter, Elizabeth, had died at birth. They came to Roslyn House, the first house on the right, coming in from Lockington Road into Lund, in 1859 as a tenant of Robert Stephenson, of Hull Bridge, feed and fertilizer merchants.

He started up a butchering business at that property which, in those days, had 31 acres of land with it. He was paying a rental of £4 per acre. (One hundred years later my father, Leonard, and I were paying £1 per acre for the land rented at Wold House on the outskirts of Lund. This was because of the repeal of the Corn Laws in the 1870s. History will tell you when that was and why).

He continued his butchering business from Roslyn House and then expanded the business, building Poplar House in Eastgate, with a proper slaughterhouse and hanging facilities for carcases. They also had a butcher's shop opposite North End Farm on North Road in Lund: three butcher's shops in total in the village. They served all the surrounding area with meat from these shops. It was not

Robert Prescott, with his second wife, Anne, taken around 1880.

uncommon to deliver 12 to 16 stones (up to 100kg) of meat to any one farm per week, as men lived in on the outlying farms—at Enthorpe Farm, beyond Lund Warren, they had such a large staff they had their own football and cricket teams. Men were accommodated mainly in the foreman's house; the foreman would be allowed his meat quota in order for the foreman's wife or the farmer's wife, to feed all these hungry men.

The four brothers were Thomas Henry, born June 7 1849; Edward, born March 19 1852; William Ouston, born November 20 1853; Robert (Marjorie Andrews' father), baptised December 25 1856, and a daughter Elizabeth, buried at Sproatley on April 16 1859, aged three days. Elizabeth, the first wife of Robert, was buried in Bishop Burton graveyard on May 18 1864.

In October 1882 (a Michaelmas Day take) my grandfather, Thomas Henry, and his brother, Edward Prescott, started farming in partnership at Lickham Hall, Scorborough. Uncle Edward, who had been working in offices in Hull, had been told to get out into the country or he would not survive. He died in 1943, surviving all the other brothers. At this time Edward and his first wife were living in what is now known as Harthill Cottage in Eastgate, Lund.

Presumably at this time the house at Lickham, with some 185 acres, was being vastly expanded from a two-bedroomed, two-up, two-down type of cottage. They added on the front portion of the house—presumably this was done by the then Lord Leconfield, who owned the property at that time. It was later bought by Edward in approximately 1920.

The farm included two cottages, Rose Cottage and the Money family's cottage, Davalon. Edward and his second wife, Helen Jane Horsley, moved there. I have no idea what they were paying in rent. The partnership continued until 1912, when it was dissolved. Party to this was perhaps the

Edward Prescott at Lickham Hall.

Above: Thomas Henry and family at Wold House.

Right: Robert Prescott, youngest son of Robert.

fact that in the latter years of the partnership Uncle Eddie (William Edward) Thomas Henry's eldest son, was delegated to bring the wages down. Perhaps the family at Lickham resented this. At the same time I believe Thomas Henry was dealing in the stock market and, later on, lost quite a bit of money this way.

In 1884 Thomas Henry took the tenancy (a Lady Day take) of Wold House, Lund, then 228 acres (again rent unknown) from Lord Hotham of the Dalton Estate. The previous tenant had been a Mr Chapman, whose thesis on his family we have in a separate file. They farmed at Holme Wold, Wold House and possibly Vicarage Farm, next door to Wold House at Lund.

Thomas Henry married Jane Horsley, sister to Helen, at some time round about the beginning of the tenancy. They subsequently had five children, William Edward (Eddie), Ernest Horsley, Ethel (who always resented only having one name), Elsie (born 1900 on with the year) and Leonard, who was Stephanie's and my father, born 1901.

At this time the Prescotts owned quite a few properties in Lund: they

Coronation Cottage, Lund—now demolished.

owned the small farm on The Green, (the farmhouse was later owned by the Sutherlands, at the end of New Row) and the 30 acres of land of which adjoined Roslyn House land, down Lockington Road.

Robert senior intended building a large house next door to this— Coronation Cottage. This was built in the garden of a large thatched cottage which stood in front of the Market Cross. This is now the garden of Coronation Cottage. It was built by Eastwood's of Middleton-on-the-Wolds, but was foreshortened as Robert was incensed because every time he visited the site the men were either in the pub opposite or drunk on the scaffolding. He had a short top put on it and left it at that.

The Prescotts were strong Methodists in those days, and it is recorded in great-grandfather's 1889 diary that Ann, his wife, would now die happy, as her beloved new chapel had opened. This is the Methodist Chapel opposite Manor House. It is ironic that it was not until the Wellington Inn public house was closed in the mid-1990s, that Tim Dulson, who had bought Coronation Cottage, was able to extend and complete the house.

Robert was buried in Lund churchyard on November 20 1890. His death was followed shortly afterwards by that of his wife, Ann, who was buried on December 29 1890.

Uncle Eddie went daily on the train from Middleton Station, to Selby Grammar School. I think Uncle Ernie went to Bridlington Grammar School,

but I am not sure. Aunty Ethel was educated at Miss Chatterton's Dame School, a small private school for young ladies in North Dalton, as was Aunty Elsie. Father went to Driffield School. All had previously attended primary school in Lund.

In 1914 when war broke out (the Great War or WWI) men from the farms were conscripted into the forces, particularly the horsemen, many of whom went with the Waggoners Reserve Battalion, spearheaded by Sir Mark Sykes of Sledmere. They were particularly important men, as they took their horses with them, and had to ferry supplies to the front- ammunition, food, etc and bring back the wounded. Consequently both men and horses were in constant danger with many, many men losing their lives at a very young age.

Above: Lund Village Green with the village cross and the pub.

Below: Alan Prescott in his soldier's uniform in 1916.

As a result of the war, Father had to leave school at Christmas, just after his 13th birthday, helping to replace the men who had been conscripted. During this period Uncle Eddie married Katherine Staveley and, in 1915, rented the farm at Lair Hill, next door to Wold House, from Lord Hotham. They had two children: Kathleen was born on April 9 1917 and Arthur Staveley on August 8 1919. Uncle Eddie, who bought the farm from Lord Hotham in 1921, farmed at Lair Hill until 1936. He said that when he left Lair Hill he had £55 in the world.

He moved to Skewsby and then to Terrington, and retired in 1943—with quite a bit of money in the bank.

Kathleen had Sheila (Vietch) in 1939: she was subsequently adopted by Aunty Elsie, who had married Oswald Harrison and was living at Woods Farm, Gainsborough, Lincolnshire. As she and Uncle Oswald could not have children it seemed an ideal solution. Kathleen subsequently married Arthur Tock and had Phillip and Susan.

Arthur, meanwhile, did an apprenticeship at British Aerospace, Brough, and was conscripted into the Navy (his life story is recorded separately). After the war he went to Cook's Precision Engineers in York, who sent him to open a branch in Cape Town, South Africa, where he stayed for the rest of his life. His gravestone and ashes are in Lund churchyard in the family grave, as are Aunty Ethel's.

Uncle Ernie married Erica (Queenie) Crick, from the Manchester area. She apparently got off the train in Middleton to start a new life (no doubt to 'find' herself) and met Uncle Ernie, who by this time was more or less farming Wold House with the aid of the then staff.

In 1921 Lord Hotham sold off all the land on the north side of Wold Road, Lund, and a lot of other farms in the area outside of his 'ring fence'. This was mainly to buy property in London. The Prescotts at Lund Wold and the Sinklers at Barff Hill, Aike, who had bought their farms, were the only farmers on the former estate who survived the Great Depression of the 1930s. Anthony Wilson (agent to Lord Hotham many years later) told me that during the 1930s times were so bad that 60 per cent of the estate had no official tenants ie no-one was paying any rent. In 1919 Uncle Ernie and Aunty Queenie moved into Wold House and farmed there until 1924.

Thomas Henry, widowed in 1922 when, on September 20, Jane died of pernicious anaemia, moved to Poplars together with Elsie and Leonard.

William Ouston, who remained a bachelor all his life, ran the butchery business at Poplars from the early 1880s until the early 1900s. After he died, on September 5 1920, Thomas Henry took over the property. During the same period Robert set up the grain and hay and straw business on Beverley Road, Hull, opposite Fountain Road. (Willy Prescott, the first son of Edward took over this business, which ran until the mid-1950s). He married Miss North and they had two children, Marjory and John. Marjory married Richard Andrews and they had two girls, Sheila (married Gerry Barton) and Barbara (married Pierce Wright).

My grandparents outside Poplars in 1920.

There was much demand for Robert's wares in the city, horses being the main source of transport.

In December 1920, there was an Agricultural Act, proposed by the coalition Government of the day, designed to support guaranteed prices for agricultural products and to maintain minimum wages for farm labourers. However, it proved ineffective and the guarantees were abandoned in July 1921, with the relevant parts of the Act repealed. The price of wheat crashed from 84s 7d a quarter (£18.80 per ton) to 44s 7d (£9.90) a drop of 48 per cent. Consequently agricultural wages dropped from 46s per week to 36s per

Agriculture Act 1920

The **Agriculture Act 1920** (10 & 11 Geo. V c. 76) was an Act of Parliament in the United Kingdom passed in December 1920 by the Coalition Government.

It was designed to support price guarantees for agricultural products, and to maintain minimum wages for farm labourers. However, it proved ineffective; the guarantees were abandoned in July 1921, with the relevant parts of the Act repealed, and the price of wheat crashed from 84s 7d a quarter to 44s 7d within one year - a drop of 48%.

The Act had established wage committees to fix minimum agricultural pay; these, too, were soon abandoned. A replacement system of "conciliation committees" was set up to mediate between employers and labourers, but these had no legal powers, and the average weekly wage fell from 46s at the beginning of 1921 to 36s by the end of the year, and to 28s a week within eighteen months of the repeal.

The next attempt to fix agricultural wages would be Labour's Agricultural Wages (Regulation) Act 1924.

week and, from January 1 1921 to December 31 1921, wages fell to 28s per week: this was within 18 months of the repeal of the 1920 Act. The next attempt to fix agricultural wages would be the Labour Government's Agricultural Wages (Regulation) Act, 1924.

Unfortunately, by 1924 Uncle Ernie was taking more interest in his Methodist preaching than his farming, although he was recognised as one of the finest ploughmen in the area. He would often walk from Wold House across the fields to the chapel on Middleton Wold Road opposite Wold House Farm, Middleton, and then walk back again—even in the depths of winter. He was not encouraged by Queenie to do farm work, as she thought he should not have to do physical work but just direct the men.

In 1924 Thomas Henry took the decision to move back to Wold House with Elsie and Father. Uncle Ernie and Aunty Queenie moved to Poplars, where he ran a taxi business and a corn milling business. They subsequently left there and went to Clayworth Wood House, Beckenham, next door to Uncle Oswald Harrison. Father then took over the running of Wold House farm, no doubt with Thomas Henry's supervision. Elsie was housekeeper.

Aunty Ethel had been housekeeper for Uncle Eddie at Lair Hill until he married. Then she went to be housekeeper to John Maxwell, of Cranswick Auctioneers, who had taken the tenancy of Poplars after William Ouston had retired. However, she soon realised he desired her for more than just her housekeeping. She quite quickly left and went to the London Hospital to train as a nurse, qualifying as a State Registered Nurse (SRN) and a State Certified Midwife (SCM). During this time she brought various nursing friends to Wold House—trying to find a wife for Father. In 1926 Aunty Ethel brought Jennie Adelaide Mortimer, my mother, to stay after she had installed a bathroom at Wold House at her own expense—£26—for which Father, some 20 years later, had to reimburse her.

One year later Father married Mother. The first thing that her father-in-law said to her was: 'Can you mek a shet? (make a shirt)'.

At that time Wold House would have a staff of the foreman, Jack East, who lived in Middleton; three men living in men's bedroom, one or two maids living in and a girl, Rachel Dove, who came up from Middleton to work in the house.

Bearing in mind that all these men folk had to be fed and watered and all laundry—bedding, etc—done, looking after them was no mean feat.

In the 1920s a foreman would be getting approximately £26 per year. The men living in would be getting in the region of £14-16 a year, paid at the end of the year. They could have a 'fess' or a payment in advance, if they were desperate.

Men used to go to the hirings in October and be hired for a year. They would have a week's holiday for the hirings—or longer if they didn't get taken on—unpaid. These men would be shepherds, bullockies (cow men), and waggoners, down to 'thod' (third) lad or 'Tommy owt' who had to do anything he was told. He would be a school leaver aged 13 or 14 years, being paid possibly £6 a year and all found. They used to say it was so cold in men's bedroom that in some winters the urine in the pots under the beds froze.

In those days most Wold farms had a four course rotation, ie year one, clean clover (white clover, no grass in it) for summer grazing for sheep; year two, wheat; year three, roots including mangolds for clamping (for feeding in the yards in the winter and for the lambing ewes penned for the first few days after lambing), soft turnips, and swedes for later on, as the swedes stood the harder weather of late winter. Swedes would

Shepherding Leicesters.

often be cut up in a turnip cutter (big chips) and fed in troughs to the fattening hoggs. Year four was barley mainly for malting (on the Wolds), undersown with clovers. The fourth year could be split with oats, mainly for feeding the horses and the cattle in the winter period.

Cattle were housed in open yards under the bedroom windows on most farms. This included the milking cows. The sheep were 'folded' on the turnips ie allocated for one day's feed; then the shepherd moved the nets progressively across the field. In a lot of cases hoggs (lambs that were born in the spring) were 'folded' in front of the in-lamb ewes, which followed behind cleaning up that which was left by the hoggs.

Summertime was more or less devoted to working the land for the turnip crop for sheep for their winter feed; ploughing several times was the main method of cultivation. Hay time was between summer cultivations and 'looking' the cereal crops, mainly for thistles and dockings. Other summer

A load of sheaves at Bishop Burton, outside what are now the college gates. The picture dates back to approximately 1900.

problems in the cereal crops were swine thistles and poppies; as the old saying goes, one year's seeding is seven years' weeding.

Harvest usually started at the end of July, with oats being the first crop to be bindered (to be cut with a binder). This would take a team of four horses, which would have to be changed every two hours as it was very hard work. A man would have to drive the horses with another man on the binder making sure that the sheaves of corn were tied correctly. After the crop was cut and tied it had to be stooked. Usually two or three men in a team would take six rows of sheaves and put them into a stook—with spring corn it used to be five-a-side, or 10 sheaves per stook, with wheat it was six-a-side or 12 in a stook.

If there were three men, one man would go down the middle two rows and set up two sheaves together in an A form, and the two outside 'wingers' would add to that. If there were only two men in a team both men would take three rows at each side. After the stooks had dried, taking perhaps a week or 10 days dependent on the weather, they would be collected by two men, one forking the sheaves onto the wagon and the second loading them. Care had to be taken to keep as much of the grain in the sheaves as possible as they would be handled many times before they reached the threshing machine.

The loaders would take great pride in trying to make a perfect load. The wagon bottom was always filled first, levelling it to the side-boards, and then there would be two to three courses of 'shipping' ie with the heads facing into the wagon down either side of the wagon, to get extra width.

After the shipping came the art of putting the front and the rear sheaves with heads of grain inwards and base outwards, both back and front. Then the binders would be put the opposite way round, gradually getting wider, the aim being to have an ace of spades shape both back and front, and the middle of the wagon would be

Unloading a wagon
onto a stack, 1950.

'shippin' shaped. When the load was completed it would have to be roped down so that nothing slipped on the way back to the yard.

When leading home from Little Wold, Hut Field and Far Field tops, you had to chain a wheel up coming down the hill so that it did not run away with the horses. This would be removed at the bottom of the hill before going up the other side.

Back in the stackyard one man would be the 'stacker' and this was always the foreman's job. He would go round and round the stack, starting in the middle, keeping the ears of corn higher than the base and ending up on the outside, which always had to be straight and tidy with all the bottoms of the sheaves facing outwards. Usually this meant going round and round until the stack was about 12 feet high, or maybe a little bit more, dependent on the size of the base. Then the 'top' would be drawn in to make an apex. When corn was a little bit tacky they would pull a bag full of straw up the middle to prevent any heating.

The stacker always had a 'pick' who would throw him the sheaves, always the right way up and the right way round for the foreman to put in place. The man teaming the wagon would always have to throw them to the 'pick'. It was easy until they got to the top of the stack, when latterly they had elevators to put the 'top' on. We had a Lister and Blackstone fold-up elevator, which could be folded in two—the length of the trough—for winter storage. I was opening out this elevator once, having to get on top to

21

loosen the chains, when I caught my toes in the tensioner at the sides and went from being perpendicular to head first to the ground. Fortunately no damage was done.

Usually, the morning after the stack was completed, while the elevator was still in position, it would be thatched with straw, starting at the eaves with heaps of loose straw just hanging over the edge, going round and round until the whole top was covered with nine inches to a foot of threshed straw. This was then was netted down and weighted to stop the wind blowing the thatching off.

In olden days the thatch would be 'bottled' straw, which was straight and always used for thatching the stacks that were very proudly displayed—as in thatched houses.

After harvest was over and all was safely gathered in, it was muck spreading, or getting the muck out of the yards and spreading on the clover leys before starting to plough and sow next year's wheat crop. The rams (or tups) were usually put in with the ewes at Hull Fair, ie October 11, to start lambing in March the following year. The gestation period was 21 weeks and three days.

Good yields of wheat after clean clovers, which were nitrogen fixing, would be seven quarters per acre (a quarter of wheat was two 18-stone bags, 4.5cwt or 225kg). On threshing days in the winter men would carry these 18-stone bags from the threshing machine, up the granary steps and stack them in the granary two high. At the end of the threshing machine would be a weigh, with four four-stone weights and one two-stone weight, plus an empty bag. These would be tied with string from the threshed sheaves and then put on the winding up barrow so the men could get them on their backs.

A good half day's threshing of wheat would be approximately 30 quarters or 60 quarters for the day (13.5 tons). The permanent grass in the park at the back of Wold House was for horse pasture in summer, the house cows and any store cattle. It was, in those days, classed as an eight-to-10-horse farm.

October 22 1927: Father married Jennie Adelaide Mortimer. The night before Father went down to Blandford, Dorset, after they had finished thatching all the corn stacks down. When they came back there had been a terrific whirlwind and it had lifted the tops off all the stacks—14 days' threshing, which had taken 14 weeks to harvest after a very wet period.

After they married, Aunty Elsie moved out and went to live with her brother, Uncle Ernie, and Aunty Queenie. She got a job as a chauffeuse, and subsequently met and married Uncle Oswald and moved to Woods Farm, Gainsborough.

March 3 1929: Thomas Henry Prescott, my grandfather, died at Wold House. It was Sunday—on the Monday Father went to see 'Brassy' Wilson, the joiner in Lund, at what is now called the Old Workhouse, in North Road, opposite the churchyard, and ordered the coffin. No doubt he would organise the digging of the grave beside my grandmother's. This is the grave on the left hand side of the path in front of the church, which has a kerb round it and encompasses various family members' ashes.

Tuesday March 5 1929: all the men at Wold House were set to, to wash and clean up the best wagon and to get the horses cleaned up. On Wednesday March 6, it was the funeral. The coffin was put on the wagon, which was pulled by the horses. Two men from Wold House and two from Lair Hill were the pall bearers. Funerals in those days were never more than three or four days after the death had occurred.

Father then took over the whole running of the farm at a most difficult time as the Great Depression was just beginning to bite. When they bought Wold House in 1921, it was £3,100 for the 126 acres. It was nearly all dale land, including quite a lot of woodland for which Father always said they had been overcharged, as the wood had been felled since purchase and had not realised the valuation.

A bank overdraft was obtained at that time, and interest rates tended to accrue on the borrowed amount. By 1951 the bank overdraft had grown to £4,100. The bank then said Father should go to the AMC (Agricultural Mortgage Corporation) and obtain a loan for this amount, which he did. It was payable over the next 60 years at £90 10s 10d twice yearly. This was approximately £1 10s per acre, which was quite a high rent even in those days. This, I am pleased to say, I saw out in 2011. Here you may well ask why did I not pay this off before, but this money was borrowed at a fixed rate of four per cent and during that period other borrowings went up as high as 18 per cent so, obviously, it was well left. It also kept our foot in the door at the AMC. The previously mentioned John Maxwell valued the farm for the AMC at £12,000—£95 per acre over the whole farm of 126 acres.

During this Great Depression Father developed a fear of going to the bank. Each week when he had to go to the bank to get wages for the men, a maximum of £10 a week, the clerk would look up in the ledger to see if they could pay out the required amount. Also during this time money was borrowed from lots of members of the family, a matter of £50 here and £50 there. Feed bills from the Robert Prescott business in Hull were not being paid. These debts were all finally paid off with interest after the war but all this scarred Father for life. He was always paranoid about borrowing money—he always said he would never go on holiday whilst he owed money. As a result, as you can imagine, he never went on holiday. They once had a two-day visit to the Lake District just before the beginning of the war. But to be fair, it was only the pure doggedness of Father, supported by Mother, which kept them in business when many farmers and businesses around went bankrupt.

In the early 1930s it was a case of finding new ways to make a living—diversification as we would call it nowadays—and the county's pig producers came in to prominence. They would supply the young piglets and the food, with the labour, straw and housing being provided by the farmer. We call it 'bed and breakfast' nowadays. The man in charge of this was called Mr Wertimer.

Pigs in the fold yard.

The covered yard, as it was, was converted into six pig pens with one long trough on the outer wall in each pen. They would be fed and cleaned out daily. The floor was concreted with a very lime-based mixture, which broke up very easily afterwards in a matter of 10 years. When the pigs were ready to go for bacon, they would go to the bacon factory at Malton, with the regular haulier being a Mr Wildbore, who was father of Val Thompson, from Scurf Dyke Farm, Cranswick.

Thinking about Malton, we have often laughed about Mr Clarkson, a farmer from Arram, who took their sheets of wool to Yorkshire and North-

24

ern Wool Growers' depot at Norton, Malton, where we all took our wool. He got down the road into Norton, and didn't know which way to go with the tractor and trailer, so he called at the little shop, and, being a bit embarrassed at being lost, bought two chickens, paid for them and then asked his way to Wool Growers. After the lady had given him directions he said he would leave the chickens and collect them on his way back. He came back a different way, and couldn't find the shop, so returned home without his chickens.

August 24 1932: Stephanie Anne, my sister, was born—Mother was 37 at the time. Stephanie went to Lund School until she was 11 years old, then went to St Philomena's Convent at Boynton, near Bridlington, to where the school had been evacuated from Hull, as the city was being so heavily bombed. After the Second World War the school was moved to Rise Hall near Skirlaugh, as tenant of the Bethell family of Rise Estate. Steph finished her schooling there, leaving at 17. She then went down to the London Hospital training school at Trueloves, Chelmsford, Essex. This did not work out, so she went to Sheffield Hallam Hospital as a trainee. I shall never forget going to see her there, driving through all the desolated steel works, which were very much in decay. It was such a depressing sight.

Top: my sister, Stephanie in 1937.

Above right: Stephanie in her nurse's uniform, 1952.

Right: Rise Hall, 1949.

Steph subsequently qualified as an SRN and then went to Hull and Liverpool to qualify as SCM. This pleased Mother enormously, as Steph was following in her footsteps.

In the early 1950s, the air station down the road from Wold House was being run as a maintenance transmitting station for the RAF. Mother would often entertain the airmen to supper and make pies, etc, for them. Peter the painter was one of these and in the summer of 1949, during one of his work periods at the air station, he painted up Wold House. Edward Whorley was another of these airmen and subsequently met Stephanie.

They married on June 23 1956. They went to live in Lydiate, Magull, Liverpool, where, by this time, Ted had become manager for Oakley and Watling, a Liverpool firm of ships chandlers. Steph continued nursing, practising midwifery in the back streets of Liverpool and the surrounding area. Many of the airmen who were stationed at Lund married local girls at that time. The air station turned into a pea-viner store then a piggery, and finally was used as a base for a second-hand provender machinery business run by 'Uncle' Fred Thompson—as the boys called him. It was demolished in the early 2000s.

Steph and Ted had Susan Alison on January 4 1960, followed by Ian Edward on March 31 1962. They moved from Liverpool to Southampton, where Ted took over a shop—a general store. Both he and Steph worked in it until Steph became too ill to carry on. They then moved to Winchester, where Ted took a job as an accountant. Steph died on October 1 1973 from a tumour on the brain. She was buried in Winchester.

Sadly Susan died aged 21 of leukaemia some seven years later. Ian met Carron Wood at Helen and Ross's wedding, in 1993. They married, now live in York and are the proud parents of Grace.

After Ted had been diagnosed with cancer, Ian brought him up from Winchester, where he had lived in Stockbridge Road since Steph's death. He died in the York Hospice. He had a naturalist funeral, which was the first one we had ever attended, and is buried at Terrington. It was a lovely service.

I, Stephen Granville, was born on November 5 1936, Mother then being 41 years old. She really was always more like a grandmother to me than a mother. She was mentally older at 65, when we married, than she was when she died aged 97 on December 14 1992. I always said that she was frightened by the fireworks on November 5. Father, who never entered village life, went into the village hall where WI members were holding the institute's birthday party and announced that their president (she was president for 32 years) had given him a son.

Grandmother Mortimer 1935.

In the winter/spring of 1936 the East Riding (Beverley Borough Council) brought mains water into the village of Lund: it was extended up Wold Road as far as the air station, which was then being built. Provision was made for a stand pipe at the road ends, so that water carts from the outlying farms could get water without going to the village pond at West End. Len Cock, Billy and Jim's brother, was part of the team digging the trench. Needless to say there were no digging machines: it was all done with a shovel and manpower.

In the May before I was born William Cock (Billy) came to work at Wold House as a cowman, or bullocky as they called them in those days, as they had started to milk cows to sell as liquid milk rather than to make it into butter. This involved building a brand-new dairy to tie up 12 cows in double stalls. Previously Mother had had to churn the milk, make into one pound pats of butter and take into Johnson's grocers in Beverley to sell. This was labour intensive and they only got one third of the price that they got for liquid milk.

The new dairy was very modern at the time and was later extended to take 18 cows. This was done to get a regular monthly income from the sale of milk. This was sold to the Milk Marketing Board, which was set up in 1933 and was the saviour of many, many farmers in that period. In those days the cows were mainly Shorthorns, which were the popular breed of the day. Milk was put into churns and left at the bottom of the drive on a stand on the roadside for the milk wagon to collect. When I was a child British Rail collected the milk and it was taken to the Glaxo Laboratories in Driffield to be processed.

September 3 1939: World War Two was declared. My first recollection on the outbreak of the war, was, presumably during the latter part of 1939, being taken, wrapped in a blanket, in the car to the air raid shelter at Driffield Aerodrome. This was just before the main gates on the roadside. I remember going down the steps into the shelter, where there were many people gathered. It seems extremely stupid driving to Driffield with masked headlights to the place which was most likely to be a target to be bombed. This was before we had our own air raid shelter, which was built in early 1940 by Eastwood Builders, of Middleton.

Another memory was of my father standing where the weighbridge office at Wold House is now, talking to one of the men and saying there would be guns lined up down the side of the paddock when I am reputed to have said: 'Are you going to shoot labbits?' This was to be the precursor of the 4th Field Ambulance Division, which was stationed on the farm and had every trade—butcher, baker, blacksmith, etc. We even had a forge, which they had in the now car park.

We had Colonel Barlass and his batman staying in the house, together with Nurse Ingleby and two men in the men's bedroom. Nurse Ingleby had come as a consequence of Mother and Mrs Watson Hall, of Scorborough Hall, forming the South Dalton Nursing Association. Prior to this Mother had been called upon to deliver babies or lay out the deceased as there was no National Health Service in those days. One memorable case being that she had to lay out Captain Byron at Kilnwick Hall: he had to be laid out in his shooting attire, with a pheasant feather in his hat.

Nurse Ingleby with Stephanie and me, 1943.

A nurse who had attended a death could not attend a birth within 24 hours, which sometimes caused problems. Nurse Ingleby originally lived at The Lodge at Scorborough Hall, but this was not satisfactory as there was no telephone. We had had the telephone installed in 1936: it was a Bakelite upright one, with a loose ear trumpet hanging on the side. This was later changed for the more recognisable Bakelite dial telephone. Our telephone number was Middle-

28

ton-on-the-Wolds 32, all done manually at the exchange at Middleton by Mrs Noble, who knew everyone's affairs as she manned the switchboard 24 hours a day.

Nurse came to live at Wold House in 1941 and stayed until 1946. She was a big 'raw-boned' lady of the utmost kindness and was dedicated to her job. She never married.

Madge, her sister, lived in Hull and was blind. She married a blind man, Joe Cawley, and they had two sons. William Guy, their elder son, was born at Wold House in 1943, on my birthday, as she was evacuated from Hull during the Blitz. The second son, Stephen, was born on March 14, 1946, in Hull. Bill was a dentist, living in Wales. Stephen was an accountant and ended up working at Buckingham Palace. Not bad for two sons of blind parents.

Mother and Nurse were always the best of friends as Mother would attend the dead or deliver babies to help out. In those days Nurse Ingleby had a very small Morris Eight car, which came in very useful as a second mode of transport when the farm Morris Oxford car broke down—which was frequently. This vehicle was bought nearly new for £12 from a garage at Woodmansey and it lasted 10 years until 1946 when we bought a Vauxhall 14/6. This was possibly an even less reliable car than the Morris. It lasted until 1953.

Vauxhall 14/6 bought in 1946.

When Uncle Eddie left Lair Hill in 1936 Wood Flat field and the grass field on the main road at South Dalton, were rented from Lord Hotham. Most farms had these 'away' fields, originally to rest stock when being walked to market in Beverley or Hull and later used for summer grazing by either store cattle or horses. These two fields were then taken on by Father, bringing the total farm acreage to 263 acres.

During the war, things greatly improved income-wise, as food was very scarce and farmers were everyone's friends. People would come out into the country to get eggs, chickens, rabbits and meat of any description. Farmers had a good black market trade in bacon as they would kill a pig on the farm, dress it and salt it down on boards on the dairy floor for two weeks. (That is why the dairy floor still gets so wet sometimes—it's the salt still coming up under the tiles, after all these years). Then the large joints—shoulders, sides and hams—would be hung from hooks in the ceiling of the kitchen to dry out, after which they would be covered in muslin and put into a bedroom for storage, until they were required.

All local farmers would be doing this and would kill pigs in roughly two to three weeks rotation in the winter. Everyone would pass round a 'fry-up' including a small pork joint, liver, black pudding, etc. The same was returned when they killed a pig. Food was rationed to a very minimum level, and those who had sufficient petrol coupons to travel into the country, would bring their wares, ie fish, bedding, carpets (or rather carpet squares and rugs), liquorice sweets—a rare treat—and any other black market goodies. Ice cream and bananas were never seen for the entirety of the war. During this period finances began to stabilise, and many of the family debts were able to be paid off.

At this time Uncle Brumfield, of Elm Tree Farm, Molescroft, was a sheep and cattle dealer as well as being Mayor of Beverley. His wife was the third of the Horsley sisters and known as Aunty Tally—Edward and Thomas's wives were her sisters.

He would supply Father with store cattle and sheep, which he would fatten. Then they would be sold and the debt paid. He once supplied us with a Shorthorn bull which had come out of Lincolnshire; from, I believe, the Hagnaby area. It was named Woldsman and was a very good bull. Because of this father chose Woldsman as our prefix for the subsequent Red Poll herd, which he started in 1953.

Threshing days were a very regular occurrence during the winter and

 always required getting in extra labour from neighbouring farms. Grain was needed for animal feed, or to sell for flour or malting. My first recollection was having the steam engine coming up the road, pulling the threshing

machine and the straw elevator or wire tied baler behind. This was always from about 5-6pm. They had to use flashlights as there was no means of lighting other than the old stable lamps.

They had to get the threshing machine set level and all in line, ready for a 7am start the following day.

Threshing days: above on a stack and below left, with a steam engine at Wold House.

The two men with the threshing machine always came in for their breakfast after they had the steam engine stoked up and the machine opened out. There were two men with the machine: one would be in charge of seeing to the engine and that everything was running correctly; the other would be the feeder, who fed the individual sheaves into the open drum on the top of the machine. He would be standing in a well behind the drum and occasionally a man would get his arm fast in the drum of the machine and lose either the arm or part thereof. Health and Safety would have had a field day had it been in existence.

Eleven men were required on threshing days: two men with the machine; two corn carriers, who each got a shilling a day more than the others; two men on the corn stack forking the sheaves onto the machine; one man cutting bands on the sheaves and passing to the feeder; two men on the straw stack; one man carrying 'chaff' and the last man carrying 'pulls'.

'Pulls' is the very short straw and threshed heads of corn. The latter two jobs were very dirty jobs—the chaff and pulls being carried in caff sheets—two hessian bags opened out and sewn together, approximately seven to eight feet square. The four corners would be gathered together after the chaff or pulls had been raked it from under the machine, and carried into the covered barn, foldyard or 'chaff hole' in the stable for the horses, to be mixed with corn for their feed. The straw was made into a stack at the bottom of the elevator, and then carted into the yard by the horse and wagons as needed. The cattle would pull the straw off the wagons, which would be left loaded in the yard. This would be done three times a week.

The engine man would knock on the engine wheel with his hammer at about 9.30am and the men on the corn stack would stop putting sheaves on-to the machine. When this had all gone through they would knock off for 'llowance (allowance or lunch): usually this would comprise of tea and a bread bun in which there was a lump of cheese. The same would happen at 12 noon, by which time the stack should have been finished for half a day's threshing. If a day's threshing was wanted the machine would have to be moved on during the lunch hour. The two threshing men would go into the house for their dinner; the other men would bring their own. The evening meal was always provided by the next day's threshing customers.

There were three brothers who were the local threshing machine contrac-tors: Harold Wood just had the ordinary threshing set and elevator; his brother, Tom, had a threshing set with a wire-tied baler with easel to push the tied bales up onto the stack, and sometimes had a bottling machine for thatching straw; Billy Wood had similar set-up to Harold, but worked more in the South Dalton/Etton direction. He was also the village blacksmith in South Dalton. There was a fourth brother, Harry, who worked on the Dalton Estate.

In a normal day's work in winter on a farm in the 1920s the horsemen would be out at 6am to feed their horses and then come in for breakfast. They would take their mid-morning refreshments with them to wherever they were working. The horses and men would come up at lunchtime. Hors-es were fed and watered first and then the men went indoors for their dinner. The same happened again in the afternoons, but this time the horses would be watered, stabled, fed and brushed before shutting the stable door until suppering-up time at 9-10pm, when they would be turned into the yard for a drink and food put in the troughs in front of them.

I always remember Father giving me the sieve with the chaff and corn in to take between two great big Shire horses to put it in the trough. No doubt they would be the quietest horses in the stable and unlikely to kick, but a lot of the horses in the stable at night would be stamping their feet, no doubt to relieve irritation, and it was very frightening to a seven to eight-year-old wreckling—as Father used to call me. Had horsepower carried on, I would not be farming now.

Breakfast in those days was nearly always cold pies, bacon and egg or bacon pie. Homemade bread was always available, being made twice a week by Mother or a maid, the flour being purchased in 10-stone bags from

Johnsons, the grocers in Beverley, usually once a month.

Men always carried cold tea in a bottle with a clip top to slake their thirst during the day. Lunch was a hot meal—always meat, mashed potatoes and seasonal vegetables—usually home-grown, followed by fruit pie—again whatever was in season (rhubarb could go on forever) with hot custard. The family had cream, skimmed off the top of the milk, which had settled over-night. There were no fridges then and all food was kept in the dairy (pantry) in a cupboard with a wire mesh door to keep the flies off. There was one pane in the window, which had a mesh over it to let in air. Tea would be cold meats, mainly bacon, pickles, fruit pies and jam and bread, all washed down with plenty of tea. Supper was a hot or cold drink with bread and dripping. Hard physical work required a lot of energy.

In the early 1940s when Hull was being bombed so badly, many of the children were evacuated into the country. Someone with local knowledge had to be in charge of temporarily re-homing mainly children, although in some cases mothers came too, particularly those whose homes had been bombed. Mother was the billeting officer for Lund and was not always the most popular person in the village as everyone had to take one or two chil-dren, depending on the amount of room they had available. Many of the evacuees, who have fond memories of being in the village and the different life they experienced from that in the centre of Hull, still keep in touch.

In the winter of 1943 there was much flooding at Lickham Hall, Scor-borough, as it had been a hard winter with a lot of snow. When the German bomber pilots, who took their bearing from Flamborough Head and headed south, saw all the water in this area they started to release their bombs and incendiaries, thinking it was the Humber. Uncle Edward, then in his 90th year, had to pump water at the back door in order to put the fire out in one of the stacks, which had had a direct hit with an incendiary bomb. It was not until the following day that they found a bomb crater in the front paddock into which you could have fitted two double-decker buses. At a similar time, Mother and Father were in bed at Wold House, with the curtains open, when they saw a German bomber—and the pilot—come between the cov-ered yard roof and the house, heading to the grass field next to Tom Fisher Wood, on Beverley Road, to put out the searchlight. He dropped his bomb short in the field we now call Shoei. A hole remained there until 1986 when John Thomas filled it in immediately he took over the farm from Harold

Wood, who farmed Town End Farm and owned one of the local threshing machines.

It was about this time that Uncle Ernie came to live with us at Wold House. Aunty Queenie and he had split up: she had kicked him out and he had nowhere else to go. She and Romney tried to carry on the farm but finances were strained. She eventually went to live with her bank manager in Devon. Romney and his wife, Doreen, then got a smallholding at Westwoodside, Lincolnshire, where they grew vegetables for the local market. This is now where they have the 'Haxey Hood' mud bath. Uncle Ernie eventually went to live with them. He died there in the early 1970s.

Poor Mrs Sharp died in Roslyn House: she was such a large lady that they could not get the coffin down the stairs so had to take her through the bedroom window. It was just after the war when a gentleman in the village, Colonel Barr, bought the house next door to the Calverts on The Green, opposite the pub, and started growing tobacco. That caused a bit of local chat. I remember the house being sold to him. It was owned by Freddie Jackson, who went to live at Clay Field Farm at Middleton. He sold the house by auction: it made somewhere in the region of £1,500—a lot of money at that time.

As the war was drawing to a close, Italian prisoners were housed in Middleton Hall, now destroyed. They were sent out onto farms and various places of work. They were not really very nice men and inclined to be lazy, although some of them were very capable.

We had one man called Merini, who used to come out of work hours and bring all sorts of trinkets he had made out of silver coins; one of his specialities was making silver rings with an initial on it. My first recollection of these Italian prisoners was of me looking out of my bedroom window above the kitchen, to see eight or 10 of them, stripped to the waist, filling manure into wagons in the foldyard. These men always had an armed guard with them.

After the Italian prisoners we got German prisoners, who were generally hard-working and appreciative of anything that was done for them. There were odd occasions when they would get a real Nazi prisoner who refused to work and he would very quickly be sent back to camp. One such came dressed in his full German officer's uniform and refused to work; he was quickly removed and we never saw him again. Many of these men were housed in the many Army camps around. Before the prisoners arrived when we had the 4th Field Ambulance on the farm at the height of the war, a lot of the soldiers would sleep in the granary or anywhere they could keep warm and dry. They told me there was up to a dozen at a time up there.

Mother never learned to drive, and was never encouraged to do so by Father as he said she would never be at home if she could drive. As a result she had to go on her sit-up-and-beg bicycle—one of the first bikes for women. On one occasion after one of Mother and Father's frequent rows, Mother took to her bicycle at 9am, saying she was off. Later that afternoon Father and I went into Beverley for something and on the way back overtook Mother at the bottom of Constitution Hill at Molescroft. She eventually arrived home. In defence of Father, he could not have got the bike into the car.

In 1943 Father bought a Standard Fordson tractor from Robert B Massey, Market Weighton. He delivered it by road, on spud wheels, and it broke down at Lair Grange gateway. This should have been a warning as it was to prove to be a very temperamental tractor. However, in harvest it could go very fast down the fields with empty trailers, doing 12mph with soil flying everywhere. Robert Massey's brother, Charlie, used to deliver the groceries for Johnson Bros grocers in Beverley. He would bring the order, which had been given to him the previous week, and Father would go into the shop on the Saturday to pay the bill.

I n 1946 Father bought from J Wood and Sons, Driffield, one of the first Fordson Majors produced. It was on rubber wheels, with only three forward gears and one reverse, started on petrol and turned over onto paraffin. There were no cabs on tractors in those days. It was only a very slow tractor, doing eight to nine miles per hour.

In the winter of 1947 we were virtually snowed in on the farm road but we could get across the fields on the tractor and onto Wold Road. Very often, if the weather was really bad, Edgar Woodall, the Fordson Major driver, would take me or fetch me back from school. By this time we had rigged up a canvas cab with Perspex windows to cover the so-called driving position. Otherwise it was a case of walking to school—wearing shorts and Wellingtons. No doubt that is why my ears are so frostbitten.

After the war the roads were in a very bad state as they were only chalk-based roads with gravel on the top. My first recollection of the road being repaired was having the road wagon and steam roller, with the tar boiler beside, parked at the bottom gate. This was pulled by a single horse, in shafts. The tar boiler had to be stoked up regularly to keep the tar hot and running. A man with a short hand-lance would spray it from side to side the width of the road. The granite chippings would be spread by hand with shovels from the back of the reversing lorry and then rolled down by the steam roller. Mr Ellerker, of Lockington, had one of these rollers. Andrew was allowed to drive it once at Vicarage Farm, when Mr Ellerker was rolling the hardcore in after the Crendon shed had been erected. Some nights I would go down to the bottom gate to see Ebenezer (Mr Johnson), who lived in Lund. He used to sleep in the road wagon, which had a coal stove in it, so that he could keep an eye on the steam engine, etc.

Winter wheat was always sown on the clover pasture, where the sheep had been grazing in the summer, after manure from the yards had been heaped in the same field and later spread, or spread straight from the yard, with three men on the wagon, spreading the muck with forks by hand. This was soul-destroying work—very heavy and repetitious. It would take four men approximately two weeks to empty a yard of manure. When the tractors came onto the scene they would pull a three-furrow plough followed by a furrow press drill, sowing three rows of corn at a time. This was called ploughing and pressing, harrows were pulled behind the press to cover the seed. There were no reversible ploughs in those days.

During the winter the arable men, after they had finished the ploughing of the stubbles, would slash all the hedges round the fields by hand with a slasher, or possibly a bill hook, if the hedges had a stronger growth.

These thorns would then all be raked up and burned. In the spring the appropriate ploughed fields that were to be drilled with spring barley, or perhaps beans, would be harrowed with gib harrows on the frost mould ploughing, usually from early March onwards, as the weather dictated.

Next would come the working of land for the mangolds followed by swedes and soft turnips, usually by the end of June or early July. First of all these root crops all had to be scruffled with one horse pulling a scruffler down between the rows, one row at a time. Latterly this was done by a tractor covering four rows, called a steerage hoe, with somebody sitting on the seat behind, steering to keep the rows in the unscruffled area. This was done three to four times before the crop was big enough to smother the rubbish. Both mangolds and turnips had to be hoed in the rows to knock out the rubbish and to leave a single plant so that they would grow bigger.

As Father always used to say: 'Turnip crops like company', and it certainly was the case. All the men would be engaged with a hoe apiece, starting at one end of the row, following in line across the field, and then returning numerous times until the field was finished. In a wet time the weeds and crop would grow faster than the men could hoe them. A soul-destroying job and hard work, as was all farm work.

Haymaking would be to a lesser degree, mainly towards the end of June, but was again two horses in a finger mower grass reaper. If it was a heavy crop it was hard work for two horses pulling a four foot cut mower. The knives had to be sharpened regularly with a carborundum stone. The hay was turned by hand with forks, put into cocks (a heap) and eventually loaded onto wagons or carts to be carried home and stacked in the stackyard before being strawed down—thatched with straw.

The shepherd was a man unto himself, as was the cowman, neither being involved with any of the other farm work barring during harvest time and busy periods, when it was all hands on deck with very long hours.

Usually the shepherd would have to have all the sheep clipped by the middle of June. There would be approximately 200 to 250 ewes and possibly some hoggs that had not been fit enough to go fat or were kept for breeding. Sometimes a contract shearer would come in to help clip by hand. When machine shearing took over in the early 1950s they used to have shearing contests, and some of the most proficient men could do 200 sheep in a day.

Dennis Clubley, whose father farmed at Lair Hill at the time and was a sheep dealer, could shear approximately this number per day with someone wrapping the fleeces and bringing the sheep to him. All these fleeces were eventually put into wool sheets—approximately 40 fleeces per sheet—which had to be stitched up at the top and then would be collected from the farm, or delivered by rail from Enthorpe, Bainton, Middleton or Kiplingcotes stations—but that one was up-and-down hill. Latterly we took them with a tractor and corncart to the Yorkshire and Northern Wool Growers' depot, at Norton, where they were loaded in bulk. We took them on a pre-arranged day so that they would be graded straight out of the trailer when we delivered them. We were paid the following week.

Grain bags were all hired from British Rail at a penny per sack, per week. This was paid by the hirer until they were returned by the purchaser of the grain, which was delivered by horses and wagon to one of the local stations, taking approximately two to three tons of corn per wagon, each pulled by a minimum of four horses, to be delivered to the appropriate merchant or miller. I can remember Thompson's millers of Hull, who would come and collect approximately eight tons in 18-stone bags, backed up to the upper granary door with two men running the bags to the step and the driver getting them on his back to loaden them. When we got the first drying plant in 1961 all the grain was in bulk. Wold Carriers, R B Massey's company run by his brother, Charlie, would collect eight tons of corn loaded in bulk in about an hour—no carrying—just the press of a button. This was real progress: we thought it was wonderful.

I always remember coming home from school on Victory in Europe day (VE Day) in 1945, to find that Mother had hung a couple of Union Jack flags at the back door. I went in and said: 'What's on? Has Uncle Ernie gone home?' My main recollection of this period before the end of the war is that Uncle Ernie was always in the house and under Mother's feet. On nice evenings in the summer he would sit on a tree stump in the park next to Middleton Woods and shoot rabbits.

In 1948 Bob and Reg Hall, of Ivy House Farm, came up from Lund one Sunday afternoon to see if there was anything interesting to do. In the gear house (tack room for horses) there was a shelf up above the corn bin on which items that were not used regularly were put out of the way. There was an old bread tin on the shelf, in which there was part of a belt of 303 bullets that some of the men had retrieved from a plane that had crashed at what is now Burdass's farm—Wold House at Middleton-on-the-Wolds.

I, having seen how some of the older boys would put these in a split gate post at the entrance to the school and then strike them, thought it would be a good lark to knock one into a four inch post in the wood. We had first to get a hammer out of the workshop—Mother caught us going out of the work-shop with me with the hammer in my hand and made me put it back. I had, however, a nail in my pocket to strike the bullet so, not to be deterred, I got a lump of chalk in my left hand and hammered the bullet point into the top of the post; when it wouldn't go any further I took the nail and struck it. There was an almighty bang and the casing of the bullet exploded and I was left with a shattered piece of chalk in my left hand and my right hand bleeding badly. With that, Bob and Reg Hall flew down the paddock on their bikes. Their father, Stan, found them half-way between North Dalton and Huggate.

Mother bandaged my hand, but it swelled badly so I was taken into Beverley Westwood Hospital. Mother, who was friendly with a Dr Boyle and his wife, who lived on site, had my hand X-rayed. This showed a piece of shrapnel in my hand from the casing of the bullet and that the tendon was cut on the ring finger of my right hand. A few months later, after I had my tendon joined together, my finger was tight down into my hand. One Sunday afternoon, while playing with Roland Boynton and Dennis Fairweather, we went crow-nesting to the wood below Bulmers, of Holme Wold, where there were always hundreds of crows—we used to get the eggs. While I was coming back down the tree, the branch broke and I caught the said finger and pulled it straight. The following day I was at the hospital—supposedly to see why the finger was not straightening. The specialist took one look at my now straight finger, looked at me and nothing more was said or done.

By 1949 the old Standard Fordson was getting outdated as hydraulics were just coming in. We bought a second Fordson Major, which had a green spot on the back axle housing: this meant that it was a higher geared tractor than the 1946 model.

Two three-furrow trailer ploughs that we had were converted into hydraulic-mounted by Hubert Marshall from North Dalton, the forward-thinking local blacksmith. This worked, but not as well as the purpose-built model. It was certainly a lot easier than the trailer models. Before we converted the ploughs, latterly one man would pull the three-furrow plough with a draw bar on the back pulling the three-furrow press drill with the harrows behind. This was the first mechanisation

Above: Jim Cock and Edgar Woodall cutting corn.

Below: Me—SGP—taking an empty wagon back to the field.

from horsepower, as one man did it all from a tractor seat. At this stage there were still no cabs on tractors, except the canvas covers which were fitted on in really bad winter weather. These were removed at the first opportunity as they were very claustrophobic. One man could plough and drill six or eight acres of winter wheat in a day.

There was no mains water or electricity on the farm, like all other farms outside the villages. As a result these were not sought after for buying or renting. Mains water came to Lund village in 1936 and electricity at approximately the same time.

We did not get electricity at Wold House until my 20th birthday in 1956.

We had a poor supply of water, via Lesley Marr, from the end of the main at the air station, which supplied Vicarage Farm. The East Yorkshire Water Board took a new main from the Goodmanham Road to Lair Hill. They then connected the main from Middleton Road at Little Wold across Little Wold, 20 acre and Little Field to the roadside and then down the roadside to the air station. This would be in 1965—it did help to have a father-in-law who was water superintendent for the Driffield area. There were three cisterns at Wold House, one 20 feet deep and 15 feet diameter at the back door, another of a similar size outside the bull box, near the weighbridge office, and one under the old cakehouse—which is now in the middle of the foldyard. We ceased milking in 1978 and it was filled in in 1979, when all the bricks went into it.

These cisterns were fed with water off the roofs of various buildings, which was then hand-pumped from the cisterns into troughs in the yard. When the cisterns ran dry for the yards, water to fill the troughs was carried from the pond, which was immediately in front of the foldyard doors at the front entrance to the yard. In a very dry time water had to be carted from the village pond or, latterly, from a stand pipe at the road ends. Clubleys of Lair Hill Farm still had to ferry water to Lair Hill Farm until the mid-1960s, when the mains were connected from Middleton Road to the air station.

The domestic water in the house was pumped by hand in the back kitchen from the cistern at the back door into a header tank in the bathroom above. Father did this and it took 200 pumps of the handle to fill it.

When it began to be too much for him to do this, he decided to stop smoking—having been a 60-a-day man. He then consumed tubes and tubes of Polo mints.

An electric pump was fitted in 1963. Water for drinking in the house and for consumption was drawn from the well, which is 184 feet deep, at the front of the dairy—now offices—in what is still called well yard. This involved drawing a large 10-gallon bucket of water from the bottom of the well and tipping into buckets, which were kept in the house dairy. This was done three or four times a week. There was a hut housing the well

Mother feeding Christmas poultry in front of the well housing.

Harvest 1952—me—SGP—unloading sheaves to a new stack bottom.

wheel that originally had a chain with which to lower the bucket. Originally there were two buckets on a very long chain—as one went down the other came up full of water. This broke regularly so was replaced with a wire rope and a single bucket.

The water level is still checked to this day by the water board so they know the level of the water table. We put a Morrison jet pump, driven by a petrol engine, down in 1952. However, when they opened the pumping station at Etton for supplying Market Weighton, Pocklington and York, it took our supply and rendered the supply useless.

This was when the water main from Vicarage Farm was mole-ploughed in across the fields. The only trouble was, when fetching the water up in buckets, a dead cat or anything else that had fallen down the well would be brought up too. When the original chain broke, which was quite frequently, everything fell to the bottom of the well and a grappling iron had to be used on a long rope to retrieve the same. This could often take a very long time.

The width of the well at the top is approximately 10 feet wide and, presumably, tapers to virtually nothing at the bottom. The well housing was removed in 1965. Steel RSJs were installed across the well top and concreted over. It is, however, still accessible. Water was the lifeblood on a farm.

I left Lund School a week after I turned 13 and went to Longcroft School in Beverley.

I had been the only boy over 11 years old in the village school and this had proved awkward for Miss Carter. I was a year younger than everyone else at Longcroft and it was a steep learning curve coming from a small village school.

There were 300 children at Longcroft: it was the first term the school had been opened. It was only half built and was not completed for another 18 months, when the full intake of 600 pupils came in.

I was fortunate in the fact that in the first term we were sorted out and I went into what was called in those days, 'the technical forms'—T11 and T12. T11 was for the older pupils who had only one more year to go. Pupils in T12, in which I was, had two or three years to go. I was fortunate in the fact that I had more or less a year's revision, as I had been pushed along at the beginning. I left school in March 1953.

I always remember February 6 1952: we were all called into the assembly hall at Longcroft School and the headmaster, Mr Dunn, told us all that

King George VI had died. Princess Elizabeth, and her husband, Philip, the Duke of Edinburgh, who were on a Royal visit to South Africa, were called home immediately. They were met off the plane by the Prime Minister, Winston Churchill. It was the beginning of the Queen Elizabeth II's reign.

Mother had arranged for me to have an interview at Askham Bryan Farm Institute at York. She and I went on the bus from North Dalton to York and then changed to the Leeds bus, which dropped us at the main gates.

Bishop Burton College was in the process of being built, so this was the last year of East Riding students attending Askham Bryan. It was the seventh course after opening after the war. Quite a few of the students were mature students who had been in the Forces and were at least 10 years older than me. I was 16 when I started in September 1953.

In April 1952 malting barley was in very short supply. The last threshing day we had was threshing all the last oats and raking barley—then barley stubbles were always raked to prevent the sheep eating too much and bursting themselves on the newly-sown leys.

This barley was obviously quite weathered and usually kept for feeding the pigs in summer. There were only six or seven quarters of it. I remember taking a sample of it to Low Gardham for Mr Stickney, of Hosdell and Stickney, corn merchants. He said: 'I think this is a better sample than the last,' and offered Father £45 per quarter or £225 per ton.

A quarter of barley was two 16-stone bags. In 2014 that price was still unobtainable. Beer was 1s a pint then. This—the early 1950s—is when the 'barley barons' were created. Many farmers grew nothing but spring barley. As a result of these good prices the Vauxhall 14/6 was replaced with Richardson's 1943 Ford 10cwt work van, as new vehicles were in very short supply.

At the same time we ordered a new Ford Consul car (MWF 280) for £612 on the road, which could not be delivered until December, 1953. They came to collect me from Askham Bryan at the end of the Christmas term in the new car. I was waiting with all the others when someone said: 'Gosh, this is a smart car.' When I realised that it was my parents' I was very proud.

Father ordered a new Fordson Major diesel tractor, with purpose-built hydraulics, which we had delivered in the summer of 1954. That in turn involved getting a new 600-gallon diesel tank, as the only other tanks were tractor vaporizing oil (TVO) tanks and were galvanised.

The old Ford van lasted quite a few years and one night I took 16 young farmers to Richardson's workshop to have a lecture on tractor maintenance. Ron Robson, the foreman, would not believe it could carry so many people.

The regular job at this time of the year was lambing. It was a matter of all hands on deck, with ewes with lambs in pens everywhere. The ewes would be in the park or the paddock during the day and brought into the covered yard at night (the front part of the current foldyard at Wold House). The cows had to rough it in the open yard for the rest of the winter. Ewes that lambed in the park during the day nearly always went to the furthest point and the lambs had to be carried up the hill. It was a relief after they had lambed and could be turned out with their mothers into either the front paddock or onto the new clover seed ley, wherever that might be.

Sheep nets, which were taken up from the sheep fold where the turnips were, were always to set round the hedge sides in the seeds fields: very often there was a shortage of nets and stakes as well as time to set them. I never particularly liked sheep although Father called them 'the golden hoof of the Wolds'.

During the lambing period it would most likely be time to start drilling the spring corn, barley, oats and maybe some beans. This nearly always coincided with lambing time, when manpower was in most demand. The cows always had to take second place to the sheep for grazing rights as they could be fed in the yards on turnips, straw and a small amount of concentrates.

After lambing time was over and corn sowing finished, I was set on to plough big field—28 acres (top half of 50-acre across the road) for mangolds, kale and turnips—the kale being at the top for strip grazing the cows. After I had ploughed it for the first time I was set on to plough it again but the other way on, across the furrows—this was called quarting.

I ploughed most of the field four times that summer before the turnips and swedes were eventually sown. But, after that, it didn't need any cultivation bar rolling. This was done to kill the rubbish as in those days there were no spray chemicals. The following year our neighbour, Dick Thompson, got a sprayer. He would spray this field of spring barley with MCPA, which was obtained from Boots the Chemist at 6s a gallon. CMPP was 8s a gallon (5p to 1s, 20s or 240d to a £1).

In June 1953 we had the coronation of Queen Elizabeth II, which was a very special occasion. I always remember going down to Benny and Marjorie Lamb's in the village to watch the coronation ceremony on a 12-inch black-and-white television screen. They had bought this television set especially to watch the event. Their front sitting room was absolutely crammed with folk from the village. The same happened in anyone else's home where they were fortunate enough to have a television set.

The cows in those days were mainly Ayrshire type: this was because Father was going in more for milk and had used an Ayrshire bull from Specks at Towthorpe Dairies in Middleton. As such they had quite long horns and no beefing qualities.

During this time the Ministry of Agriculture and Fisheries and Food (MAFF) was beginning to give grants for various

An Ayrshire bull.

things, to increase productivity on farms. One of these grants was a calf subsidy on beef type calves, which the Ayrshires certainly were not. The calf subsidy in those days was £4 for a steer calf and £3 for a heifer calf. It could be claimed after the calf was eight months old, and had to be certified by the calf certifying officer.

Douglas Hutchinson, farmer at Elm Tree Farm, Holme-on-the-Wolds, was the first to do this job. This involved punching a hole in the right ear of the calf if it was up to standard. The Ayrshire heifer calves were definitely not suitable, so Father decided to buy a Red Poll bull calf from Sharps, of Throstle Nest Farm, Pocklington, who used to live in Lund. The farmer was the brother-in-law of our foreman, Jim Cock, and had just started with Red Polls.

Whilst I was at Askham Bryan, Jack Ibbotson and I went to see a herd of milking Red Polls at Mrs Fawcett's at Tadcaster. She was the then secretary of the Northern Counties Red Poll Breeders Association. She had approximately 50 cows, all nicely bedded up with barley straw, looking extremely contented and milking very well. It was whilst we were at Askham Bryan that Thornton Ibbotson, Jack's father, bought Cawkeld, for £28,000.

Later on in the summer of 1954, I took Mother and Father to see this herd. Father decided to buy six maiden heifers, none of which turned out to be any good. At the same time he bought a Suffolk ram lamb from the college farm and that proved to be a useful ram. We then bought three Red Poll in-calf heifers at the York Red Poll Society show and sale in the July, one of which turned out to be very good and produced a bull calf, Woldsman Wonder Boy—the foundation of our herd. What an excellent bull he turned out to be.

Food rationing was officially ended in 1954, farm improvement grants were brought into being and officially organised by MAFF to encourage food production in all departments of agriculture and horticulture. These continued until 1984 when everything was put into reverse gear.

After I left Askham Bryan it was straight into new farm work for me. I had been well initiated with milking cows and getting up early at Askham Bryan, and was guided towards dairying.

First of all, instead of buying all the concentrates ready compounded from Barkers & Lee Smith's in Beverley, which was always a heavy bill to pay—very often nearly out of hand—we decided to mix the raw materials ourselves with our own corn. This we did—by hand using shovels—in the cakehouse until we got a ground-level mixer installed in the mill house. In those days we had no electricity so the roller/grinder mill was driven by belt from an overhead shaft with pulleys on, from an Amanco petrol/paraffin engine. This could also drive a choppy cutter for cutting straw to feed to the cows, or a turnip cutter to cut turnips.

It was in the spring of 1955 when Tom Mitchell, who farmed at Enthorpe, died. I was working in one of the fields across the road from Wold House when his hearse came down the road with the cortège following, for his funeral in Lund Church. The farm was sold later that year to Horace Taylor, timber merchant from Driffield, for £32,000 for the 500 acres plus the 40-odd acres of mature woodland. He kept the woodland, and sold the farm on to Tony Sellars.

By that time the Ayrshire cows had to be TB tested. Most of the older cows failed the test and had to be sold, mostly in the open market or fat if they were not in calf. Some of the first Red Polls we got were TB-free when we bought them, but were infected by being with the Ayrshires. As these cows went out, we bought in Red Poll heifers in calf from Rawreth Estates

WI Rally 1948

in Essex, several other young cows as available or bought at the York sales and two from Mr Crossley, the agent at Lord Hotham's—he had come from Lord Hastings in Norfolk and had brought these two with him, as he was allowed to have house cows and a small amount of grass for himself.

During the war period there was the War Agricultural Executive Committee (WARAG) formed by the Government and made up of the more progressive farmers in each area. They would come round onto the farm and advise the farmer what to do, which crops to plant and to plough out grasses and sow with wheat to get more production. If you did not co-operate or improve your production you would be turned off your farm, whether you owned it or not. It was all organic farming in those days as no fertilizer could be imported from abroad—and it was impossible to increase the yields without fertilizer.

After the end of the war, when imports were allowed, fertilizers were used very sparingly, Cross Bone Fertilizers, of Bridlington, was one of the local merchants who would produce some of the early compounds, which were in the region of eight per cent nitrogen, 10 per cent phosphate, and 12 per cent potash (8.10.12). These were all in 1cwt hessian sacks and soon went hard if not kept very dry. Later on, in the mid-1950s, Robert Stephenson, of Hull Bridge, Beverley, started producing compounds of much higher analysis, ie 15.10.10 and later up to 22.11.11. These were applied at a rate of 3cwts or 150kgs per acre on all spring corn, with winter wheat getting a smaller amount. The permanent grasses were also given the same amount as the spring corn. By 1970 fertilizers were packed in 1cwt (112lbs) polythene sealed bags, which kept it dry.

The only problem being with these bags and the increasing rate at which fertilizer was being applied was the number of individual bags which had to all be man-handled. This was soon superseded by 30 bags on a pallet. This entailed us having some device, a forklift of some sort, to handle these pallets. This was the time when we bought a McConnell 'tail slave', which worked on the rear hydraulics, with a straight up and down duplex mast with a forward and backward tilt. A very neck-aching job. This was soon followed by us buying a Sanderson forklift, direct from Roy Sanderson himself, after Von and I went down to Skegness to see him. We bought it for £8,000 delivered. We now have

1978 Sanderson teleporter with duplex mast

three forklifts, some of the most useful pieces of equipment on the farm. When men were filling manure by hand it was always a constant gripe: 'I wish they could invent a mechanical muck fork.' Now they have.

I joined Bainton Young Farmers in 1955 as an intermediate member. At the first rally in 1956 I won the Intermediate Dairy Cow Judging and then went on to represent the East Riding Young Farmers judging dairy cows at the Dairy Show in London for the next five or six years.

This was no mean feat as there was tremendous competition for all stock judging classes, both at county and national level. The highest I achieved was first individual in Jersey cattle judging and seventh in Shorthorns. Overall I was third in the national competition. There would be more than 50 teams entered, as many counties had two teams in, including Yorkshire. Devon or one of the Welsh Counties nearly always won.

In 1956 Lesley Marr, the new owner of Vicarage Farm having bought it from the Church Commissioners, helped us get the water supply to Wold House, via Vicarage Farm, in a one-inch black alkathene pipe mole-ploughed in. He promised us that when Mr Fenton retired he wanted us to take the farm. In 1957 Mr Fenton took his nephew, Bethel Fenton, with him to pay the rent at the offices of Todd and Thorpe in the Land of Green Ginger, Hull, handed in his notice and asked Mr G W A Todd if his nephew could have the tenancy. Mr Todd agreed to this. When he reported back he was reprimanded—Mr Marr telling him that he had already promised the farm to Father.

We took over the farm on April 6 1958. We had to pay the agreed rent, which was £3 per acre. This was a very big amount for the times, as we were paying less than £1.50 to Lord Hotham for the rented land at Wold House. This brought our total acreage to 409 acres. Billy Cock, his wife and daughter, Joyce, went to live there. They remained there for two years until Mrs Cock became ill and they went to live in a cottage in Middleton.

June 23 1956: Stephanie Ann, my sister, married Edward Ernest Whorley in Lund Church. Bob Broadley was best man, and Raymond Cogswell and I were groomsmen. Vera Cogswell was chief bridesmaid and Gill and Phillipa Spencer (the daughters of John and Marjorie Spencer, of Driffield) were bridesmaids. The reception was held in the village hall, with Mrs Snowden from Kirkburn doing the catering. After a honeymoon in the Isle of Man they went to live at The Willows, 31 Wynstay Avenue, Lydiate, Liverpool, where Steph continued nursing.

It was a momentous year, as we had electricity installed. Gone were the lamps. The Government of the day decreed that they would supply all the outlying rural areas with electricity. We were very fortunate that we were able to get a three-phase supply connected that year and on November 5 the lights were turned on.

The cost of wiring up all Wold House and the farm buildings, such as they were, by Hale's electricians, of Beverley, was £263. The first thing to be electrified was the milking machine vacuum pump. This was followed very quickly by the purchase of a hammer mill for grinding the corn for the animals. The old Amanco engine in the mill house was quickly scrapped.

In the autumn of 1957 we ploughed all the stubble land at Vicarage Farm, as Mr Fenton only had Bob Witty working for him because Mike Dixon had left after harvest. We also ploughed up the grass field next to Hall's field at the back of the farm, which had been grass for more than 40 years—since Mr Fenton originally took the farm—and sowed it with winter wheat for his following crop.

Mr Fenton had his farm sale on April 3 1958. All small tools and implements were set out in the field above the pit, approximately five acres of stubble: the rest we had ploughed out. Ullyotts Auctioneers conducted the sale of horses, cattle and sheep, which were penned in the stackyard or foldyard, and auctioned through a ring. Normally the sale would have been in a grass field, but there was no grass field available.

We bought several items: harrows, small tools, etc and when I went to pay for these we went in through the front door to the sitting room on the right, Geoff Ullyott and his brother, Dick, were taking the money seated behind the solitary table standing on the brick tiled floor. There was no electricity. Geoff Ullyott was Peter Ullyott's Father.

The first thing we had to do when we took possession was to get electricity installed. Billy Cock, his wife and daughter had to do without until we had it wired, again by Hales of Beverley. The electricity board had to bring the supply up from the road, which was done after harvest. The foldyard was immediately filled with pigs, which we had bred at Wold House. These were fattened and then delivered by me to the bacon factory at Malton. We did buy quite a few store pigs from various sources.

During this period I met Yvonne Carr, a member of the Bridlington YFC, on July 25 1958 at the Driffield Show Dance. I took her home that night to Bridlington, backed into a concrete post whilst turning round in Mill Lane and dinted the chrome steel bumper quite badly. I got home at approximately 3am and was up again at 5am. I took the car out of the garage at the front, into the old workshop in the stack yard, took off the bumper, hammered it out straight and re-fixed it. Three months or so later Father said: 'Have you noticed the bumper on that car? The chrome is going rusty.' He never knew.

It was during this time, when I was chairman of Bainton YFC, that I received a cup for the club winning the county quiz competition. Subsequently I appeared in a photograph receiving the cup from Lord Halifax, who was our county president. When Von went to get a copy of the photograph from the Bridlington Free Press office the girl who gave it to her said: 'Is that his father?'

It soon became obvious after we took Vicarage Farm that, even with two binders (the latter one being a power binder, in other words driven from the PTO of the tractor and purchased as result of getting Vicarage Farm): the days of sheaves were limited. It was a wet harvest and we had to get Tom Wood in with his combine to combine a small amount of the barley. This entailed bagging the corn on the combine and then picking the bags up off the floor with a trailed Reffold sack elevator, which pulled a trailer behind to stack the bags on. This had to be repeated back in the stack yard, teaming the bags up the elevator into the granary—or any shed that was available. If the bags got wet at the bottom the grain would grow into the bags. Obviously other ideas had to be explored.

By 1960 we had bought our own 780 Special Massey Ferguson combine, for £1,760, less an early ordering discount of £60 cash in pound notes sent through the post. The same applied for the Massey Ferguson pickup baler: I can't remember how much it was, but we got £40 back in cash for that, too.

The only problem being with these pick-up bales was that they were very numerous and needed to be under cover: they got very wet if stored outside in a stack. The buying of the combine caused problems in the fact that we had no shed or building big enough to house it out of season. So I set to on farm improvement grant number one to build the original combine shed, which is now the old part of the workshop.

This was built of nine inch by 18 inch breeze blocks: after we got to eaves height we had to employ a bricklayer to do the apex and Sissons, the joiners, to put on the roof. They also made wooden-framed, galvanised sliding doors for each of the two bays.

This was the first building to be erected on the farm since the farm was taken in 1884. The grant on this was one third of the standard costs, which, in the end, cost us about £200 after the grant was obtained. This shed was later extended in 1973 to its present size, up to the Dragon boiler.

January 4 1960: my sister, Stephanie, had a baby, Susan Alison Whorley. Mother went over to Magull, Lydiate, near Liverpool, to help Steph for a couple of weeks.

At the same time, egg-laying hens housed in deep litter huts were coming very much to the fore and Woods of Driffield supplied ready-made deep litter huts, 18 feet wide in eight feet long sections. We bought sufficient for a hut 40 feet long by 18 feet wide, which was big enough to house 250 hens.

This proved quite lucrative in the early days as egg production was scarce. Tom Soanes, Clive's father, used to come round every week with his three-ton covered lorry to collect the eggs to deliver to East Riding Packing Station, which was situated off Hengate, Beverley, opposite Jacob's Well.

Mother was a member of East Yorkshire Egg Producers at that time; she got quite a nice nest egg from accrued shares when they were taken over by Yorkshire Egg Producers and moved to Mill Lane in Beverley. I extended the poultry house after we married, doing all the work myself, building all the sections up in the granary and putting on the roof.

After we bought the combine, which was a bulk combine, corn had to be bagged off from it onto a trailer in the field. This was about as labour intensive as the bagger combine. After the 1960 harvest it was apparent that we had to have a more modern set up.

Again Ministry of Agriculture farm improvement grants and Harry Bowes, their machinery adviser, came into play. The first question was: 'How many acres of grain do you grow?' 200 acres. 'What yield do you get per acre?' 30cwt—or one and a half tons. 'Therefore you need 300 tons of storage capacity.' The next question was: 'What sort of a drying plant would you like?' Father was very much against having a continuous dryer with a flame as this was a fire hazard, so we elected to have Simplex bins with electric heated fans. The next problem was we had to put up a building to house the new drier and the grain pit, elevators, etc.

The building was erected by Ron North, of Woodmansey, with whose foreman I had been at school. The main building that housed the grain bins was 30 feet wide by 75 feet long, and we put on a lean-to at either side. I insisted that the lean-to main beam should be a single RSJ—they had never used a single beam before, it was always a prefabricated truss. This idea was very quickly adopted by all other steel erectors.

This building cost £1,800 with, again, a third of it in grant to come off. The drying bins were all blown from the electric fan at the end of the tunnel near the elevator shafts. These took grain from the intake grain pit which would hold eight tons—just two cart loads of corn—when full. Theakstons of Driffield helped us erect the bins and the drying cylinder in the four ventilated bins. They supplied and installed all the elevators, conveyors and pre-cleaning equipment together with the catwalk, bulk loading facility, ladder, etc. All the bricklaying work was done by Eastwood's of Middleton, and the total net cost of the whole old drier was £7,500, which again was where the AMC came to our aid. This was borrowed over 10 years, at 10 per cent interest.

T he first year—the 1961 harvest—we just filled all the bins in the drier with one cart load over and Father, with a wry smile on his face, said: 'You've not done so bad.' Praise indeed.

The following spring of 1962 we had all the lambing ewes inside in the lean-tos, with individual pens down both walls of each lean-to and a ewe and her lambs in each pen. After a day or so they were moved into a communal pen as others came in to lamb and then out into the paddock. It was ideal lambing in there because it was light, dry, comfortable— and easy to clean out with a fore-end loader.

In the summer of 1963 Bainton YFC held a Wild West Dance in the drier shed, as it was one of the biggest sheds in the area and had a concrete floor. There were between 400 and 500 young farmers there: no trouble at all.

October 7 1961: Yvonne and I married at Bridlington Priory at 11am— it was a very wet morning. William Lamb was my best man, and Richard, his brother, one of the groomsmen. We have always been pleased to think that that was one of the last happy days for Richard, as he died from leukaemia on January 20 the following year. Edward Whorley and Uncle Tommy Carr were ushers. Margaret Thompson was chief bridesmaid and Lesley Howell and Sheila Sharp were bridesmaids.

We had our reception at the Spa restaurant at a cost of 7s 6d per head. We hired a Ford Anglia car from Richardson's in Driffield. However, the guests didn't know this and all thought that we would be going away in the Ford Consul. It being a wet day some of the guests covered the Consul with soap flakes, which gently bubbled up. Father and Mother had to drive the car home like that.

We were going round Driffield showground corner at 4pm, off on our honeymoon—all done between 11am and 4pm. We spent our first night at

Our wedding at Bridlington Priory on October 7 1961.

Warwick, and then went down to Newquay, in Cornwall, and toured the south coast for the rest of the week.

During the previous spring we had felled all of the trees in the shelter belt, both to the west and to the north, and these were sold off. In the autumn of 1961 Davidson's, of Pocklington, replanted trees at four feet intervals in rows four feet apart. Father spent a lot of time during the next four years mowing between the trees to keep all the rubbish down.

At this time we had Father, me, Billy Cock and Edgar Woodhall and were desperate for another man. Labour was difficult to get: the local councils could always pay more than farming could and the only way to attract men was to have a house to offer them. Vicarage Farm, where I had intended us to live after we got married, had to be offered to Alf and Evelyn Dowson together with their sons, John and Peter.

Vicarage Farm house was in poor repair and it was difficult to get repairs and improvements done, as Lesley Marr had died and his son Andrew had just taken over at 18 years of age. Mr G W A Todd had also died and his son, Tony, had taken over, so everything was in a state of flux. We ended up having to live with my parents as there was no other option and money was very tight.

I'm afraid it was not an easy time for Yvonne, adjusting to farm life, my parents there all the time, not a great deal of privacy and away from everyone she knew, but she coped admirably and from then on we were a partner-ship.

It was a matter of us sticking together and coping with the ups and downs of farm life.

In the autumn of 1961 Mr Cooke-Buttle, who farmed Lund Warren at that time, bought some sheep at one of the Northumberland markets and they brought foot-and-mouth disease with them. This meant that all his stock—cattle, sheep and pigs (if any)—had to be slaughtered and burned. Jack Watts' sheep at Wold Dyke Farm had to be destroyed as well.

As a result, restrictions of movement of all animals within a five-mile radius were enforced. At the time we had pigs, which we either bred or bought in, fattening at Vicarage Farm for the Malton Bacon Factory. As these went for bacon we were not able to replace them. Therefore we filled up with calves and cattle, which we had bred and could not move, so this was the end of pig-keeping at Wold House.

Mr Cooke-Buttle died in early 1962: the farm was sold to a Mr Greaves, but he only kept it for 18 months and then went bankrupt. It was bought by Maltas Farms Ltd in 1964 and they stayed for the next 50-odd years—the longest time that farm has been in single occupancy for this last century as it seems to bankrupt people.

It was about this time that Mrs Fawcett retired from being the secretary of the Northern Counties Red Poll Breeders Association, and I took on the job—with the help of Yvonne.

In the previous year, 1960, the Royal Agricultural Society of England (RASE) in conjunction with the Red Poll Cattle Society had organised a national judging competition for probationer judges at Cambridge, and each area—of which there were eight in those days—entered a team of three.

Arnott Weightman, Neville Henderson and I made up the northern team; Arnott and Neville were both from Durham. Neville and I both slept in the Red Poll Society caravan the first night, as judging was early in the morn-ing. We had to judge classes of bulls, cows and in-calf heifers, four in each class. Our team won the overall competition and I got the highest individual score, so felt my Young Farmers' training and judging had put me in good stead.

T he first winter we were married I spent any spare time in the granary building 12 more sections for the deep litter hut and could usually manage a couple of sections a week. When spring came we had a bricklayer from Driffield come and extend a level base for the deep litter hut. I had already made a false end with an adjoining gate. We then took the original end to the new end, putting up new roof trusses between each section and then adding an asbestos roof and guttering.

Ian Edward Whorley made his entrance on the March 31 1962: I had taken Mother to Liverpool in the van as I was taking Dick Sharp to Cheethams in Hyde, Cheshire, to see, and subsequently buy, nine strong heifer calves. I picked these up on the way back from Liverpool, having collected a spare wheel after getting a puncture, which had happened on the way there, repaired in a garage in Tintwistle.

In April, we bought a new Super Major (4105 WF) and new Super Dexta (4106 WF) for £600 and £500 respectively. It was the first time Richardson's had delivered two tractors to the same farm on the same lorry.

In the summer of 1962, we had Alf, John and Peter Dowson working on the farm, together with Billy Cock, Eric Higgs, from Cherry Burton Hostel, Father and me.

It had been a good spring, and we had got on well with the arable work. We spent a lot of time concreting the open foldyard where there was a raised drain across the middle, from the barn side to the dairy. This not only caused a lot of problems clearing the muck out but also held water in summer as the drains were higher than the yard level, having put in the new drain from the drier (first one). All this was done by hand with sand, gravel and cement mixed in the concrete mixer, recently purchased second-hand, from Eastwood's.

Lickham Hall, August 8 1964.

Alf and Eric were chief shovellers into the mixer, with Peter Dowson carrying water and fetching cement. John Dowson was barrowman and I was laying with John's help screeding off every five or six barrow loads. We got all the foldyard done before harvest: this was all done with the cows coming in twice a day for milking in the milking shed. All this work was done on standard costs, which basically paid for the materials. The labour was there in any case.

In June that year, Uncle Alan at Lickham asked me if I would go down and clip his sheep, as he could not get anyone to do them. I did this: it was the first time I had ever seen sheep ticks. Naturally I was asked in for lunch, and

LICKHAM HALL FARM
SCORBOROUGH
NEAR BEVERLEY, EAST YORKSHIRE

SALE OF LIVE AND DEAD FARM STOCK
including the entire
PEDIGREE SCORBOROUGH HERD OF

BRITISH FRIESIAN
CATTLE
the property of
Mr A PRESCOTT

which

DEE & ATKINSON

will Sell by Auction on

TUESDAY, 6th NOVEMBER, 1962

Sale to Commence at 1-30 p.m. with Implements
followed by Poultry, Sheep (at 2-30 p.m.), Cattle,
and Horses.

Auctioneers' Addresses:
The Exchange,   14 North Bar Street,
Driffield. (Tel. 3154/2)   Beverley. (Tel. 82621)

during the course of the meal Uncle Alan said he was going to retire in the autumn: if we wanted we could have the farm for £25,000. I came back home, full of enthusiasm, to tell Father we could have the farm for £25,000, to which he replied: 'Never deal with relations.' End of story.

The farm was subsequently bought by David Brotherton, of Whitwell-on -the-Hill, who had just come out of university. His mother wanted to set him up and this was the first farm that came available. He bought it privately for £26,000 on the January 6 1963. At the same time Uncle Alan sold Rose Cottage to Mr Burrell for £850. Father and I went to Uncle Alan's sale on November 6, when he sold all his cattle—Friesian cows—the top cow making £67.

Mr Brotherton sold the two paddocks at the back of the cottage to Mr Burrell for £400 in 1970. Uncle Alan gave George Money, who had been his cowman for donkey's years, the choice of the two cottages: Rose Cottage (where he, his wife and family were then living) or Davalon, (named for David, Alan and John, their sons). George and his wife chose Davalon, as, by that time, there was only John at home and they thought the house would be big enough for them as it was only two-up and two-down. Uncle Alan gave them this as a mark of gratitude. John Money died in 2012 and the house was subsequently sold by auction to Mr and Mrs H Thomas for £172,000. Both Alan and David said it was only fit for knocking down.

It had been a very dry summer and, as a result, the turnip or root crop in low 22 acre (bottom of 50 acre), did not grow very well—only at the top end where there was more moisture and it had been sown earlier.

It was a catchy harvest after a dry summer and we struggled to get all combined by the end of September. Lambs helped us finish combining the hillsides in 20 acre. Peter was baling with the Massey Ferguson baler most of harvest with Alf on the sledge. On October 16 I had to bale the hillsides in 20 acre after Lambs' combining. Mother and Von came to bring me a cup of tea about 5pm and Von said: 'I think it's time we were going to hospital.' Dr Nye had already said it was a small baby as it was due a fortnight earlier. I finished the hillsides with just the bales left to collect.

I took Von into East Riding General Hospital, Driffield, and went to the maternity ward where Sister Hardy took the small case I was carrying and said: 'Goodnight Mr Prescott. Ring in the morning.' I was dismissed.

I rang at 7am to be told that nothing had happened and then at 8.30am they rang me to tell me we had a son. Andrew Richard was 9lbs 13ozs. He was born bottom first (extended breach), having been induced. He had a lump the size of a hen's egg on the back of his head and a bruise across his nose. It was thanks to Mr Bibby, the East Riding gynaecologist, that he was born alive. A very proud moment. The next generation of Prescotts had arrived.

Von stayed in hospital for 10 days, as was the norm in those days. We had an electric fire in our bedroom for the first time as we had the cot in our room, which was called the ice box.

It was becoming obvious that our 780 combine hadn't sufficient capacity to cope with the increasing yield, so we ordered a new Claas Standard combine from Barrett of Bainton. This was £4,000, less the trade-in for the Massey Ferguson combine. This would be delivered the following spring.

January 6: Andrew was christened in Lund Church. We were in between vicars at the time so Canon Duckwith, a dear man who had been a prisoner-of-war held by the Japanese, took the service. Stephanie and Ted Whorley and William Lamb were Andrew's godparents.

The 1962/3 winter was very severe: it had started to freeze between Christmas and New Year, and the ground was frozen a good 12 inches below the surface. We had the ewes folded on turnips in the low 22-acre and Alf had to shepherd these sheep daily, giving them hay and corn only, as the turnips were frozen solid in the ground and could not be eaten by the sheep. In the end the nets were set round the whole field and the sheep given free run. The frost eventually began to ease a little on March 3. It had been a continuous hard frost since the end of December and, as a result of the thaw, everywhere was very muddy. Barrett's decided to bring the new combine by road from Bainton—as a result the combine got blathered up for a start.

That year I had entered two Red Poll cows in the Scottish Dairy Show, in Glasgow, to compete in the milk trials competition. We shared a transport with the Fullers from Kirby Moorside (the Lund Herd) and also Arnott Weightman (Butterwick Herd).

Tom Young, of North Dalton, took me and the two cows to Kirby Moorside, and then we had Turnbull's Transport to pick up the rest. We had to go down Sutton Bank, which was only just passable be-

Claas Matador Standard combine, 1963.

Aerial picture of Wold House. 1963, showing the new drier (1961) and the deep litter extension (1962). The shelter belt was felled and replanted in 1962.

cause the frost was so bad. Eventually we went across the A66 Bowes Moor road which, in those days, was only single carriageway, joining the A74 at Carlisle.

We eventually arrived in Glasgow at 6pm after a very hazardous journey. Fortunately, there had not been a lot of traffic on the roads. I got first for the intermediate class in milk and inspection and third with the senior cow. That started me off showing. The next show was the Newark and Nottingham Show, where the marquee in which we were housed, blew away so we all went home immediately after the judging. The Lincoln Show followed in June.

That spring, as with the last, Father spent most of his time working in the shelter belt round the stackyard, mowing in between the newly-planted trees. Now he had a companion; Andrew sat in his pram, rocking back and forth and chattering to him in his baby talk. Grandad thought the world of Fella, as he always called him.

During the summer we had Eastwood's building two bins in the barn, with an elevator pit to empty from a central point in the passageway. These two bins would hold a good 30 tons of barley each and were fed from the conveyor in the apex of the granary roof, which went from one end to the other. We could hold another 150 tons of grain in the granaries, which could be used for animal feed. Two or three years later John Dowson was putting the last ton or so of barley into the granary above the mill house when the floor collapsed, with all going into the mill house below.

We were going to the Yorkshire Show in July 1963 when Von was violently sick in York. That was when we realised she was pregnant with Helen.

Chapter 7—1964-1969

A ll this time Von was going with her father to see her mother in the White Hart Hospital in Harrogate. Her mother was suffering from Addison's disease and had been on massive doses of steroids which, in turn, had softened her bones so much that she was hardly able to walk. She came to us for a little while but had to go into hospital in Driffield after Christmas. She died on January 20 1964—sadly she never saw Helen.

In February I took father-in-law up to the Scottish Dairy Show to show three full-sister cows. We went along with Fullers, of Kirby Moorside, and Peter Aconley, a Friesian breeder, who was taking one cow.

I got the championship with Woldsman Rosalie, and first with heifer-in-milk, and inspection. She gave seven gallons of milk at 5.9 per cent butter-fat, which was higher than either the Friesians or Ayrshires. We missed out on the Glasgow Corporation Cup for that class, as the judge was of the Friesian persuasion. He knew we had a 21-point lead on milk points over the Friesian heifer and it would not have done for us to win.

It was later on that summer when the judge's brother-in-law, Frank Chapman, of York, came to buy two Red Poll heifers to go to Romania that I told him of this experience, not realising to whom he was related. That summer really set us off on the showing circuit, going to Newark and Nottingham, Lincoln, Great Yorkshire, Wetherby and Malton shows. That autumn we exported Woldsman Ringo to Brazil: he was out of one of the three cows shown in Scotland.

During February I was taking Von each Monday to see Mr Bibby in Driffield, as he didn't want her to have another big baby. She went about five weeks on the trot, each time taking her bag with her.

March 9 1964—Monday morning: we were busy sorting sheep in the foldyard, so Father took Von into Driffield. Of course this was the time he told her to stay. Von said Father took her to the ward door—the wards were wooden huts from the war—where he stood shuffling from one leg to another and said: 'You'll be alright from here will you?' and shot off.

I rang at 1pm and was told nothing was happening and she had had her dinner. Helen Jane was born at 2.55pm, weighing 7lb 10ozs, having been

Woldsman Rosalie—1963 Glasgow Dairy Show champion.

induced. The afterbirth weighed 5lbs 8ozs—the largest known to Mr Bibby, who had suspected twins. It went round the various teaching hospitals afterwards as a specimen. I rang at 4pm and have never lived it down that she was born ages before I knew. We were very happy to have a little daughter, making a pigeon pair.

Just after Helen was born we bought a new Ford Zodiac (95 BWF), which replaced the Ford Consul that we had bought second-hand only a year previously but had proved to be very unreliable: it would go so far and then slowly grind to a halt. You would wait a few minutes and off it would go again. The garage was beat with it—and we were fed up with it.

The Zodiac cost £1,200 new and was top of the Ford range. The same summer we bought the green Thames one-ton van, as the old grey Ford van packed up at the top of North Grimston hill—known now to the family as 'pork pie hill'. It broke down as I was returning from Yorkshire and Northern Wool Growers with 20 new sheep nets in the back. I had bought a pork pie and a steak and kidney pie (10d each—or 4p in today's money) at a shop in Norton on our way back. I had Andrew, 18 months, with me: he devoured the pork pie whilst I was being towed home by a very kind driver from Taylor's Timber Merchants of Driffield. He did not know who I was or where I was from—he just followed my indicator instructions from behind.

August 9: Helen was christened in Lund Church. As it was in interregnum we had Canon Duckwith taking services. Her godparents were Margaret Shipley and Margaret and John Prescott.

Woldsman Ringo—exported to Brazil.

Lund Warren Farm, Lund—487 acres—was sold privately to Maltas Farms Ltd for £100,000. David and Margaret Maltas and their four boys—Brian, Roger, Timothy and Geoffrey were from Roos. Greaves had to sell the farm after buying it from Cooke-Buttle some 18 months previously.

We had a brief trial with the Danish Red breed, and inseminated 10 cows with Madsen, out of which we only got three calves. AI in those days was not very reliable. In 1964 the Barber sisters from Kirby Overblow were retiring from farming; they had two pure bred cows from the original import, so we bought these and two or three cross breeds as well as their cattle wagon.

By this time the cowshed, where we had 18 cows tied up for milking, was becoming too small and we had to have two sittings for milking. We also needed to re-cover the front part of the foldyard as it was in need of a lot of repair. We took the plunge to re-cover the front part of the yard and also right over the existing cowshed and the foldyard. This we did in two parts, the back part being done first followed by the front. Naylor's of Driffield did this: we had to build brick pillars up to strengthen the existing walls and to get extra height. This was done by Hoggard's builders of Driffield. (I learned a long time later that Leo Hoggard was Val Thompson's stepfather). Grandad Carr and I did all the wiring with strip lights.

The first half at the back was put up under Sir Alec Douglas-Home's Tory Government in August and the second half in October/November under Harold Wilson's Labour Government. Getting this yard covered was marvellous. The cows were milking a lot better in the winter even though they were strip-grazing kale in snow.

All this time, from 1954 when we started milking the Red Polls, we had been milk recording. The number of cows being milked with bucket units was beginning to take too long so it was decided to put in a four-point herringbone parlour, which again was done by Hoggard's of Driffield. It had a pit in the centre, which saved a lot of hard work bending down and carrying milk. It took quite a while in the autumn of 1965 to install the parlour because of the groundworks needed.

Eric dug a very deep trench in front of the garage to accommodate a drain from the pit, which was continued across to the foldyard wall, in readiness to connect to the house sewerage much later. At first the milk was piped straight into milk churns against the house wall. The milk was cooled by a rotary-in-churn cooler. The churns were then put into the fridge in the cooler house at night only. The following year, 1966, we put in the 500-gallon bulk milk tank—we just managed to fill it in two days at spring. Billy took to the new system very quickly.

The tanker came up to the farm daily to collect the milk. This necessitated strengthening the road all around the front of the buildings and making a longer turning circle at the front for the tanker to back in. We put a drain in at the outside of a kerb in order to take all the surface water, and then concreted in front of the now office and old dairy, right round the front of the now weighbridge office.

1965-67

Von's father married Lil Casey in June that year; she was someone he had known before he married her mother. She had been married twice before, lived in Staithes but hailed from Stockton-on-Tees. She had no children and not many relatives—just a sister, Edie, who still lived in Stockton with her husband, Norman. They came to the wedding. Jack Gregory was Grandad's best man. Canon Duckwith married them in Lund Church. Uncle Tommy was commissioned to keep the drinks flowing—Uncle Tommy said he would have run out of money long before Canon Duckwith was topped up. He was a grand chap.

Andrew started at the Lund playgroup—all the mothers had got together and set up a playgroup for three mornings a week at a cost of 2s 6d a morning. They employed Muriel Massey, of Middleton, to be in charge, with all the mothers helping one week each on a rota basis. Nicholas Snowden and Paul Walker started at the same time—they seemed to have a ball.

Every year we bought 200 day-old Rhode Island Red/Light Sussex male chicks to rear for Christmas as well as 200 pullet chicks, same cross. These were all sex-linked, cockerels coming out white and the pullets brown. Von used to feed them in the park. Then at Christmas we used to dress them, usually on Von's birthday, it being a week before Christmas. They were sold to various people for many years. Harold Peck, from Beverley, always took the surplus. There was always an argument as to how much he was going to pay, particularly with the cull hens when they went as boilers. In those days a six-to-nine pound caponised cockerel would be 3s 6d (about £1.50 at today's prices) per pound, oven-ready including giblets.

Geese took more doing, particularly plucking. Billy, and anyone available, used to sit in the 'slum' plucking poultry with the fire roaring up the chimney, burning up the feathers. The geese used to have to have their feet scalded and skinned and put in the back opening of the goose for presentation. The kitchen was a bit like a butcher's shop with Mother and Von dressing poultry as fast as they could go. Many years later, when we were in Chile and going round a market, we stopped at a stall selling poultry and Margaret Shipley said: 'Who would ever want to buy chicken feet?' David Harrison, as quick as a flash, said: 'Someone who wants to scratch a living.' Recollections of scalding geese feet.

November 2 1966: Father was 65 and, as such, could draw his state pension. Mother, being six years older, could not draw a pension until Father had claimed the married person's pension at 65. She would not have got a pension at all if Father died before he had claimed his so, very reluctantly, he claimed it. However, in those days, you could not draw the retirement pension if you were still in business so he had to hand over his share of the business to me.

Unfortunately, as far as Mother was concerned, his share of the partnership and business, which was originally left to her, was now given to me and no provision was made for her at all. Blakeston and Lundy, who were his solicitors, should have made him aware of the fact but omitted to do so. So much for solicitors.

During the harvest Father became very ill. We were touched when Eric, the hostel man with learning difficulties, came to the door with a jar of malt extract, for which he had walked into Beverley to buy, to give to Father.

Father, by this time had taken to sleeping downstairs in the chair in the sitting room in front of the fire. He got progressively worse with the emphysema and eventually died at 3.30am on December 27 1967.

Billy was off ill at the same time with flu so I had to go down to his house that morning and fetch him up to do the milking. We were all ill with flu. Grandad Carr and Lil were staying, as was Molly Course and her father, who had only one leg. He became very ill at the same time; Molly took him home and he died in January 1968.

Father's funeral was on the December 29 1967. The church was full, which was a nice tribute, and just Mother, Steph, Von and I went to the crematorium in Hull.

Steph came over from Liverpool, and I met her in Hull on Wednesday December 27. The following day Mother, Steph and I went to the solicitors in the afternoon—Mother was upset, as she got nothing. Steph got £2,000 out of the farm—with the overdraft being £4,000 and a new bank manager taking over on Monday, January 1 1968. I got the freehold of Wold House Farm, 126 acres with a 44-year mortgage. It was not a wonderful Christmas for the children and a good job that Grandad Carr, Lil and Molly were there. Margaret Snowden, Rosalind Walker and Margaret Maltas were very kind having Andrew and Helen: all the children played together a lot anyway.

To complete the picture of that unforgettable Christmas, John and Anne Dowson were married in Bradford on Boxing Day and then came to live with Alf and Mrs Dowson at Vicarage Farm.

Andrew started school at Middleton in the autumn. He went to the old school on Front Street; they had to walk in twos round to the village hall for their dinner. Vicky Burdass had to look after him. Later they moved into the new school on Warter Road. It was open plan and very up-to-date.

1968

January 1: Mother and I tried to go to Malton Hospital to see Uncle Eddie, but only got as far as Fimber roundabout as the road was closed being beneath six feet of snow, as was the Sledmere to Malton road. Emma Du Pre, sister of Miss Carter (the Lund School ex-headmistress), died at the same time as Father and her funeral was on New Year's Day.

January 2: two men came from the Midland Bank Trustee Branch, in Hull (Midland Bank were Father's executors). They took over the administration and charged £600 for the pleasure. Never use a bank as a trustee— they always take their expenses out first.

Uncle Eddie, Father's eldest brother had visited just before Christmas when I was sawing logs into the coal house (the old 'stores'). I asked him if he would like some logs. I put him two bags in the back of his van and he went in to see Father. After half an hour he came out, looking very shocked, and said: 'I shan't have time to burn all those.'

He drove back to Malton and had a small stroke on the way. He ended up in hospital over Christmas and died on January 3. Uncle Eddie was 14 years older than Father. Mother, Von and I went to York Crematorium for Uncle Eddie's funeral—there were only 13 of us there. Uncle Oswald came up from Lincolnshire. Mother caught the train down to Bournemouth afterwards to go to stay with Molly Course and help her.

It was at this time that we realised that if we wanted any more children now was the time. Yvonne had been reluctant to have another child whilst we were living with my parents but we felt that time was moving on and now the house was ours. Mother was less than pleased when we told her we were having another child.

Stan Shepherd, from Birds Eye Foods, came round wanting to know if we were interested in growing peas in the summer. We agreed to grow 50 acres of peas in the field across the road. We had our inaugural meeting at the Rose and Crown pub, Beverley, in early March. We elected Cliff Wilson, of Cliffe, as chairman, John Dunning as secretary and Peter Blacker as treasurer and Beverley Pea Growers was formed. We all had to put in £2 per acre to buy our cutters. In those days we were growing 1,000 acres in the group, which had about 22 members. This was a new venture—Birds Eye had only started growing peas in this area the year before, freezing them at the Hull factory.

We were also persuaded to grow eight acres of Brussels sprouts in the field next to the paddock. These were a nightmare to grow and we had to have contract labour in to hoe, top and de-leaf, cut at the base at harvest, and then load onto trailers, which we delivered to Hessle Road in Hull by tractor.

We got the last loads loaded on the Sunday before the weather broke. We had to have three tractors to pull these loads out of the field on the Monday morning. They returned £200 per acre gross which, in those days, was a very good return but I quickly realised that they were a very catchy and labour-intensive crop. The peas did quite well, yielding 35cwt per acre and netting nearly £50 per acre. They were harvested before grain harvesting started and we were able to cultivate the pea stubble, hulm in and have an excellent seed bed by October 7, when we drilled it with winter wheat.

Now that I was completely in charge we quickly disbanded the flock of sheep with David Maltas buying the majority of the ewes with lambs at foot. The cull ewes went into Driffield Market, and all the sheep nets, stakes, troughs, feeders, etc went into the Driffield implement sale. The cash from disbanding the sheep enterprise paid off the outstanding Barkers & Lee Smith bill and quite a few other long-standing debts. It proved to be one of the best moves we could have made, as it released more land for arable crops such as peas and wheat.

Alf, the shepherd, was absorbed into the general farm work. The hostel man, Eric, was no longer required, and that saved on wages—we had had to pay for his transport each day and these costs kept rising. We were sorry, Eric was mentally handicapped and was doing the only sort of work of which he was capable and which he was quite happy doing. He would always find a job to do—even if it was one you didn't really want doing.

Work began to be more streamlined: there was more straw to bale and yields were getting bigger. It was at this time, through the pea group, that we joined what we called the Wheat Yield Efficiency group (WYE), where we would go round members' fields where wheat was grown after peas, and discuss methods, etc.

From then on yields went from two to four tons per acre by 1984, when the whole farm—600-odd acres—averaged 84cwt per acre. By the time harvest was over we were getting to the stage that it was obvious the Claas Matador Standard was not big enough to cope with our needs, so we did a deal with Charlie Barrett to buy a new Claas Senator, top of the range at £4,000, with the Standard thrown in as part-exchange.

July 16: we had the crane booked to start erecting the second-hand Dutch barn we had bought from Theakstons. All the steelwork cost £600, and there are five 20-foot bays. It was a pouring wet day and John and I were up the ladders all day, bolting the stanchions to the trusses. We had everything tied to trees in the wood, posts, tractors, all on long ropes, and eventually got all the purlins on by night. We finished by 6pm getting all the steel work secured.

The same day Anne, John's wife, had their first child, Karen. They were then living with Alf and Mrs Dowson and Peter at Vicarage Farm. It was then that we managed to buy numbers 39 and 41 South Street in Middleton-on-the-Wolds, then five and six Pantgarth, for £1,250 from Mrs Dulson, with the proviso that she could remain a tenant in number six for her lifetime. Eastwood's then had to put in a new bathroom, toilet and utility converting the old coalhouse and attached sheds. John, Anne and Karen moved in just before Christmas.

It was about now that we finally persuaded Andrew Marr that the foldyard at Vicarage Farm was not a lot of use in its present state, so he agreed to us getting prices for covering the whole yard. This we did, and Naylor's of Driffield finally covered the yard in two 40-foot spans with a valley gutter down the middle—a big mistake, never install a valley gutter. We went halves with the cost. The total cost of Naylor's bill was £2,400, of which we each paid £800 after grant.

Friday **October 18 1968**: I took Von into Driffield hospital but Mr Bibby said he had come to her twice in Driffield, so she had to go to him at the new maternity hospital in Beverley. Angus Granville, who had lots of dark hair, arrived into the world at 6.30pm weighing 7lbs 4ozs. We were delighted to have another son. Mr Bibby, leaning against the wall viewing the situation, said: 'Right, now have you had enough?' so that was our little family completed. Every night when I went in to see Von and Angus I gave them the latest update on the Brussels sprout saga: we used to call him the Brussels sprout kid—perhaps that's why he never liked them to eat.

On the very same day Stephanie was having a second operation for a brain tumour; the surgeon said if she did not she would not live for another six months. This operation would not cure her, but would give her some respite, perhaps for up to 10 years—it was, in fact, five years.

Angus was christened in Lund Church on December 1 by the Rev Arthur Lawes, a family friend as well as vicar of the parish. His godparents were Liz Wells, John Richardson and Ben Goodwin. On December 27 we took Andrew and Helen to the Christmas party in the village hall and it started to snow heavily, so we had to leave early. It was a good job we didn't delay, as we got as far as Hall's first gateway at Corporation Farm and came to a full stop in a snowdrift. I had to walk home, leaving Von and the children in the car. The only tractor easily available was the Ford with the rotavator on, which was a good thing for ballast as it levelled a bit of the snow. I then towed the car home with Von behind the wheel. We were not out again for about a week.

1969

As a result of buying the new combine, Barrett's invited me to go on a trip to the Claas factory in Germany. I took Ben Goodwin from Skipsea, who was Angus's godfather, Dick Webb and Mr Bird from Hornsea area. We went on February 11. It was snowing a blizzard as we went up Middleton Wold road, and we got a puncture at Kipling House so had to change the wheel.

We tried every garage on the way to Doncaster to get a new tyre, to no avail. As it was still snowing hard we decided to head off to Luton. My passengers said: 'We'll never make it.'

Ken Grantham met us at the airport and greeted us with: 'Where the hell have you been?' With that we parked the car, threw our bags on the plane and were off. We came back to Luton two days later after being at the factory and a night club where we drank 14 bottles of wine between 10 of us (it must have been weak). We came back on a wing and a prayer—with no spare wheel through slush and snow. I went into Barrett's the following morning to get a new tyre, but fortunately it was only a four inch nail straight into the tyre. The night after we were supposed to be going to Pocklington Hunt Ball but didn't as it was snowing so heavily.

February 17: Von and I went into partnership with the business. On February 19 we asked Bill Atkin from Pinkney's solicitors, Bridlington, to bid on behalf of us for Alwyn Middleton's 52.426 acres of land at Lund, giving him a limit of £18,000.

He went to the sale at the Conservative Club, Beverley, and ended having to pay £18,250, exceeding the limit we had set. He came back to the farm in an absolute sweat—so much so that he had made a mess of the blank cheque we had given him for the deposit and had to come back for another. It had made £348 2s 5d per acre, which was an unheard of price; it was generally agreed in the area that it would bankrupt us. The previous July, Ken Walker bought Albert Hunsley's 31.128 acres of land on Lockington Road, originally farmed by Robert Prescott in 1859, for £8,600—£276 5s 8d per acre. This land is now Paul Walker's. The same day the specialist said Andrew had to have his tonsils out.

This money was borrowed from the AMC—£18,500 at nine and a half per cent over 15 years. I took out a life insurance policy to cover the outstanding amount should I die before the expiry date. I quickly realised how easy it was to borrow money and, at that time, inflation was running high.

We quickly uprooted the trees all around the paddock at the crossroads and all the dividing hedges between the fields, of which there were six. We bulldozed the bank at the roadside at the crossroads into the field as it was a very high bank. All the hedges and tree roots were put into the pit on the main road side. I think it was the talk of the neighbourhood: prairie farming—52 acres in one field. There were 16 acres of newly-sown clover ley in the middle of all this but, as it was not very good, we ploughed it out. There were 12 acres of winter wheat which we left.

Mr Benny Lamb and Horace Marshall and William Lamb were driving sheep up Wold Road, and he was not very pleased that there was no roadside hedge. The council had already told us not to obscure visibility by replanting trees or hedges on the corner.

Helen started school at Middleton and just about drove Liz Walker mad. She ended up tying her to a chair to stop her wandering round the open-plan school. She was just interested.

By early April Billy Cock had gone down with flu and was off work. One Saturday morning I went out to milk but all I could do was get up and sit down on the box in the dairy, having absolutely no energy whatsoever. Fortunately 12-year-old Stephen Woodall from the village was coming up to earn a bit of pocket money. He ended up milking for two weeks and looking after the stock until Billy returned to work. Luckily it was over the Easter holidays.

Von called the doctor and he diagnosed me with jaundice (hepatitis). I was in bed for a fortnight until one Sunday morning when I went with Von to fetch the children and Geoffrey and Tim Maltas from Sunday school. We took the Maltas boys home and, after going to see the cows on Far Field tops, returned to Wold House to be greeted at the front doorstep by Dr Clements. He handed me a letter and said: 'Take this to Beverley Westwood tomorrow morning and expect to be admitted.'

I was there for six weeks' enforced bed rest, as that was the only known cure then, except for some vile medicine I had to take. David Maltas, who was a very good neighbour, came down most days to help Von running the farm.

After I came out of hospital it was hay-making time in Little Wold; the first thing I did was to walk across Park to see what it was like. It was the first walking I had done for two months.

Pea vining was immediately before harvest and John Dowson went as one of the cutter drivers for swathing the peas in front of the mobile viner, working 12-hour shifts, swapping night to day shifts weekly. This usually took about five weeks, but was good money for the men, as they were on overtime rate for the whole of the period. In a dry year it was easy, and a short season, but in a wet time it was a very different story.

The whole 'circus' moved from field to field, governed by Birds Eye field managers. Latterly John Dowson went as fitter in the mobile workshop with an experienced mechanic. They had to sharpen the knives for the cutters, as well as doing any running repairs to the machines. In our 'red' group there were four cutters, four viners, one high lift cart and a field manager per shift. These were trailed viners in the early days, pulled by usually a four-wheel drive tractor loaned by farmers in the group, and paid for separately.

Harvest was much easier that year with the new combine, which John Dowson was driving. We had also got a new Claas baler, which was a higher density model than the Massey Fergie, but it still involved gathering up the many thousand bales after they had all been stacked in heaps of eight by Tom Reed, John Horsley and Mr Harper, who Von fetched from Lund. They were a wonderful team: they were all aged around 80 but thoroughly enjoyed themselves—working at their own pace but still getting the job done and earning a bit of pocket money.

After combining all the corn it was time to collect all the thousands of bales, each one being handled many times. At first we had a bale gripper on the fore-end loader, which could put eight bales on at a time, but nearly always had to be loaded by a stacker before being taken home on a trailer to be made into a stack in the stackyard. This was the worst part and hardest work of harvest. As everyone was tired this was the last straw—literally. But it was not as bad as when they were sheaves and much more rewarding.

During all this harvest time Von and Mother were busy providing lunches for however many men were working at any given time, twice or even three times a day dependent on how late they were working or going for spare parts from various quarters, mainly Barrett's of Bainton. It was hard work for everybody. This was as well as looking after the children and being part of the taxi run rota to Middleton School, one week each taken by Margaret Snowden, Christine Walker and Von. At one time they had seven children in the car. This continued for 10 years without any problems. No seat belts: just pile them all in.

By Christmas 1969 we had central heating installed. We had no time clock or thermostat to control the boiler at that stage so, although there was snow on the ground we spent Christmas Day with the windows open as we were all so hot. Grandad Carr and Lil were there of course. We had the thermostat fitted in the middle of January.

W e had Major Agnew and his manager to stay and they bought a bull—a pure Danish Red, which was out of one of our pure-bred Danish cows. They stayed the night and as Helen, almost six, was going to bed she kissed us all, turned to the major and his manager and said: 'Night boys' and tripped off. We all killed ourselves laughing—she was a card.

Herbert Appleton rang, asking if we were still interested in buying a house in Middleton as 10 South Street was vacant and we could have the three cottages—6, 8 and 10 South Street—for £1,500.

We needed to secure a house for the future as it was impossible to get a man if you didn't have a house to offer him, so we accepted his offer immediately and the houses were put in our joint names.

We immediately set in motion improvements to the three houses as the toilets were at the bottom of the gardens and there were no indoor bathrooms. Eastwood's put in a common drain across the three properties for the sewage, and then proceeded to build onto each house a bathroom, kitchen and rear entrance with a flat roof. Number 6 was occupied by Amy Norman and number 8 by Mrs Horne, whose son, Ted, had worked for us when I was a baby before he joined the Forces as a career. The rent for these two houses was controlled at 7s 6d per week and could only be increased annually by 2s 6d per week. After the improvements had been done a year later the rent was 10s, or 50p in today's money.

Andrew and Helen had started horse-riding classes at Jean Lawler's at Bainton: I think Andrew liked mucking out and laying concrete for them better than the riding.

January 17: two years and three weeks after Father's death we received a cheque from the Midland Bank executor and trustee company for £223 18s 3d, the balance of his estate.

In the spring Paley and Donkin, of Cottingham, carpeted from the front door up the stairs, along the landings and down the back stairs. The year previously I had knocked a way through from the back 'men's bedroom' to opposite the bathroom. There had been a door there years before, but my grandfather had it bricked up to prevent any fraternisation between men and the maids. The new car-

LICKHAM FARM

Dee & Atkinson
DRIFFIELD and BEVERLEY
EAST YORKSHIRE

pet was a wonderful achievement—there was no longer a 'runner' carpet, held by brass rods at each step or the hall tiles to be washed and polished at least weekly. The carpet came with underlay and fitting and cost £2 19s 9d (£2.98) per square yard.

The Conservative Party won the General Election. Thank goodness to see the back of Harold Wilson. Most unexpectedly Ted Heath was Prime Minister.

June 17: Andrew Marr and Tony Todd, his agent, came to see me regarding a rent review on Vicarage Farm. The rent went from £3 per acre to £5, which was a bit severe. They agreed to damp-proof the house and suggested getting Eastwood's to 'tank the house out'—in other words line all the downstairs walls with horizontally corrugated bitumastic fibre, which would be rendered over with sand and cement with a skim finish.

They also said they were going to try to buy Alan Walker's 101-acre plot of land next door to Clay Field at Middleton and asked if we were interested, to which I responded: 'Yes, we are.' To this Andrew Marr said he would take a very dim view of it if we bid against him. In the event it made £46,000 and British China Clay bought it. The same people also bought Bainton Heights Farm—400 acres for £140,000.

After we had bought Road Ends field, Bill Pinkney said he could sell us Bainton Heights for £140,000. I thought that was a bit too much of a stretch for us. My yardstick was that we should be able to pay the annual AMC fee out of the current profits, before we bought the said land, and that would have been a bit too much. With hindsight…

I went to Dee and Atkinson's saleroom in Driffield, where they were selling several farms: Bainton Heights—403 acres, made £140,000 to British China Clay; Alan Walker's land at Middleton—101 acres made £46,000 to British China Clay; JSR Farm at North Dalton—92 acres made £30,000; Wilkinson's Eastfield Farm, Cranswick—222 acres made £49,000 to Hubert Thompson; Stabler's at Rotsea was withdrawn at £75,000 for 405 acres.

Whilst they were there I asked Mr Todd who had bought Lickham Hall the previous day at the sale. He said that it had been withdrawn, as there were no bids. The 16-acre field on Beverley Road had been sold for £3,000 to Peter Johnson.

This made me think. Andrew and Helen swam at the Francis Scaife Pool at Pocklington, and this particular night I had gone with Von to take them. As we came back down Middleton Wold Road, I suggested that we call and see what Mr Brotherton would take for Lickham. He was not in so we left a card. He rang me the next day and I offered him £35,000 lock, stock and barrel—it was 168 acres in all. Two weeks later he rang and accepted our offer. The crops were valued at £6,000.

We paid Mr Brotherton a deposit of £3,500, and took over more or less straight away at the end of July. There were 14 fields all; 13 acres in the bog were uncultivated, just growing weeds and seven feet high bulrushes. The barley crops were full of wild oats and the field on the roadside next to Taylors was oats—of both varieties—with a small patch of winter wheat of about five acres. The whole place was a mess.

I combined it and put the corn into the drier shed, with the aid of a six-inch augur, on top of above-ground laterals, covered with hessian. There were six bins in all with a total of about 200 tons. The bit of wheat, about 20 tons, we brought home.

The best thing Mr Brotherton had done to the farm since he bought it was that he had re-roofed the rear part of the house and put up the new drier and Dutch barn—a useful shed. We also took over 10 or a dozen cats and had to come every day to feed them. The corn was estimated to us at £30 per ton, which was the going rate before harvest.

By the time we had finished harvest the corn had doubled in price to nearly £60 a ton, so that was a bit of luck.

It was about this time that we sold, for £2,000, the gardens next to 10 South Street for a building plot for two houses. It was sold to a Mr Barrett, whose address was the Black Bull, Escrick. He said he wanted to build one to live in and the other to sell to cover the costs. In the event he squashed three houses onto the site, taking a bit more land from each side to make this possible. The boundary wall into Eddie's garden collapsed under the strain shortly afterwards. We tried to get him to pay for the extra land he had taken and the damage he had done but, as our solicitor Bill Atkin said, he was a man of straw. So that was that.

I had a strange experience whilst on the combine at Lickham; I was coming down towards Leconfield, in the field on Railway Side, roughly down the line of the now new hedgerow, when the combine was making such a noise I thought it was going to blow up. I managed to get it out of gear and the engine stopped and with that a Vulcan bomber came overhead coming in to land at Leconfield Aerodrome. I could have touched it with a short stick—nothing wrong with the combine at all. The end-of-runway lights were at the bottom of Lounts' fields on Arram Road.

As soon as we had finished harvest I sprayed the whole farm off with four pints per acre of Gramoxone as it was full of wicks everywhere. Next we got Clifford Watts in with his bulldozer and he knocked up all the intermediate hedges, barring the one next to Clark Field, which was all grass at the time and did not get sprayed. Watts also bulldozed the pond in on Railway Side and the pond behind the stack yard.

John Sleight came to work for us at the beginning of October. He and Margaret Starkey were married on November 7 and went to live in the house at Lickham. It was a bit primitive with the water pump, which was always leaking, under the sink in the kitchen.

We bought a new Ford 5000 from Richardson's of Driffield (VWF 657J) with a three-furrow reversible plough and John ploughed the whole farm with this during the winter. The following year John and Stephen Woodall dug an open dyke in the 13 acres of bog, from the beck at the lowest point straight up towards Taylors, and left it open for the summer. Stephen was ferrying two and a half inch wide half-sleepers from back to front of the tractor as John dug out the dyke. By the time he got to the electric power line it was virtually dry. The rubbish was rotavated after we had sprayed it off with Gramoxone. By the end of the summer it was completely dry and during the winter John and Stephen potted the open dyke with six-inch drain pots. There was a spring just towards the house from the dyke, which John dug out and filled with chalk. We put a 20-foot steel pipe from the chalk into the new dyke drain. We sowed the 13 acres of bog, which was unusable before, with Italian rye grass in spring 1972.

1971

February 15: sterling was decimalised from pounds, shillings and pence (240 old pence to the pound) to pounds and pence. We were assured that it would make no difference to the pound in our pocket—but it did.

As a sample of the bills we used to receive: February 26 1971: paid Barrett's bill of £584 for 1968/9. He used to only send a bill every year or maybe two—the trouble was, you dreaded it when it came.

In March we bought a second-hand Massey Ferguson 135 (MFW 451F) for £650. We swapped the 1962 Super Major model (4105 WF) for a 1965 10/60 Nuffield (CWF 796C). These were approximately worth £300 each.

March 13: John and Anne Dowson had their second daughter, Anne Marie. At the same time Andrew and Helen were going to Jean Lawler's at Bainton for riding lessons, at a cost of £5 a morning for the two. We had a portrait of Angus done by Mrs Varley, of Etton, to match those she had done of Andrew and Helen, at a cost of £7.35.

At the same time we had a rent increase from the Hotham Estate: from April 6 1971 the rent would be £6.75 per acre for the 138 acres we rented from them.

In the spring of 1971 we sowed all of Railway Side and in front of the house down to the bog with spring barley, which came out a very thick crop. When Von, the kids, dogs and I walked across it in May, a cloud of dust rose: mildew as we had never seen it before.

That summer we bought a giant Matador combine from Barrett's for £1,800 second-hand. Originally it was from Holtbys of Ferriby. John and Tom Sleight combined all of Lickham with that and came up to Wold House as and when.

We started draining the very worst places in the autumn of 1971, with the aid of farm improvement grants. First of all we did the bit below the stackyard, putting an outflow straight into the Scorborough Beck. A new main outfall into the beck on Railway Side, six inches down to four inches, was to be added to later on. We also put in laterals straight into the beck next to Clark Field, where Mr Brotherton had drained it at 22 yards; we put in intermediate ones, so the whole lot was drained at 11 yards. John Binnington from Hornsea was the surveyor and drew up all the plans, Richardson's from Holderness did the first two schemes and Arnott's from Leven did the rest of the drainage work. In fact between 1971 and 1983 the whole farm was drained at 11 yard intervals.

1972

This was the year we joined the European Economic Community—known as the Common Market. At the time there were only six member states and it was designed to be a common market—and no more than that.

January 6: Uncle Allan from Lickham (then living in Wylies Road, Beverley) died aged 80. I took Mother over to see Aunty Ethel and fetched her back in the evening. The funeral was held at Scorborough Church on January 10: the church was full.

We bought a pony named Black Tiger from Taylors at Cottingham for £80: it was very quiet and thin, but after a week of better feeding it suddenly came to life and threw Helen off at the bottom of the front paddock. As a result Von had to rush her to Westwood Hospital suffering from a broken wrist. Andrew could ride it but it was now very strong. Subsequently we sold it to Anne Cooke at Mount Pleasant. They changed its name to Kes and it went on to win lots of jumping classes: they knew what they were doing.

In **June** I went with David Maltas and the Aldbrough Discussion Group to Boots Farm at Nottingham. The following day we went to Scotland with David and I bought 29 store bullocks for grazing at Lickham.

We bought a new automatic Ford Granada in April paying £2,000 less £525 for the Zodiac trade-in. At the same time we got a bill from Eastwood's for £3,000 for the improvements to the three cottages in Middleton. We also got a tenant for number 10—a Mrs Clews.

Iris Taylor finally finished working in the house; Von had been ferrying her to and fro twice a week since her family had moved from Lund to Beverley. Muriel Ellis from Middleton started work for three mornings a week, when one or other of us would fetch her and take her back. She was Percy Ellis's wife, who worked at Jack Soanes' Central Garage in Middleton.

1973

January 15: we bought a new Commer 22cwt van from Aldred's in Driffield; it was pale green, £955 on the road with the registration FBT 628L. This replaced the old Thames dark green van and was mainly for John Sleight's use at Lickham.

In **March** Billy Cock retired. It was a sad day as he was part of the family having worked for us for so long; he had started in May, 1936. He had me following him around when I was a child and then our three in turn: he made them small pitchforks and one or another was always in his wake with a wisp of hay on their fork. He was very patient. To start with he had all his meals in the house but when he moved to Vicarage Farm he went back home to Mrs Cock to eat. They had nearly three years there before Mrs Cock became ill, when they moved to Back Street, Middleton. He walked to work up through Middleton Woods and if the weather was bad either Von or I took him home. He came to milk just mornings only until we got a man—Denis Rugg started in April but didn't last very long: two months in fact.

Andrew went to Cundall Manor Preparatory School in April and was quite glad to have left Middleton—headmaster John Goodrick had moved to a school in Willerby and Middleton had had three different head teachers in a year.

It was not easy leaving him but Cundall's headmaster Jeremy Valentine, helped by his wife Sue, ran a brilliant school: we like to think that Andrew was very happy there. We paid £190 for the first term.

John and Mr Sleight started demolishing the covered yard at Lickham in the spring, knocking down both the milk house and bull pen in the corner of the yard and cleaning up the entire yard ready for Crendon erecting the

Andrew ready for a new school pictured with Angus and Helen.

Aerial view of Wold House, 1973.

new building. The total cost of that was £3,181 with the total grant being £1,368.67; this was done on actual costs. Arthur Day's price for installing two 750-watt halogen lights was £50. At the same time we agreed to erect a 90-foot by 30-foot Dutch barn at Vicarage Farm, again with Crendon at a cost of £1,824. This was all done before harvest in July.

In addition we had to make better provision for drying increased amounts of corn as the four small bins could not cope with the heavier yields. We installed central cylinders in the four bigger Simplex bins with a tunnel down the back side of the bins and a separate delivery to each bin. The total cost of this was £1,660; there was no grant on the fan itself, but there was grant on the tunneling, etc, which was £321.

In **June** Hargreaves tarmacked the farm road from the bottom gate round the front, into the stackyard past the workshop and up to Park gate. They made an excellent job of it. The total cost was £1,727.10 with a grant of £568. 48 towards it; it was well worth doing.

At this time we bought a 16-foot Welton Miravistor caravan with a 14-foot awning in very good condition for £580 from some people at Willerby. Subsequently we sold the awning for £50 and bought a new 16-foot one from Navarac in North Dalton.

As we fetched Andrew home from Cundall at the end of his first term, we called at Swinton Grange, near Malton, to see Eddie Jowsey, who was looking for a dairyman's job as Col Berens, who milked Ayrshires, was going out of production.

We arrived about 6pm when he had just finished work and Pauline, his wife, who was pregnant, had six children all ready for bed: the house was spotlessly clean.

He got the job and moved into 41 South Street, Middleton on September 11 1973. He had said he never stayed anywhere longer than four years but he stayed with us for 21 years and had two more children.

Angus in the milking parlour with Eddie Jowsey.

Eddie ruled his family with a rod of iron but he had a soft spot for Angus, who used to gather up an armful of clothes and take them out into the cowhouse in the morning where Eddie, who started at 6am (always had done and always would), dressed him and chattered to him.

In the **July** of this year Ted rang to ask if we would fetch Steph for a couple of weeks as she was not well. We had a terrible journey; we thought the tumour had got a real grip. She was ill on the way up and, 475 miles and 14 hours later, we got her to Wold House. It was all pretty horrendous.

She was very ill whilst with us and had to go into hospital in early August. She was desperate to see Ted and the children after about a month and insisted on going home; she had to be transported in an ambulance with the ambulances meeting half-way and swapping the patient over.

She was at home for a few days and then telephoned asking Mother if she could come back. Mother went to Von and asked: 'What do we do?' Von said that we couldn't have her as it was not fair on the ambulance service, which had been so good.

Steph died on **October 1**. Ted rang and asked Mother if she wanted a church service and naturally she said: 'Yes.' Mother, Von and I went for the funeral; there were Ted's parents and his brother and wife at the house, so

Vicarage Farm in 1974—when the rent per acre doubled.

we all went to church together. There was one person in the church—our cousin Raymond Cogswell, who was over from South America where he worked on an estancia for Vestey Foods, the big meat company.

His mother, who was very close to my mother, had told him about Steph's death so he just came and we were very glad to see him. Ted had not told Steph's nursing colleagues or any of her friends when the funeral was so, of course, they did not go. It was all very sad.

September 4: Angus started school at Middleton. It was Von's week on school run; she came back very down-hearted, Angus being the last one to go to school.

September 5: we started to burn Road Ends wheat straw after we had baled two headland swaths and dragged round the outside. We backfired down Clark's hedge side and then along the bottom. Once we got onto the main road side the wind took the fire across the field and by the time we had got to the top end of the field, the whole field had been burned. We went round the field to make sure there was no stray fire left burning and then went home.

When we got into the stackyard at Wold House the ash was just beginning to fall there. That was one hour after starting to fire; I have never seen anything go so quickly in my life. It took longer to back fire than to burn the whole field.

The Maltas family bought the 800-odd acre Hunterheck Farm, at Moffat in Scotland, for £220,000 in September. Brian, the eldest son had been at school at The Barony, Dumfries; he loved it there and has stayed ever since.

October 18: Angus had his fifth birthday party; he had been to Angela Bulmer's birthday party a couple of weeks earlier, so she came to his. Von mentioned in her diary that Angela had said: 'I love Helen; I wish I lived with her.'

John and Alf Dowson swapped houses on **October 24** that year, Alf and Mrs Dowson moving to 39 South Street, and John, Anne, Karen, and Anne Marie, going to Vicarage Farm.

The whole of that summer Andrew and Helen had been going to the Francis Scaife pool in Pocklington to learn to swim and, in the October, Helen joined the Dolphin Swimming Club there. That involved more trips to Pocklington for Von as Helen swam two or three nights a week—and sometimes more—both away and at home. Helen learned her tables on the journeys to and fro and was commended by Mr Sykes for not needing to use a calculator in class.

We finally got the mill mix and cubing plant finished off in the mill house, which had been an ongoing project for the previous two or three years, and we managed to claim a grant on that, a matter of some £900. It was a bit of a slow job to operate and never 100 per cent successful.

1974

New Year's Day 1974 was the first year that January 1 became a Bank Holiday.

In February Marrs doubled the rent for Vicarage Farm from £5 to £10 per acre set for the next three years; this was quite a hike. They had just bought the 355-acre Bainton Balk for £356,000. They kept it for six years then sold it in 1980 to Peter Hepworth for £1.2 million.

Andrew was helping Eddie to castrate some calves. When they had finished he asked: 'Will they be heifers now?' Eddie told me that he had been a good help and when I gave him £2 wages for his work he burst into tears.

Francis Jackson had us grow seed corn for ACC and we grew 52 acres of

Zephyr across the road and another 52 acres of Midas at Road Ends.

The Post Office at Lund closed around this time. After delivering mail around the village Joan Gurney had cycled round the Wolds; she always arrived with us by about 9am and had a cup of tea before carrying on to Clay Field and Horn Hill Top. The round was then put onto van delivery and we have never ever received the mail as early as we did when Joan was delivering. Originally it had been deemed a walking round but when she walked it with the 'man from the Royal Mail' he quickly agreed that she needed a bike as he was exhausted.

We started putting up an extension to the workshop that year; I had bought 10 stanchions at a sale at Holme-upon-Spalding Moor and Norman Colley made the clear span trusses to fit the old workshop size; we put up 15-foot wood purlins between. I built up the walls all the way round, with a window in each bay round the back and large sliding doors all across the front side. I also built an inspection pit in the second bay.

We got it completed by harvest, just back-filling the sides of the pit before we concreted. On a very wet day in harvest, John came haring back to the farm with the combine and parked over the inspection pit with one big wheel on the loose back-fill. The weight of the combine pushed in the pit wall. We had to get Bill Fussey to lift the combine up and pull it backwards. That was before the floor was concreted. The total cost of the extension on standard costs was £4,492 and we got one third of that back in grant. The farm improvement grants were invaluable; people who did not take advantage of them were soon left to realise the error of their ways.

June 15: my father-in-law retired from work. Latterly he had been superintendent of the East Yorkshire (Wolds Area) Water Board. He had joined Bridlington Borough Council as a plumber when he came out of the Royal Engineers in 1946 and had gone through all the changes the water industry had faced. He ended up as water superintendent but was much happier when he could work with the men out in all weathers.

As he was a trained plumber/electrician, he was most useful to us and did a lot of the wiring and plumbing round the farm after Von's mother died. He also helped with corn-carting in harvest, glazing windows, etc and helping me lay blocks in the extension to the combine shed (now the workshop). We got on very well.

June 26: we bought a Mercedes car (NVN 700M) for £2,700 with 8,000 miles on the clock, with our car going in part exchange for £1,000. It had been a director's car and was a very good, reliable vehicle—the only problem being it was a long way to go to Pickering to get it serviced.

Just after we bought the car we took the caravan over to Southport and had a few days with the children there before Mother and Mrs Farnaby arrived on the train at Lime Street Station, Liverpool. Helen went with me to collect them. I was unfamiliar with Liverpool city centre so asked for directions from a black man, who was standing at a bus stop in the pouring rain. He said: 'You take me, I show you.' He knew the way on foot, but after he had taken us through the Mersey tunnel and back again, he got out and left us to it. Mother and Mrs Farnaby stayed for a week and then we fetched them back.

We got approval from MAFF to convert the deep-litter hut into a calf-rearing house, which would accommodate 66 calves in total by the time we had finished it at Christmas. By the following spring it was filled with calves but unfortunately that was the only time it was ever used as the calves got very expensive and the disease problem from buying in so many from different sources was calamitous.

The middle of July was when the pea viners moved in. They started in Chalk Road at 6pm on a lovely day. It had been wet so there had not been any peas vined for a day or two so it was good that it was an excellent crop with a lot of peas. There were not many fields left so they were pleased to have a good crop to go at. Lickham peas averaged 2.26 tons per acre for 31 acres; they seeded down three acres, we had 84 acres in all vined so averaged 2.70 overall at £191 per acre, which was marvellous.

Andrew had been trying to get Angus going on his little red two-wheeler bike and on that day he made it. Was he fussy! He could now go from a standing start. Andrew, Helen and Angus had built a 'caravan' out of the old scalding tub, a door and a box and fastened polythene bags round for walls. It was quite good really.

We ordered a new Howard baler from RBM—a low-density, big baler, which only had three strings on. John Sleight used this after we had virtually finished combining and baled all up much faster than usual. We paid RBM £3,625 for the Howard baler, gripper and sub-frame, and one tonne of twine. On September 4 we sold Richard Dawson 100 tonnes of wheat at £60 a tonne. On September 12 we finished harvest in record time with all bales being led; it was much easier than having to physically handle the thousands of small bales.

We limed half of Railway Side at Lickham—the first and last time.

September 20: John and Margaret Sleight had a second daughter, Jennifer, at Beverley Westwood Hospital. The Sleights were very good friends as well as employees.

In **October** Von and I had a few days in Scotland; I was buying bullocks, and got 55, mainly blue greys, from Lockerbie for £3,601. At the same time we saw some new tractors for sale on the roadside outside the R Lloyd tractor showroom at Newbridge, Dumfries. I enquired as to whether they were for sale and was asked, very sarcastically: 'What do you think they are here for?' I explained that we had one on order in Driffield for the last 18 months and still had not got it.

Once home I was told by Richardson's that we were number 13 on the list and they had had three delivered that year. I replied: 'I can get a new one for the price of a telephone call', and was told to go ahead. So I did.

Lloyds delivered a new Ford 5000 GSM 330N for £3,272.40 which included eight per cent VAT and delivery. Richardson's, who were asking full list price, plus 15 per cent and eight per cent VAT, were not amused. The waiting list for tractors in this area was quite common but disappeared within a couple of months, along with the price premium.

At the end of October we sold Holderness Farm Supplies 80 tonnes of wheat at £65 a tonne.

Christmas Day—another trauma: Eddie brought Darren to help him feed up and milk but unfortunately Darren left the mill house door open; the cows got in and gorged themselves with the result there were five dead cows between December 26 and 31.

1975

January 6: We paid Humberside County Council £78.75 for the Land Rover, van and three tractor licences. In addition we paid £2 for a petrol licence—that was for the 500-gallon petrol tank and pump; the tank is just outside the garden wall at the front of Wold. The rates for Wold House were £151. We bought a power hacksaw from W and J Oliver's in Hull for £259.20. At the same time we were doing a very good trade selling steers and heifers, which we had reared in the calf house. They were averaging just over £120 each plus the calf subsidy, which was £1,984 for 72 heifers and 56 steers. Brookfield Allen came to give us a pep talk on farm safety. Eddie went to sleep during the proceedings.

Just after Christmas Andrew and I went shooting rabbits in the fields at the back of Vicarage Farm, which were all grass at the time. The first night I shot 39 rabbits with the .22 rifle. After that we had various drivers and passengers spotting rabbits—John Richardson, a friend and Angus's godfather, Von's father, Keith Lander and other school pals of Andrew's. We shot 138 rabbits and 31 hares between January and February. One night after that I took Andrew, Keith Lander, Hopkins, Hogg, two of Thompsons and Hyatt back to school in thick fog.

During this time John Dowson and I were making and hanging all the doors on the new extension to the workshop. Late February John Sleight spread 4cwt per acre of 22.11.11 fertilizer on all the grasses.

March 7: Andrew was confirmed in York Minster by the Bishop of Selby along with other boys from Cundall and York Choir School. Afterwards we all attended a reception at St William's College.

At this time Helen took her entrance exam for The Mount in York and Queen Margaret's at Escrick. She wrote and accepted a place at Queen Margaret's and we paid the deposit; then The Mount wrote and offered her a place.

March 14: we received a cheque from the FMC for £2,552 for 14 steers. These were the first of the blue greys that we bought at Lockerbie. Then another, on March 22, for £3,887 for 18 heifers and five steers. They had been reared in the calf house.

During March we were all working flat out cultivating and drilling for spring barley; I was sowing 4cwts (200kg per acre) of 22.11.11 fertilizer. John Dowson was drilling barley at 1.25cwts (10 stones) per acre of mainly Zephyr barley or Midas for seed for either Dawson's or ACC. Alf was rolling behind.

We received a cheque for £8,544 from Holderness Farm Supplies for seed barley. We pulled a hedge up between the two grasses at South Dalton, next to Tom Fisher Wood, after Watts had buried all the concrete and bricks, etc which the Army had used for their searchlight base during the war. We then drilled it with Midas seed barley.

We went on holiday to France with the caravan, needless to say getting lost. We stopped to ask a chap the way to the site we had booked onto, and he did no more than pedal like mad all the way in front of us until we got there. When we offered him some money he said: 'No, the English were very good to us in the war.' We were very touched. We went round Paris and saw all the sights: when we went to the Sacre Coeur Angus insisted on buying a leather cowboy hat from a vendor on the steps. Well, that was fine until we got it inside the car; it smelt disgusting, as if every dog in Paris had weed on it: he had to hang it out of the window. We toured all round and had a really good holiday, all together.

May 1: we bought a second-hand Massey Fergie 29 combine drill from RBM in Market Weighton, for £325. Richardson's serviced the tractor we got in Scotland.

May 6: John Sleight drilled Maro peas at Lickham, 30 acres on Railway Side near the road with the new drill.

May 12: Von and I went down to Roy Sanderson's at Croft near Skegness, and we ordered a purpose-built forklift unit with a 14 feet duplex mast (this had to be changed to a triplex mast when they had got it manufactured), a corn bucket and a muck fork attachment, for £7,400 plus VAT. We were entertained to lunch at Roy and Jean's council house—a far cry from the empire they built up, which was eventually taken over by Priestman's in Hull. This was the first proper forklift that we had and it replaced the McConnell tail slave, which was on the rear hydraulics of the Ford 5000. A very good buy. We have never been without a forklift since.

That month we went to London with Joe and Audrey Huxtable, with whom we were very good friends. Joe and I went to the Red Poll Council meeting at the Farmers Club, with the girls going into London while we were at the meeting.

We were increasing our pea acreage so we sent a cheque off to Beverley pea growers for £230 to increase our quota to 120 acres annually, which was what we were growing that year.

In early May, Mother and Aunty Farnaby had a fortnight's holiday in the Isle of Man. Twelve steers that went to Doncaster averaged £200 each: there were only nine left in the winter fattening yard.

Andrew did the Lyke Wake Walk at the end of May, it was 42 miles, and was completed in 24 hours. They had two snow storms in the middle of the night. We met him at Ravenscar at 2.30pm: he was exhausted and slept all

Vicarage Farm in 1979 showing the lean-to extension.

the way home, had a bath, was in bed for 7pm and slept all night.

Bills did not come as promptly in those days as they do now—I paid Harry Ellerker £7.50 for rolling Vicarage Farm stackyard, three years previously.

Most of **June** was spent making hay in the four fields behind Vicarage Farm, also in 20 acre, and we also bought 27 acres of hay to bale from William Lamb at Lund for £750—provided that Mr Lamb senior agreed to this, which he did. That same June we baled just over 1,000 bales of hay with the new Howard baler, which was ideal for hay.

In anticipation of a good harvest we bought 160 feet of grain walling from Lockwood's, of Wold Newton, for £706. We sold this two years later to Lount's at Leconfield. During this time John and I were making a calf creep, a photograph of which subsequently appeared in the Farmers Weekly, together with straw feeder racks, etc.

June 24: at the mid-summer Driffield implement sale we had sold the previously mentioned Nuffield 10/60 tractor for £310 and the Lister multi-level elevator for £150; this was because we no longer needed it with the big Howard bales.

We entered the Claas baler but it was withdrawn at £180. The weekly wage bill at that time, for five men —Eddie, Alf, John S, John D, Mr Sleight and a bit for ourselves—came to £300. At the same time we bought 34.5 per cent Nitro Shell at £51 per tonne from Yorkshire Fertilizers. We also had the AIS plane to spray the wheat at the front of Vicarage Farm for rust.

Von was over the moon as the Lund WI won the cup at the annual WI Rally—most prestigious indeed. She didn't come home until midnight; they had been drinking champagne at Joan Helm's.

In **July** of that year we put a lean-to on the side of the Dutch barn in the stackyard at Vicarage Farm. Norman Colley made the single span and the stanchions and we dug the holes with Starkey's digger, which John S had borrowed. There were six bays, thus seven holes for stanchions. We got seven cubic yards of concrete from Readymix for £85. The Maro peas at Lickham did 1.92 tonnes per acres (tpa), Dalton grass did 2.23tpa and Little Wold peas did 3tpa. We baled the pea straw in the latter and got 800 small Claas bales from it. It was a very dusty job, not only making the dry pea hulm (straw) and stacking it but also when feeding it out. We never did this again.

In **August and September** Sissons at Beswick, Bernard mainly, painted up all the doors, windows, etc, down at Lickham, and did on-going repairs as he went round. John Dowson started combining Wood Flat Zephyr barley and got 41 tonnes off the whole field. The following day John Sleight started combining wheat at Lickham on the Railway Side, with Andrew and Ian Whorley on corncarts. Sanderson's brought the new forklift, LAT 549P, it only had a duplex mast, as the triplex mast was not available at the time and would be fitted later. A French boy, Jean Andre, came to stay to improve his English and, hopefully, improve our children's French.

August 19: We got a cheque for £11,900 from Beverley Pea Growers for this season's crop. The same day I won £50 on the Premium Bonds with one of three Premium Bonds given to us with the Calixin chemical for spraying crops, which we had bought the previous year. They had only been in for three months.

We finished combining all the corn on August 26 and sold 60 tonnes of

Atou wheat for £70 a tonne, to Albright and Wilson, from whom we bought fertilizer. This was collected the following day. I think it was for seed, as it went to Brigg. At the same time Richardson's came to put the third clutch that year on SBT 954H—this was the tractor that Alf drove. We finished gathering up all the bales on August 30: three weeks from start to finish. Wonderful.

September 9—a landmark day: Helen started school at Queen Margaret's, Escrick. We took her at tea-time and got diverted but managed to arrive at the Dower House, which was Helen's boarding house. Here we were met by a porter who opened the boot and took Helen's trunk indoors. We met the matron, her housemistress Miss Morrell and Miss Meeke: we felt we were leaving her in safe hands. Helen was quite calm when we left her, and waved us off, which made it a lot easier for her mother.

The last week in September Garry Hyde was here cutting all the hedges at Lund, Dalton Grass and Lickham. On December 5 we paid his bill of £235: he had made an excellent job.

September 21: we went to watch Andrew playing rugby at Howsham Hall Preparatory School, just outside York, and he came home for the night. The following morning I fetched Helen from Queen Margaret's, and took them both back to their respective schools in the evening. Andrew could come home every other weekend, but with Helen it was her first time home since she started. She seemed happy enough. She was only allowed a weekend out twice a term.

Eddie was finding 41 South Street in Middleton a little bit cramped for his family; Stuart had left home by now but Teresa had come along. We had Eastwood's put on a third bedroom, big enough for three boys, with a flat roof over the kitchen, toilet and bathroom at 10 South Street and they moved in October.

Grandad loved being on the farm and particularly taking the boys rabbiting—his latest was teaching them how to set snickles to catch the rabbits, rather than putting a net over the burrow hole and using the Jack Russell—I sometimes wonder if he was trained as a poacher in a previous life...

October 3: we bought a new Ford 7000 from Richardson's, of Driffield, (LKH 615P) for £5,090. I went with George Thompson and a crowd of chaps to France and Belgium with the Burgess Feeds trip, visiting various farms and mills, etc. A very interesting five-day visit. We went on the ferry from Hull and returned the same way. The day after I returned, Von, Mother, Angus and I went to Lockerbie for the day and bought 10 heifers and 16 steers for £2,625. The haulage on these was £84.24. The following day a Mr G W Nicholson from Morpeth, Northumberland, came and bought eight Red Poll cows for suckling purposes for £1,600.

October 17—Andrew was 13: he rang to say he was pleased with his presents—particularly the sheath knife from Helen and Angus. We took Aunty Ethel back to Scarborough that night.

October 18: Angus was seven; he had a party and had a marvellous day.

November 3: we took Andrew, plus two pig huts, which we had bought from David Brumfield (we had put new floors in both huts) for Cundall to start keeping a few pigs as Jeremy Valentine, the headmaster, was keen on the boys looking after animals. The goat had the other pig hut. Andrew regularly milked the goat—and then drank the milk. It was an excellent school. Sanderson's came and changed the Duplex mast for a triplex mast and put in a new wiring loom, which had burnt out.

The bonfire party on the fifth was in Lambs' field, behind the pit on Beverley Road. There were five Lambs, six Snowdens, six Peter Walkers, four George Walkers, four Helms, six Clarksons and four Prescotts—and they said that Lund was a dying village. When we took Helen back to school we saw Miss Morrell, who said that Helen had settled down well, so that was a relief.

December 1: I took Grandad Carr and Andrew and John Dowson by car to Smithfield Show at Earls Court in London. We left home at 5.45am and arrived back at 11.45pm. It rained solidly the whole day, but we had a good time. It was about this time that we started doing the extension to the sideway at Wold House. All the surplus stuff in the sideway went into the defunct calf house and we put a steel RSJ from the boiler house wall into the front bedroom back wall. For the next six months any spare time was spent building the inside wall and the wall across to the men's bedroom (latterly Ben's bedroom), making a new bedroom over the boiler house and a bathroom over the new dining room.

December 9: we bought nine Friesian steers from Frank Taylor at Scorborough for £1,000: we would pay him in the middle of January.

I n **January** we made an outside yard for the new lean-to in the stackyard at Vicarage Farm and put in there the 43 weaned suckler cows and the Charolais bull from the grass fields behind the stackyard. At the same time Bill Walker, the FMC representative, came and I signed a contract to supply 160 fat beasts in the next six months. Mr Stabler, the calf certifying officer, came and punched 53 steers and 46 heifers for calf subsidy. The steers were £18.50 each and the heifers £16.50 each. Grandad, Andrew and I dug the trench from the boiler house to the drain down the lawn and put in a salt-glazed drain to take the effluent from the new bathroom; we built an inspection chamber over the existing drain at the junction.

We sent nine heifers to the Fatstock Marketing Company (FMC), Doncaster; they made £1,606 net. We sold the last of the wheat at Lickham to Dawson's for £64 per tonne for February delivery. Suzy, the pet Jack Russell, had four pups, one of which was Jaws—which Rachel Shipley cajoled her father into having. I have never seen such flashing eyes from a 10-year-old: her father was putty in her hands.

That winter we had signed a contract with Barkers & Lee Smith to contra our beef cube contracted price for £65 per tonne up to the end of December. We would supply wheat and barley to contra this at the going rate. In January a new contract for another 60 tonnes at £69 per tonne was agreed. Ten steers went to Rotherham for FMC for £2,161. We paid Richardson's £2,000 for tractor repairs.

In **February** I saw John Wilson, bank manager at the Midland Bank, Beverley, and he increased the overdraft to £40,000. We sold Zephyr seed barley to both Albright and Wilson (fertilizer suppliers) and Dawson's at Market Weighton: 60 tonnes made £3,721. We paid £21.28 including VAT to Tom Helm for the 1974/75 valuation fee. The total fertilizer usage for this coming year was 12 tonnes of 0.20.20 at £83 a tonne, 60 tonnes of 22.11.11

Vehicle	Registration	Month	Year	Make
Car	NVN 700M	August	1973	Mercedes
Van	FBT 628L	January	1973	Commer
Land Rover	AWF 804B	January	1964	Rover
Forklift	LAT 549P	September	1975	Sanderson
7000	LKH 615P	October	1975	Ford
5000	GSM 330N	October	1973	Ford
5000	VWF 657J	January	1970	Ford
5000	SBT 954H	January	1969	Ford
5000	JWF 783E	August	1967	Ford
5000	HWF 251D	January	1966	Ford
135	MFW 451F	March	1968	Massey Ferguson
Senator	PBT 294G	August	1969	Claas
Matador	DWF 513C	August	1965	Claas

Vehicles and tractors etc that we had on January 1 1976

and 40 tonnes of 34.5 per cent nitrogen at £51 per tonne.

We took a coach to Bradford to see the pantomime Goldilocks And The Three Bears. There were 49 of us; the seats were £1.50 each and the coach was 85p each.

At that time we were contracted to the council to do snow ploughing with the forklift when they called upon us. Both John Sleight and John Dowson took turns at this as there had been quite heavy snowfalls. We had all the kids in the area tobogganing down Park Hill.

Spring was very early and we had got on working the land that was for spring corn in February. We started drilling on the March 2 and finished on March 5. John S was using the combine drill down at Lickham for Midas feed barley, and then finished off in Wood Flat. Then John D was drilling at Wold House with the straight seed drill, with me putting fertilizer on with a spinner in front of him. We paid Chas Wood £550.70 for auditing the 1974/75 accounts, also Eastwood's £1,590 for putting the third bedroom on 10 South Street.

March 31: Grandad, Andrew and I started putting down foundations for the greenhouse at the end of the combine shed, facing the house. We got the greenhouse from Elthringhton's in Hull. They delivered it the following week, for us to erect.

April 4: we started to drill 52 acres across the road with Scout peas; the same week Hargreaves tarmacked the drive and stackyard at Lickham.

April 12: Von, Andrew, Helen and Angus and I set out for Rotterdam in a second-hand station wagon I had bought. We had loaded four five-gallon drums of diesel inside the station wagon and covered them with a board and blankets. Angus thought this was great, as he could lie out on it. Needless to say it was loaded to the gunnels with luggage and food for our trip alongside the Rhine with the caravan.

We were just leaving one site when we stopped at the gate, where two Germans were standing, one smoking a cigar. He looked at our station wagon, then at his cigar, and said 'Stinkum'. We visited Alan Drusellier, who had the champagne company Ayala. He entertained us to a seven-course lunch the following day, after giving us a tour round the cellars: Angus got drunk and was quite merry.

We went round Rheims after that and then back to the caravan. Angus slept. When we came back on the ferry I said: 'Let's do as we did coming out, have our meal in the harbour then we can watch as we go through the lock gates.' We did this but as soon as we got into the English Channel it was very choppy and Angus was the first one to feel sick. I followed him up to our cabin and there he was, hanging over the loo with his skin going backwards and forwards over his ribs, just like a young pup, being sick. That was enough for me, I was next. Helen sat it out on deck and was perfectly fine. When we came home we found out that Andrew had been made a prefect at school.

In early **May** the river board dredged the beck from Scorborough through to the railway lines. Then they decided to cut off the horseshoe in the beck in Clark Field. We carted all the dugout soil up to the shed at Rose Cottage, filled in the hollows from the shed to the moat, and levelled it all up.

There were 51 bullocks left at Vicarage Farm, and we marked 31 of them to go in the following week to Doncaster and Sheffield. They made £6,835.72 (£220 per head average).

We had Sissons decorating in the house; I took down the chimney stack above Mother's bedroom to below roof level, and at the same time we took down the chimney stack at the end of the house, near Helen's bedroom, to floor level in the back kitchen and put a window in where the chimney breast had been. Whilst Sissons were here, we had Clubleys here making good the roof. They put us onto Burton and Sissons in Bridlington, who would put a flat roof over the new bathroom and the bedroom that used to be the sideway and was now going to be turned into a dining room. I paid Bernard Sissons £1,084 for painting up at Lickham that autumn. Bounce, the Labrador, got fastened in the boiler house and ate through the diesel pipe, there was diesel everywhere. We had to get Sam Archer to come and make good the damage.

June 22: Andrew passed his entrance exam for St Peter's; Jeremy Valentine was very pleased with him as he had just missed a distinction in mathematics. The same night I went to a meeting at The Vicarage with Col Phillips, re knocking down the forge, which he had bought for the church and which was going to be rebuilt through the council youth scheme.

At this time of the year holidays were usually taken by employees before we got into the busy harvesting season, usually one man off at a time. In most businesses there were only two weeks' paid holiday per person. Usually they took one week off and used the other week for odd days off when needed—in other words 10 working days per year.

June saw us going round like bluebottles, John D started pea vining on June 26, John S and I baled hay in Hut Field and Far Field tops. Angus had to miss his swimming as Von was opening the garden fete at Kilnwick at 2.30pm: she was presented with a bouquet by the daughter of Beryl Smith (Percy Wharram's daughter from Lund). She rushed back to collect Angus and myself and we were off to St Peter's where we joined the headmaster and other parents. Andrew had been taken with two or three other boys who were also going to St Peter's. We had a look round and I think poor Andrew was overwhelmed with the size of the school, the prospect of another four years at school and leaving Cundall, which he loved.

Before going home we went round the Minster, up into the roof and then onto the walls of York. In the evening we left the children with Mother and went off to Thompsons at Flamborough for supper. A full day…

In the spring we had ploughed up the front paddock at Wold House and levelled up all the 'lands' as best we could, also down at the bottom of the paddock where it was very badly landed. Then we direct reseeded it and baled it for hay.

July 5: we had the honour of being the first farm visit on the first International Red Poll Conference, which was to be held in Nottingham University. Mrs Ellis, Madge Heseltine, Alice Farnaby, Lil and Grandad were all helping. Mrs Hesletine came out with a tray of white coffee and they all wanted black.

They had a ride round the farm, saw the cattle and then came back for lunch in the drier; all went well and they were very fussy. They had to go to Mrs Fawcett's at Tadcaster, Charlie Kidson's at Wakefield and back to Nottingham for the night. They didn't leave us until 3.30pm.

Peter Ullyott and I went to the two-day conference a week later at Nottingham University. In the evening of July 5 we collected Christophe Repanau, from Epenay in France, from York Station. He brought three bottles of champagne which they produced. Folk were all over—gleaning peas after the viners had finished in 52-acre.

The next day at breakfast I asked Christophe what he usually had for breakfast. He replied: 'We produce champagne, we drink champagne.' I said: 'Well, that's OK—we produce milk, so drink milk.' Von and I took him that day down to the Royal Show at Stoneleigh in Warwickshire, where we met all the overseas visitors we had had the previous day.

July 7: we entertained our former vicar, the Rev Lance W Foster, and his wife. He had been the vicar of Lund and Lockington for about seven years in the mid-1950s. They were a very well-liked couple, so we invited the Fishers and the Steeles from Lockington, the Middletons and Snowdens and the current vicar, the Rev A Bromley and his wife.

July 9: we traded our old Howard baler in for a new model. RBM allowed us £3,000 for our old baler and that left a balance of £1,500 to pay. The following day it was Andrew's sports day at Cundall and at tea time we all came home.

Shortly afterwards the phone went: Anne Thompson from Bainton Station, whose two sons, Richard and William, often shared transport with us to Cundall, rang in a panic. Her horse, Foretell, had fallen, back-end first into a cesspit. Could we help? I went with the Sanderson forklift; the vet, Warwick Chinn, was already there when I arrived, plus three police cars and the fire brigade. The vet managed to scramble in beside the horse and get a belt round behind its front legs and I lifted him out with the forklift as fast as possible. He lay flat out on the ground whilst the fire brigade hosed him down and when he was cleaned he got up. That Sanderson was worth its weight in gold.

Subsequently Anne sent me and the vet a bottle of whisky each.

July 12: whilst Peter and I were at the conference, Von took Anne Thompson, Richard, William, Christophe, Andrew, Hyatt, Hopkins and the two Price boys to Cundall for the last time; it rained all the way. That station wagon had its uses.

July 14: my cousin, Arthur Prescott, who lived in South Africa, came to stay. He was the son of Uncle Eddie from Lair Hill. The day after, David Hastings, my second cousin—Cynthia's son—came to stay. Christophe was still with us (I sometimes think we run a free boarding house); in the midst of this Von developed German measles.

July 24: we left the children in the care of Aunty Farnaby, as Mother was staying with her niece, Diana, and Von and I went down to Kemerton, Worcestershire, to Adrian Darby's where I bought seven heifers for £250 each. Adrian is married to the daughter of Sir Alec Douglas-Home, the former Prime Minister, who was there. We were introduced to him: it was strange seeing him in the flesh.

July 25: we started combining Aramire barley in Chalk Road field and got approximately 32 tonnes. The following day John and Mr Sleight combined Zephyr barley in front of the house at Lickham and I baled Chalk Road field and got 102 bales. Andrew, Alf and David Hastings led and stacked the straw in the Dutch barn at Vicarage Farm. Von had Mr O'Hara, her old boss from her days at Bridlington Town Hall, and his wife to lunch—Mrs O'Hara used to teach Von at school. They had apparently enjoyed themselves seeing it all.

July 29—we had an all-change: Diana, Denis and Phillip Warry brought Mother back and took David Hastings home to Oxford; Adrian Darby came and stayed to lunch.

That summer turned out to be the driest since records began. It brought everything forward. Jean Andre Calvair, the French boy who came via Mrs Outred, came to stay for a couple of weeks and on the same day we received a cheque for £7,700 for peas so far from treasurer Peter Blacker.

August 7: Mother opened the garden fete at Cleone Bloom's bungalow in Scorborough. We finished combining on August 10, the same day as we had started in 1974. The following day Susan and Ian came to stay; Von fetched them from York. Andrew and Jean Andre were leading bales at Lickham all day and didn't come back until 10pm.

August 14: Mother was 80 and 14 of us went out for a meal to celebrate. We tried a new venture that year; Peter Beale came and direct-drilled Little Wold with stubble turnips and a week later John Dowson put on 2cwt of 34.5 per cent nitrogen.

Richard Dawson bought 35 tonnes of wheat for September movement at £80 a tonne. During this time John Sleight was baling with the Howard baler for Irelands, Farnabys, Holtbys and Bishop Burton College. They got 904 bales for the college.

August 20—a memorable day for all of us: Von took Jean Andre to catch the train at York, together with Andrew and Helen. They put Jean Andre on the train—with Helen going on first with his case. There was someone sitting in his seat so Von and Andrew followed in order to sort it out and with that the whistle blew. Andrew shot out of the door followed by Von but Helen was trapped behind a large lady. The porter slammed shut the door, the train moved out and Von said to him: 'My daughter's on that train.' He replied: 'Well, it wouldn't stop for the Queen herself until it gets to London.'

With that he went to the office and telephoned through to the train to tell the guard, who found Helen in tears. Jean Andre refused to speak to her— and didn't speak all the way to London. The guard looked after her and when they arrived bought her a sandwich and a drink and generally kept his eye on her. He put her on another train for the return journey and when some youths got into her carriage he came along and moved her. British Rail was excellent.

In the meantime Von and Andrew went and bought his new uniform for St Peters, had lunch and returned to the station to await the 2.30pm arrival of Helen, who had been to London and back on a four pence platform ticket. 'Oh! That Helen,' as Father would have said. Bless her, it was not her fault.

The trio then went off and bought Helen a new school coat. Von wrote a letter to the Yorkshire Post saying how kind the men on BR had been to Helen on her unplanned trip.

That weekend, **August 21 and 22**, Von and Marie Reffold were judging at Ripley Show on the Saturday so, en route, dropped Mother and Helen at Nurse Ingleby's at Wetherby. (Von judged at quite a few shows in the summer.) On the Sunday, Grandad had free tickets for Butlins so, as there were 10 of us, we went in the station wagon. We left the children—Sue, Ian, Andrew, Helen and Angus—at Butlins with £5 to spend between them and Mother, Von, Grandad, Lil and I went onto Filey Brigg; it was a beautiful day.

We received a cheque from Beverley Pea Growers for £850 for John's pea harvest wages. After we had cleared all the bales and dragged round the hedge sides we started burning a lot of the stubbles; it made a really good job cleaning up a lot of weed, seeds etc. When Alf came to work he asked if we had heard Radio Humberside news—the story of Helen's trip to London had been on.

August 28: Von, the three children and I went off to Scotland in the caravan for a week's holiday prior to Andrew starting school at St Peter's.

September 7: we took Andrew to St Peter's and got lost trying to find his dormitory—it is such a big school. We were met by Mr Crane, his housemaster, and Mr McDonald; both seemed OK. A gang of 15-year-olds was coming haring up the stairs, heading for the new boys' dorm; they saw Mr Crane and turned tail, meek as anything. Andrew had been working solidly all the holidays amongst bales and spreading manure, so school may have been a rest for him.

September 9: Helen returned to school for her second year at Queen Margaret's. Angus also returned to school that day, this time in Muriel Moody's class. The house certainly felt strange without them. Von had a rota arrangement with Margaret Snowden and Christine Walker, each taking a week for transporting the children to school and it worked marvellously well; it was Margaret's week that week.

September 12: with it being so dry all summer there was no grass in the fields at all, so we slept the cows in for the first time; the same at Lickham the following day. Tim Smith from Fakenham came to see the hay in the Howard bales: he wanted to export these to Holland as they were in a similar situation to us having no fodder at all. It was a matter of how many could he get into a curtain sider. They would be £40 a tonne, but they only got one load, as they could only get seven and a half tonnes on a 40ft curtain sider.

David Brumfield came to see the young Hereford bull, agreed to buy it for £400 but wanted it weighed first, so I took him to Barkers & Lee Smith's weighbridge in Beverley—it weighed 15cwt.

September 26—Sunday: the Marr family arrived—Andrew, Elsa and the four children. Mr Marr had come to tell us that he was putting up the rent to £16 per acre.

Before the Marrs we had already had David Maltas, Denis Clark and Arthur Prescott's friend, Brian Alridge, and then the Reffolds arrived. Von took them into Hut Field to gather mushrooms only to discover someone had been in before them and cleaned the lot up.

September 28: I took Grandad Carr, Mother and Von to Lockerbie to try to buy store bullocks but the prices had absolutely rocketed to £50 a cwt. At the same time we were getting just over £30 a cwt fat so we came home without buying any. We were back by 5.30pm. I think this was the last time we went up to Scotland to try to buy bullocks. By this time the weekly drawings for wages, including for ourselves, had gone up to £400 a week.

Lund had won the Best Kept Village competition for Humberside: Lord Halifax presented a seat and a plaque and we all had tea in the village hall. After this we took Helen back to school for 8pm: she did not get out as much as Andrew, who could now come out after games each Saturday. He would run the length of York to catch the bus from Piccadilly to Market Weighton, where one or other of us would pick him up. We would take him back on Sunday evening.

October 5: John Sleight started drilling wheat on Railway Side at Lickham. After he had finished there he drilled all first and second crop wheat at Wold House before starting sub-soiling in Clark Field at Lickham: Arnott's had drained it and we had pulled up the hedge round the little paddock next to the moat. He then ploughed it and we all helped work and drill it between November 1 and 10.

October 29: Alf Dowson officially retired; we gave him a cheque for £50 and a clock. He had been off sick all September and was really more than ready for retirement but came back to work part-time. He was still living at 39 South Street and stayed there until he died in 1981. Mrs Dowson stayed there rent-free until she finally got a council bungalow, at which stage Helen took it over.

The bonfire that year was in Alwyn's paddock; Alec was renting it then.

We went down to Lambs for supper, then Angus would insist on going back to see the bonfire with George Walker and me. Von took Mother home and discovered that I had the house key in my pocket, so she had to climb in through the dining room bay window. I went and got the Sanderson muck-fork to push the bonfire up and it was 11.30pm before Angus and I returned, looking like sweeps. We had to have a bath before going to bed.

Mary Varley had finished the miniatures of the three children so Von went to collect them; they were really very good likenesses.

We were at last getting on with the work out the sideway, Grandad and I were wiring up a new fuse box in the passage with a new main back to the meters in saddle room. We altered the entire central heating piping round to put into the floor of the new extension. We also took down the old boiler house roof to extend the existing walls up to eaves height. A few days later we installed an RSJ from the boiler house wall to the sitting room wall over what would be the patio doors.

November 27: we had the YFC County Ploughing Match in the Road End 52-acre field. There were 52 competitors, several demonstration plots in Mr Thompson's Bramble Butts field and food was served in Clark's barn. We had 12 judges to lunch and Margaret Soanes brought Keith Lander along—he still came to stay even though he was at Pocklington School and Andrew was at St Peter's. Andrew brought Paul Close home and I took them all rabbiting in the evening, which they all thoroughly enjoyed.

December 2: we had a very sad funeral for Derek Pilmoor, who had died, aged 18, when he ran into a tree on his motorbike. Von's cousin, Stan Pilmoor, and his wife, Dolly, had adopted the boy when it seemed that Dolly couldn't carry a child to full-term. They went on to have two daughters, Lesley and Susan.

December 6: John D managed to break one of the roof trusses in the foldyard roof when he lifted the high-lift cart too high, so we had to lift it up and bolt it together with light RSJs. It is still the same today. On the same day Uncle Henry Prescott, Alan's brother who was a bank manager in Hull, died. We went to his funeral on December 8 at Cottingham. There was not the long delay in those days between death and funeral.

On the Saturday Andrew broke up and we took Angus to see Father Christmas in Leek and Thorpe's. York was packed.

Burton and Sissons came and put the flat roof on the sideway; they had the first layer of felt on by 6.30pm. They finished it off the following day and made the slates good at Wold House and Vicarage Farm.

Maurice Robson arrived and bought approximately 40 tonnes of Mink seed barley at £96 per tonne and approximately 45 tonnes of Hobbit wheat at £82, to go after Christmas. The same day Helen broke up from Queen Margaret's so we were back to full strength. I took Andrew into Hull and bought him a motor bike for £40; he was thrilled, and bought himself a helmet. The same night 15 carol singers from church came for supper, and after we had cleared up I took Von and Mother to church for the midnight service, which was packed.

Christmas Day went off well with no disasters. Andrew and Helen spent the afternoon riding up and down the front paddock on the new bike. As usual we entertained: Nurse Ingleby, two of her friends and all the Maltas family came to tea. Another day we all went to Lickham to tea with the Sleights. We even had Lesley Howell, a friend of Von's pre-married days, over and the Shipley family too.

January 11: Messrs Marr and Todd came to lunch; they put the rent of Vicarage Farm up from £10 per acre to £20 per acre. They agreed to let us pull up the hedges—surreptitiously—between the two back fields as are now, down the side of Vicarage Farm drive and between the field next to paddock and Middle Field. They also agreed to give us a tenant right on rebuilding and surfacing the farm road and to pay £60 per year shooting rent for the land at Wold House.

By the beginning of March we had to have all safety cabs fitted on tractors that didn't already have them. We bought two cabs for the 5000s and one for the Massey Fergie tractor; there was one left to be sent for a 5000. I sent a cheque for £874 to Alexander Duncan for the first three on January 17. The third one came later in the month. At the same time we received a cheque from the FMC for a bonus on the contracted cattle of £129.50.

Von and I went to Frank Taylor's to get some furniture. Andrew Taylor had been delegated to clear furniture from the RAF camp at Leconfield when it was changing over from the RAF to the Army School of Driver Training. A leg of every piece of furniture was supposed to be broken, but by the third day it was pouring with rain and the sergeant in charge was fed up, so Andrew just brought the furniture home as it was. He gave all the neighbours whatever they wanted from the pieces of whole furniture. We took some and used it for various purposes. The big table in the farm office today is one of those pieces.

January 31: Natalie Jowsey was born, so Eddie had 10 days holiday to help out. No paternity leave in those days.

In early **February** John Dowson was filling the Sanderson up with diesel, whilst he was loading manure, and spilt a drop of diesel on the exhaust; with that the whole machine burst into flames, burning out all the wiring and the alternator. Sanderson's had to totally rewire the machine and the cost was covered by insurance: the National Farmers' Union (NFU) paid up after Tom Julian and an inspector had been to view.

March 3: I went to the estate office at South Dalton to meet Mr Northern, who was put in to arbitrate on the rent and we agreed to pay £17.50 per acre from the £10.17 we were already paying.

March 5: we had the Houghtlings from the USA came to stay, via a visit to Bishop Burton College. We have corresponded with them ever since.

March 9—Helen's birthday: I sowed 58cwt of 22.11.11 on Chalk Road field and Mr Sleight harrowed up after me. John Dowson sowed 10 stones per acre of Aramire barley and Grandad rolled it down after that.

March 12: we had Pat Miller aerial spreading 34.5 per cent nitrogen on 30 acres of winter wheat at Lickham and approximately 63 acres of hillsides and dale at Wold House, and got five tonnes on the whole lot. We moved 25 cows and their calves from the grasses behind Vicarage Farm to Middleton Tops.

John D and Andrew pulled up the hedge between the field next to the Park and Middle Field in one hour. The following day John D dug the hedge up from Vicarage Farm stackyard to Middleton wood: I was leading the hedge, roots, etc into the pit with the high-lift cart, which I managed to turn over. Fortunately no damage was done.

Andrew was very keen to take either his mother or myself on his motorbike. Von, much to her surprise, really enjoyed their trips with Angus on his bike with the dogs. I took him on the motorbike to Beswick to get the wallpaper book so that he could choose his bedroom wallpaper.

At the end of March we had the first meeting of the village Queen's jubilee committee in the village hall at which I was made chairman. This was the first of many meetings to be held to arrange our celebrations. We agreed to have 5,000 draw tickets printed to sell to all and sundry in order to raise funds for the event.

In early **April** John Sleight ploughed out the grass field next to Park, now 35 acres. Andrew harrowed after him with two sets of gib harrows, one behind the other. John D drilled it with Ark Royal barley after I had sown 110 bags of 22.11.11.

April 6: Bernard Sissons finished decorating the new wing and the back passage after all the alterations and improvements had been done, six months from the day we had started work. The following day John D was drilling Lofa Abed barley in stackyard field at Vicarage Farm, but got snowed off. I paid Burton and Sissons £514.08 for putting the flat roof on the new build and plastering all the internal walls.

Mr Stabler, the calf certifying officer, was with us all day, and punched the ears of 45 heifer calves, 53 steer calves and 15 bull calves at all three farms. I sowed 170cwt of 22.11.11 on 52 acres at Road Ends and Andrew harrowed in after me with two sets of gib harrows. This was how he spent his Easter holidays. John D drilled 63cwt of Zephyr barley.

We started to sow Scout peas in the 50 acre across the road; it was the third time that this field had been peas, ie 1968, 1973 and 1977—the first year 50-acre was peas Lord Hotham allowed us to pull up the cross hedges between 28-acre and 22-acre (now 50-acre) and between 25-acre and 27-acre (now 52-acre). These peas did very well at harvest, doing just over 2.5tpa. They were Scout peas in Wood Flat too, all except the hill. They did a similar yield. The peas at Lickham that year were by-passed, as they had got over ripe.

April 20: we had a really good sale of cattle: Chris Waite took 58 steers and heifers from Lickham into Beverley Market, as stores, and they made £10,092.84 (£241 each).

The same day eight steers and four heifers went to FMC in Chesterfield, and 10 steers and two heifers to FMC Bedale. The ones to Bedale made £3,182 (£261 each). The same day we paid Pauls £5,360 for beef nuts, Miller's £245 for the aerial spraying and Alexander Duncan the balance of £291.27, which included the last cab that they sent. The two Johns fitted the last cab on to JWF 5000.

April 29: we had our Northern Counties Red Poll Breeders Association (NCRPBA) dinner at the Chase Hotel at York. At 10pm, after our meeting and speaker, our chairman Benny Bradshaw, from Reighton, stood up and said: 'Oh well, I'd better get home and have my porridge, if I have it at night it saves time in the morning before I milk.' We were all in stitches because he meant it. A couple of months after he died, aged 92, his elder son, Teddy, told us that he was now the head of Bradshaw's Mill in Driffield and that he had never signed a cheque in his life before—and that was at 67-years old.

In early **May** we were having a lot of problems with pigeons on the peas, both in 50-acre across the road and down in Wood Flat. We had Mike Lazenby shooting pigeons and also the Kitchen brothers from Etton: I had to sack the latter, as Mike said they were shooting at him. Later in the month we went to the wedding of my cousin, Brian Prescott, to Julie Baxter, from Bainton. He was living with his parents at 8 South Street in Middleton, which his father, Edward Prescott, had bought.

I was made chairman of the parish council and the first task I undertook was to rotavate the whole of Queen's Mead that was not level. It was overgrown with rubbish of every description and was always a bone of contention at every parish council meeting. I continued rotavating this ground all the summer to clean and level, as we thought to make a play area for the children. By 1979 the elm trees on the road side all had Dutch elm disease and had to be taken down.

May 26: Von and I went down to Knepp Castle in Sussex, to stay the night with Sir Walter and Lady Burrell; we were going to see a bull, Knepp Quartet. It all turned into an interesting experience; we arrived 4.15pm to be met by David Meadows, the farm manager, who sent us up to the house, where the butler received us and showed us into the study.

We had afternoon tea with Sir Walter and Lady Burrell. They were charming and took us to see the bull and the rest of their herd. They were a very good-looking lot and it was all most enjoyable. On our return we had very large drinks and then dinner, all served by the butler of course.

When we retired to bed there was a portrait on the staircase of Sir Walter's father, Sir Merrick Burrell, who I thought was King George V. Sir Merrick had a mortgage on Lickham in the 1880s.

The setting was wonderful but the quantity of food was a lot less than we were used to. Lady Burrell was the daughter of Lady Denman, the founder of both the WI movement and the Family Planning Association. After dinner the ladies left us and Sir Walter closed the door behind them—and locked it. We sat down to drink and talk business. I agreed to buy the bull for £350. He turned out to be a very good buy.

On our return home the following day we drove straight through the centre of London, past the Houses of Parliament, Trafalgar Square and Piccadilly. We called to see Liz and Jack Wells at Newark on the way home before seeing an Austin Princess car at Walkington garage that George Thompson had told us about. The bull did not lie down in 10 hours. We turned him out into the grass at Lickham and he was as calm as you like. On our return I took Mrs Farnaby home—she was a brick, always came and stayed with Mother if we were away, as Mother would never stay at Wold House or with the children alone. Mrs Farnaby spent a lot of time with us at Wold House and loved the children dearly. Von went off to a produce meeting at night, so it was a fairly full day.

We sold the Land Rover station wagon (PAT 468M) which had been problematic ever since we bought it; it had been converted to diesel from petrol and had not been properly done. It had been used as the village bus for WI outings and children's transport and we had many happy memories of it—even to the several breakdowns. There were no child protection checks or rules on numbers of passengers in those days. We sold it for £2,538, including VAT; this was roughly the same price that we had paid for it. We bought a dark red BMC Austin Maxi (BVY 295R) as a runabout for Von.

The next big event in the village was the Queen's Silver Jubilee celebration on **Sunday June 5**. It was a national Bank Holiday long weekend, starting on the Sunday. We started off with a service, which was the same service in every Church of England across the country; it was good as there was a full church.

We had a comic cricket match in Walker's field. In the evening we called for Christine Walker; she was in a tizzy as all their heifers were out and she couldn't get hold of George. I volunteered to go and see what I could do. I met Mr Thompson and then George appeared so we all went and rounded them up. We then went to the pub for the darts and dominoes.

June 6: it poured with rain all day. Mrs Farnaby wept with disappointment as we were to have a party in her garden but it was far too wet. All had to be transferred to the Lambs' grain store: the table looked super with all the flowers and fancy plates, etc. In the afternoon we had It's A Knockout—this time in the Lambs' foldyard. We had planned for all these events to be outside, but the weather decreed otherwise. The huge slide gave the children more pleasure than anything.

In the evening Stella and Peter Harvey, assisted by Liz Walker and company, put on an excellent Old Time Music Hall in the village hall. Many in the audience were in costume, adding to the atmosphere and glamour. Afterwards the ladies served supper to at least 220 people. Needless to say Von was in the thick of it. It was 1.30am when we got to bed.

June 7: Mike Lazenby and Ron Downes were in charge of the spit and fire for the barbecue: they got 4cwt of coke red hot. The lamb was given by the Lambs, the pig was given by Alec Snowden—I said I was not giving a bullock. Whilst this preparation was carrying on, there was a wrestling match on The Green, which was extremely funny: Chris Thompson, from Bainton station, and Mr Sedman were the wrestlers and put on a very good show, although Mr Sedman ended up with three stitches in his forehead.

Von and Joan Helm did the ice cream, and there was a bygone exhibition, a mummer's play, Punch and Judy show and—the highlight—a fancy dress competition. Much work had gone into the costumes by many and there was a lot of entries. Helen went as Elizabeth Fry and Angus was the Knave of Hearts—Grandad had painted him sandwich boards to wear and he looked very good. In the decorated bike competition Helen came second. She and Andrew, with help from Booey, had built a most spectacular aeroplane round her bicycle.

All then went back to Lambs' barn for the barbecue and the prize draw. The ladies had cooked 320 chicken portions; there was 80lbs of lamb, 70lbs of pork, 40lbs of sausages and 60lbs of mushy peas and all was consumed. There was a disco, and then the draw for 70 prizes took place. It was a highly successful weekend. We got to bed at 2am.

This letter was delivered to every household in the village, after the Queen's Silver Jubilee, and was the forerunner of the Lund Link newsletter. We printed and delivered letters round the village informing the villagers what was going on. It seemed to help bring the village together and was the catalyst of the Best Kept Village, etc. Then, in 1984, William Lamb and Yvonne went to a meeting explaining how to do the job properly, and after that Lund Link was born.

Wold House
Lund, Driffield
June 10 1977
Dear All,

As chairman, and on behalf of the members of the Parish Council, I am writing to thank you most sincerely for all you put into the various activities to make the Silver Jubilee of our Queen such a happy and memorable time for us all in Lund.

I was the co-ordinator for the event, and thanks to everyone using their initiative my job was made very easy. I am sure that no other community in the country could have had a happier or more successful jubilee. The co-operation and enthusiasm of all the factions of the village was tremendous, and I personally never remember a time when everybody joined together with such a will to make an event such a success. I am proud to be associated with all of you, as are my parish council. We could never find a better village to represent. We are proud to be your parish council.

It is difficult to select individuals to praise, but we must thank Mr Middleton and the vicar for the Sunday morning service, which was packed to the doors, Mrs Bradley, at the Wellington, for the cricket match which, although it was cold, was most entertaining. Also the darts and dominoes on Sunday evening. Mrs Bradley and her helpers have done stalwart work throughout the events.

On Monday, Mr George Walker and all his helpers worked like Trojans, at very short notice to ensure that 'it's a knock out' took place, which it did with great success. The slide certainly being a major attraction, and worthy of all the work involved in erecting and dismantling twice.

The children's tea party was a loud success! The venue again, having to be moved at short notice from Mrs Farnaby's garden to Mr Lamb's grain store. Every child in the parish was given a jubilee mug and a crown (coin) in a presentation box, as mementoes of this happy time

Mr and Mrs Harvey's tremendous work and effort with the Old Time Music Hall was well justified, as the evening was a fantastic success, the excellent and well-trained cast, and their willing helpers, really pulled out all the stops to make sure it was a night to remember. The audience joined in with a will, and many came in costume, adding greatly to the effect.

The students, who led the adventure project on Tuesday morning, really did a great job, the children entering into the spirit of the thing with a will, and as a result thoroughly enjoyed themselves.

Mr Ken Westoby and all his supporters and helpers put on a wonderful afternoon of entertainment on the Tuesday the town crier, Jack Bransgrove, tying the whole thing together with professional ability! The bygone exhibition created great interest, the arts and crafts were well visited, the stocks, the mummers, the Punch and Judy, the slapstick, the decorated bicycles, the fancy dress, the ladies bonnets, the professional wrestlers, carrying realism to the point that three stitches in the forehead of 'gentleman Jim'! The bal-

loon race (still underway), fortune telling, apple bobbing, horseshoe throwing, Aunt Sally—the list is interminable! It was just a great afternoon.

The barbecue was undoubtedly a marvellous success, and here I must mention Mr Lamb, Mr Downes and Mr Mike Lazenby, not only for the work that they put in at the barbecue, but beforehand, making the spit, etc. The fire was lit at 10am and by mid-day we had four cwts of red hot coke on the fire! The two carcases (very professionally wired onto the spit) were then put on to roast, these being donated by our two county chairman (NFU and YFC) Mr Lamb and Mr Snowden.

After seven and a half hours of continuous basting (by numerous natives) both the pork and the lamb (not our host!) were done to a turn (literally). We all then commenced to devour 320 chicken portions, 70 lbs of lamb, 80 lbs of pork, 40 lbs of sausages, pounds of peas, and 800 bread rolls! The quality of the food and the standard of cooking was perfection.

Here I must pay particular thanks to, in the words of our own Leonard Sachs, the indefatigable ladies of Lund, who provided food, cooked food, helped, cleaned and scrubbed, often looked gorgeous and kept us mere males on the right path! They are indeed wonderful.

The grand draw, our only money-raising effort, will, we hope, keep us solvent, although it is too early to say. Thanks here again to all those who bought and sold tickets; we had 10,000 printed, most of which were sold. The draw took place at 9pm and many thanks to all those who made it go so smoothly, for the display and ferrying back and forth of the prizes (70 of them) and by no means least of all to those who gave such super prizes. The disco afterwards was enjoyed by the majority, thanks to our disc jockey and also the Wellington to help us to enjoy the spirit of the occasion.

I must make one special thank you to Mr and Mrs Lamb who allowed us to use their home and farmstead ad lib, without which we would have had much greater difficulties.

Thanks also to Messrs Walkers for putting at our disposal the football field and their grain store should we have needed it on the Tuesday. Thanks to the village hall, the Oddfellows Hall, the Wellington, and all those who put their homes at our disposal for meetings, etc, and particularly Mr Bill Aspey, who has kept us well informed with the jubilee news, as this has helped everyone to know how things have progressed stage by stage, and kept interest mounting.

Thanks also to all the people, particularly Mr Bernard Calvert and Mr Ivan Marshall, who helped us prepare and clear away afterwards all the different events, whose work is unheralded, and to all those who have done their bit in keeping the village clean and tidy and making it a village to be admired.

We are having a meeting in the village hall on Friday June 17, at 7.30pm at the Old School, when it is hoped all the money will be in, and the majority of the bills presented to our treasurer Mr Peter Harvey.

One thought I have had was that anyone who took some good photographs or slides of the celebrations might like to lend them during the winter for an evening show, also any ideas on how we might commemorate this jubilee in the village with surplus money, if any, would be welcome.

Thank you everyone, we are proud of Lund, and we are even more proud of the folk who live there.

Sincerely

Stephen Prescott

(Chairman, Lund Parish Council)

The whole of that spring and summer John Sleight was doing a very good trade in getting muck out at all the neighbouring farms with the Sanderson forklift—Farnabys, Holtbys, Clarksons, Sellars, Irelands and the Maltas family at Roos.

June 20: Angus fell off the steps at the front door whilst he was trimming the honeysuckle—we had gone indoors to watch the news. It was a Monday night and we ended up in Hull Royal Infirmary for X-ray and check. He had three stitches in his forehead. The same day I had taken Peter Ullyott to Brough for the train to London to go to the Red Poll Council meeting and annual meeting at the Farmers Club. Peter was a total embarrassment on the Tube; he had his usual cap on, unstudded so it stuck up, and was saying, in a loud voice: 'I hope thou knows where thou's going.' The city gentlemen lowered their papers to look and the expression on their faces said: 'I didn't know it was Smithfield this week.'

August 9: I went into Hull to buy a go-kart for the boys and a Honda 50 motor bike (YKH 76J) for Helen. I had a nasty shock as we had to pay £4,400 income tax to the Inland Revenue. I suppose we must have made a bit of money or we would not have had to pay this. This was slightly tempered by getting a cheque for £11,296 for that year's peas. However, we had to pay AIS £2,735 for summer chemicals.

It had been a very wet summer and, as a result, we did not start combining until August 23: the previous year we had all finished and put away by this date—there are never two seasons alike. We started in Chalk Road field, at Vicarage Farm, which was all Aramire barley across the front. We got 100 tonnes of Hobbit wheat from 30 acres on the Railway Side at Lickham.

September 1: Grandad and I went down to Bentall's at Maldon in Essex for a new fan with more volume for the drying bins. We left home at 4.30am and got back to the farm by 3.45pm, having travelled 450 miles.

Arthur Day's men fitted the fan and had it running by 11pm the same night. We paid RBM £1,210 for the fan. It was a very catchy harvest and drying corn was a problem. Grandad worked full-time in harvest on the corncart and Andrew was the main baler man—at 14 years old. The day after, Eddie broke his arm and was off work for two weeks, just when it was the busiest time. However, he did come back in the afternoons to relieve Helen, who was looking after the drier.

The 35-acre pea-land wheat at the front of the house at Lickham did approximately 120 tonnes, which worked out at just over three tonnes per acre.

September 12: Helen went back to school; this time she moved from Dower House to St Aidan's, which was in the main school. Fenella Thompson started that day and she was also in Hall House, so it was nice for them both. Andrew went back to school the following day, but he was home again at the weekend and baled the field next to Park—100 bales—on the Sunday. Eddie got back to work full time on the Monday and we finished combining on Tuesday September 16.

September 19: William Binnington's and Mrs Calvert's funerals took place at 2pm and 2.45pm: the brother and sister were aged 82 and 92 respectively. Mr Binnington had been foreman at Walkers of Manor House for donkey's years -from the time the Walkers came to Lund in fact. Mrs Binnington had the Post Office. Mrs Calvert lived in the house opposite the cross on The Green, and was the mother of Bernard Calvert, who worked on farms all his life, latterly at Snowdens. He delivered the newspapers, maintained the village green spaces and many gardens round the village. He never stopped.

Later that week we finished gathering up all the straw at Wold House and stacking down the side of the drive—of which Von strongly disapproved. We then had Scorborough and Lund Harvest Festivals one evening after the other. Both churches were packed; you had to get there early to get a seat.

It was at this time that Alan Walker, of Middleton, sold off the grass field in the middle of the village for housing. John Dowson was off work seeing about getting a mortgage to buy a house on the estate. They built 120 houses there on the 12 acres; in the beginning the houses next to the main road, at the top of the hill, were selling for £7,000 each. This was in 1973 when the first houses were built. By the time John got his house they had risen to about £9,000. Needless to say the writing was on the wall regarding John's continuing employment now he would be moving out of Vicarage Farm.

At the end of September we sold Fishers the Atou wheat for seed at £100 a tonne. At the same time I sowed 119cwt of 0.20.20 on the 50-acre pea land across the road. John then sowed 58cwt of Maris Kinsman wheat.

October 7: it was our wedding anniversary so I took Von to the Beansheaf at Pickering for a meal. Alone.

I sowed 11cwt of 9.24.24 on 52 acres across the road, with John drilling Hobbit wheat after me. Mother, Angus and I went to Queen Margaret's for the official opening of the new canteen. Von went to St Peter's for prize-giving and then we all met for lunch at the Little Chef at Pocklington. We had a very long wait; it closed down not long afterwards. They built a new roundabout on the site in 2013.

We received a cheque for £1,112 for John D's wages and mileage for the pea harvest from Beverley Pea Growers.

Jack Ingle, Bentall's representative, came up the same day to see about a new Goldhanger drier set up. It was obvious after this last harvest that we needed to get more storage space for corn and a better system for getting the corn dried at harvest. The ventilated bin plant was becoming overloaded and outdated.

He took me round to see various similar plants, the first one being a Bentall grain drier only at Parks and Simpson's farm at Wetwang, which we would eventually buy seven years later. The drier had been newly installed that harvest and there were still no doors on the sheds, the corn just being dropped on the floor from the overhead conveyor in the apex of the building. The same evening, Von and I went to the Bainton YFC annual general meeting; I was in the chair, as Moore Beachell (David's father) was ill. Von and I had been asked to judge the Club of the Year competition throughout the winter: this entailed visiting every club in the county, of which there were 19. It proved to be a most interesting and enjoyable experience.

Chris Atkinson, from Nafferton, came with his mobile seed dresser, dressing seed corn for ourselves and quite a few small orders that we had. I paid the £1,204 half year's rent at South Dalton and Todd and Thorpe £1,550 for the Vicarage Farm rent.

We had to have Eastwood's at Lickham to rebuild the wall at the front of the foldyard; John S had forgotten to lower his tipping cart when coming out of the yard at harvest and pulled the door track and doors down. John D knocked up the hedge down the side of Chalk Road at Vicarage Farm, mainly to prevent the road getting blocked with snow in the winter but also to eliminate tyres being punctured by the thorns when the hedge was cut.

November 4: we finished drilling all the winter corn for the year: we had 120 acres of winter wheat at both Lickham and Wold House, plus 20 acres winter barley—that was in 20-acre after we had ploughed out the grass. I ordered 50 tonnes of 22.11.11 at £89 per tonne and 11 tonnes of 0.20.20 at £76 per tonne from Francis Jackson, of Albright and Wilson.

November 14: Mother, Von and I went to Uncle Ernie's funeral at Haxey Church, in Lincolnshire, where he had been living with his son and daughter-in-law, Romney and Doreen, at their market garden. The following day we went to Mr Tock's funeral in Middleton—he was Kathleen's father-in-law—and I buried Thor, Andrew's three-legged guinea pig, under the cherry trees in the orchard. We also went to see Billy Cock as he was very ill.

Von got eight turkeys from Twydale Turkeys in Driffield, to give to the men and Mrs Ellis for Christmas. Jim Beal, the RBM (originally Robert B Massey) representative, brought a quote for a Goldhanger drier and equipment, elevators, conveys, dresser, etc all incorporated in the main building—a total 600 tonnes of storage—for £36,035.

We added four more bins the following year as we still had not sufficient storage. This meant that now we could sell off all the grain sides, etc, which we had had to accommodate corn down each side of the old drier—approximately 300 tonnes at each side. The original idea was that we should keep all the seed barley in the old drier and the new drier would accommodate all the seed wheat, which we were growing more or less across the whole farm.

I paid Steve Stephenson £3,027 for autumn chemicals and Roundup.

November 22: Ridings Constructions, from York, started preparing Vicarage Farm road, stoning the potholes on the side of the road and grading it with a machine before putting on a base coat of one and a half inch stone, from the back door at Vicarage Farm to the end of the stable and right down the road to the entrance.

The whole process took about a week to do, finishing off with a three quarter inch bitumastic top coat, rolled down with a heavy roller. Riding's bill for the total cost was £6,270, of which we got a farm improvement grant of £1,254 and a contribution from the landlord of £600. It was money well spent. When Andrew Marr saw it he said that he didn't know they had extended the motorway to Vicarage Farm.

During this time we had Redshaw's, from Driffield, spreading manure at all three farms, from the yards and from the manure hills outside in the fields, for about two weeks at a total cost of £560. We were filling with the Sanderson, and we were using one of our spreaders as well.

At the beginning of **December** Dawson's paid us £10,086 for 127 tonnes of Aramire seed barley. Von and I went down to Smithfield Show in the car: we left home at 6.10am, parked in Earls Court car park, spent the day at the show and were back home by 8.30pm We had a very good day.

Getting to the Christmas period, it was the usual round of carol services at all the schools; Angus's being the first at North Dalton Church. Then the villages carol services at Lund and Scorborough.

December 14: I went to the Exchange Salerooms, in Driffield, where Dee and Atkinson were selling John Farnsworth's 256-acre Manor Farm, Goodmanham, which made £370,000 to T A Stephenson at Arras. It was then farmed by John Stephenson from Goodmanham Wold but it was soon sold on to Talbots. This is where Chris Towse worked until they had completed the sale.

John Dowson was on holiday the same day, moving house from Vicarage Farm to Greenfield Road in Middleton. I ordered 42 tonnes of 34.5 per cent nitrogen from ACT at £71 per tonne, for delivery in January. This was all stacked in the combine shed, now the workshop.

December 16: Von and I went to the Guildhall in Hull to see William Lamb hand over the chain of office at the end of his year as NFU county chairman. Angus broke up at Middleton-on-the-Wolds School that day, Helen had broken up the day before and Andrew broke up the next day, which was well synchronised. I paid the YEB £1,173.88 for electricity for the three farms.

As usual we had Molly Course up for Christmas as well as Grandad, Aunty Lil and Nurse Ingleby. Cynthia, Stan and David Hastings came from Oxford to stay a couple of days after Christmas. We had bought Helen a portable typewriter, so she was well pleased.

I t was becoming more obvious that we could no longer continue milking the cows, as we needed to at least double the number of milking cows and then would need to upgrade the parlour. Moreover, we could not produce the same amount of grass as the western side of the country because of the rainfall, so we took the decision to take the 'golden handshake' of £12,000 and discontinue milking.

At the same time the MAFF was beginning to implement the Farm Horticulture Development Scheme (FHD), which involved Frank Watts, our advisor, sitting down and drawing up a six-year plan to spend money and obtain grants for improving productivity and profitability of farms. This was like giving us an open cheque book to receive these grants. By the time we got to the sixth year we were struggling to find something to spend money on. This was, of course, assuming we were making any money. We put down a farm weighbridge, at an estimated cost of £25,000, and laughed, thinking that never in a million years we would take up THAT grant. But we did.

We went to the accountant, Charles Wood, to agree the accounts for 1976/77 and paid him £856.10. He suggested that we paid Andrew and Helen £235 each and Angus, aged eight, £32 in wages for that year. This was not just lip-service: they had earned it by working during the holidays. We paid ACT £384 for 5,000 litres of tractor diesel, ie 0.0768p per litre and received a cheque for £1,009 from Shoulers for five fat cows

Later in **January** John Sleight fetched 300 beech hedge plants from Henley's at Market Weighton, and he and John D planted them behind the orchard from the dugout to the wood end at Wold House.

I went to Mrs Swallow's funeral at Middleton Church. After the service we all had to wait in the church whilst the grave was re-dug, as the sides had fallen in because there had been so much rain.

We paid Francis Jackson £5,035.50 for spring fertilizer.

When Molly Course went back to Bournemouth after Christmas, she took Mother with her. Grandad and I went there on January 25, calling at PEGRO at Peterborough to leave two samples of peas to get germination tested, etc. Then we called to see Adrian Sherriff at St Albans to see his stock and have a look at Capps Duke, a bull we swapped for our Woldsman Roman, plus £100, which Adrian would deliver the next week.

We got down to Molly's in the evening. John D, in the meantime, gave in his notice to Von, which I had been expecting as he was obviously losing interest in the job and was getting ready for a change.

Grandad and I had two days tiling Molly's kitchen finishing at 11.45pm on the second day. We had to get a new tyre for the car before travelling home on January 28. Grandad, Mother and I left Bournemouth at 8.55am and were home by 2.45pm after calling at 20 St Mary's Road, Doncaster, to pick up John Beaumont's Jaguar to bring it back home for short-term storage. We got home to find that Suzy, the Jack Russell, had had four pups to Etherington's dog. We kept one—Robin—and sold the other three for £15 each.

At the beginning of **February** Peter and Caroline Brown came round with Arthur Newlove, woodman, to see if we would mind them putting a gate in Park hedge next to Middleton Wood, so that the horses could go through a gate rather than try and jump the hedge—Peter was master of the hunt. Several years previously a lady rider had come off her horse and broken her arm after trying to jump the hedge.

Mike Taylor and Rex Harland, from Spofforth, near Wetherby, came with Jack Ingle regarding erecting and assembling the new Bentall Goldhanger drier. Jack Ingle brought four sets of plans for us to approve or otherwise. Funnily enough Jack and I had drawn up, quite independently, virtually identical plans over the weekend, and that is the building which stands now—with a different work area.

Bert and Alan Cheetham came over and bought nine pedigree Red Poll in-calf heifers and three in-calf Danish Red cross cows, at £300 and £250 each respectively. On February 11 we had a very hard frost, which was immediately followed by a very heavy fall of snow. John S was quickly commandeered by the Beverley Borough Council to clear snow in the car parks in Beverley. He also pulled a car out at the bottom of Constitution Hill at

5.30am; he obviously saved someone's embarrassment as the driver gave him £5—a lot of money then: he still talks about it now.

I went into Barclays Bank and paid Andrew's plane fare to Indonesia into John Beaumont's account: Ian Beaumont was a pal of Andrew's and often came to stay at weekends, as his parents were in Indonesia, working for Caterpillar. He had invited Andrew to go over there with him for the Easter holidays. Von was very dubious, as he was only 14, but I pointed out that next year they may not be there and let him have the experience. They were moved the following year.

The grain sections, which had been sold, were all dismantled after we had removed all the seed barley down each side of the old drier—the new Bentall drier parts started arriving and were put in there for the time being.

John Dowson was leaving after 17 years working for us; we were sorry to see him go but had to replace him. We advertised and eventually employed Peter Fisher, who would get married and go to live at Vicarage Farm. Chris Towse from Goodmanham was also employed, provided he could get transport to get to work. In the beginning he had a provisional licence and a 50cc Honda, which got him to and from work. Then he graduated to a car and passed his driving test.

March 1: Millers Aerial Sprayers came to spread fertilizer. They spread 34.5 per cent nitrogen at 1.5cwt per acre on Wood Flat and 20 acre before bursting a wheel on landing. The following day they finished spreading the same on 102 acres across the road and all the wheat at Lickham. Blooms also brought up a load of nine tonnes of nitrogen to spread on their land at Scorborough. Our landing strip on Middleton Tops was very good.

March 3: John Dowson finished—the old order changeth. He went to work for Richard Briggs, at the Land Rover Centre in Middleton; he was there for about a year before moving to work for Rowlands (Naverac at North Dalton), where Anne, his wife, worked. He stayed there for two or three years and then set up with Anne selling sheets, towels, duvets, etc at markets.

A couple of days later Von was judging public speaking at Market Weighton. She did this for many years and we trained the Bainton team as well. At this time Von was president of Northern Area YFC and used to go with Paul Butler to attend meetings at Scotch Corner and various other places. Young Farmers had always formed a big part of our recreation. We always laughed, as I judged stock, Von cookery, Mother handicrafts and Grandad horticulture: we could have covered a show by ourselves.

March 6: Peter Fisher and Chris Towse started work at Wold House and were immediately put to work clearing up in the workshop with Eddie and John Sleight; Chris getting used to the layout of the farm. We made our formal application to MAFF for grant on the new Bentall plant.

March 13: we had Aunty Hilda Duggleby's funeral at North Frodingham; she was the last of the children born at Lickham to Uncle Edward and Aunty Helen (Nelly) and she would also be the last bride from Lickham. She had married Douglas Duggleby, who lived at Arram at that time. They went to live at High Farm at North Frodingham, and had Frankie and Edward (Gill and Rosemary's father).

The next day the YFC county organiser, Mitch, came to discuss Club of the Year awards. First was Holme-upon-Spalding Moor, second Driffield, third Bridlington and fourth equal Muston and Roos. Beverley was sixth.

March 18: Andrew broke up early in the morning for some reason so we fetched him home and later Mother, Von and I went to Helen's confirmation in the school chapel at Queen Margaret's. Afterwards we went to The Chase in York for a meal, which was very enjoyable. The following day Angus, Aunty Farnaby, Von and I went to school for Helen's first communion—and then they broke up.

March 20—a big day: Von and I took Andrew to Doncaster to collect Ian and Nigel Beaumont from their grandparents' home, which was their UK base. We took them to catch the London train at Doncaster and off they went to Indonesia. Andrew had a fantastic time, returning two weeks later with his case full of bananas. He had travelled—alone—from Indonesia to Singapore, where he was met by a Caterpillar representative who took him to a hotel for the day, saying he would collect him in the evening and take him to the airport. As soon as he had gone, Andrew went outside, hailed a betcha, or rickshaw, and went all round Singapore, returning in time to be collected and taken to the next plane. It was a wonderful experience for him, which he has never forgotten.

The following day all of us were freeze-branding all the cows, in-calf heifers and maiden heifers—easy identification for the new regime. Bernard Sissons started painting 41 South Street, ready for our holiday lettings. I paid Bernard £1,777 for decoration and repairs at Wold. All of us were taking up trees in the wood where the drier was going and replanting them down the side of the paddock to make an avenue. We planted two beech trees, 100 metres from the garden wall below the two lime trees and put some round Park pond hole. We then levelled the base in the stackyard for the new building and put the rubbish and scrapings into Park pond hole.

March 29: we started drilling Ark Royal spring barley in Little Wold. Andrew rang from Indonesia; all was going fine.

At the end of March we had two Americans, Bob and Rosie Anderson, to stay via Bishop Burton College. Helen read a lesson at the Easter service and the following day Arnott and Betty Weightman came for the night.

As it was the end of the tax year in April, Eddie started working a normal timetable, the same as the rest of the men. Before this he had been staggering his day off so that he got a weekend every six weeks but now, if he worked weekends, it was overtime. I took 1,350 empty fertilizer bags into Lees in Driffield, all slit at the top: so long as they were in good condition you could get half a penny each for them—and it got rid of them. You could take old newspaper and large paper feed bags in as well.

April 11: it was the Maltas's silver wedding anniversary. David had arranged a party at the Old Mill at Stamford Bridge, totally unknown to Margaret, as she would not have gone. Von had to persuade her to get her hair done and invest in a new dress—on the pretext that the four of us were going out to dinner and she should push the boat out.

We went to the hotel, and Margaret, who is very sharp, said: 'Oh, look, that's Roy Knight's car there.' We all coughed discreetly and got her indoors, to see all the five boys standing on the staircase at a couple of steps interval. She was totally amazed, went up the stairs and into the room, to see a roomful of their friends and acquaintances waiting. She thoroughly enjoyed herself. We three each heaved a sigh of relief; she could just have easily turned tail. Roy and Esther Knight stayed with us for the night—Roy was the auctioneer for Harrison and Hetherington at Lockerbie and Carlisle.

The next day Andrew returned from Indonesia. We met him at York Station in the afternoon, with his suitcase full of bananas: he was full of his amazing experiences in a country so different from his own and it was difficult to comprehend. He had come back a week before Ian as he wanted a bit of time at home before returning to school. The same day Tony Fieldsend, a friend of John Beaumont, was over for a three-week holiday and was borrowing John's Jaguar for the period. He returned it to us to continue storing.

April 23: John started drilling Scout peas in the four front fields at Vicarage Farm. RBM representative Jim Beales came up and I paid him £33,591.47 for the Bentall bins, drier, elevators, etc. I had never written such a large cheque in my life.

At that time we were buying new-born suckling calves at £50 a time to put onto the Red Poll cows that we had been milking previously. The same day Robin Hood, Turner's Digger contractors, started digging out the cesspit down the paddock. Eastwood's men bricked it out. Unfortunately they cut through the two-inch main water pipe feeding the farm so we had to have emergency repairs done. This meant going into Driffield and getting a two-inch straight connector. This pipe runs past the corner of the cesspit, from the bottom gate to the front garden wall.

They then starting digging out the elevator shaft for the new drier, and spreading it all over the base for the new Bentall bins. Every five feet there was a three to four inch layer of flint. They went down 20 feet into neat chalk for the elevator shaft and then started pulling out for the wet pit and the holding bin pit. All this chalk spoil made excellent hardcore for putting under the bins, where we had dug out the soil after removing the trees.

At the end of the month John and Mr Sleight were working land for peas at Lickham. Eastwood's finished building the settling chamber for the farm sewage and surface water before starting building the elevator shaft for the new drier. They then continued building the dividing wall up between the holding bin and the wet pit. During all this time we were getting Ready Mix Concrete (RMC) at £40.75 per cubic metre. We had a dozen loads just for the base and work bay area alone.

May 4: Von took Mother to the funeral of one of our evacuees: the Mann family had been evacuated with us for a period of time and we kept in touch with them afterwards. Mr Mann was one of the pilots on the Humber, and it was his wife who had died.

So far that spring it had been quite a catchy time and, as a result, it was too wet to get on spreading fertilizer, so we had AIS, our chemical supplier, spray all the wheats with Cycocel and Derosal using their helicopter.

Mother was one of the first to be into the helicopter for a ride—surprise. She thoroughly enjoyed herself and we all had a turn eventually.

The next day Von, Peter Ullyott and I went down to the Red Poll Council meeting and annual general meeting in London, where I was made president elect. The same day we had 300 breeze blocks delivered for Eastwood's to build out the pit walls. Watts brought two big loads of face gravel to back fill the blocks after they had been filled with concrete and reinforced.

It continued to be quite a catchy drilling time and Chris finished drilling the peas in Air Station field on May 10. Beverley Pea Growers had bought a controlled droplet application (CDA) sprayer from Horstine Farmery to use within the pea group; unfortunately it didn't catch on. A week later John drilled 35 acres of Scout peas at Lickham at the beck end on the Railway Side

May 20: Angus was poorly with measles and had to stay in bed. Unfortunately I caught them from him and was worse than he was. Every time I smelt food the pain in my neck was excruciating.

May 25: we received a letter from the estate office telling us that we had been successful in getting the summer grazing rights on 29.5 acres at Holme Wold for £1,056 until November 1. Chris spread 75cwt of 34.5 per cent nitrogen on this in the afternoon of the same day. The following day he sprayed as much as possible with MCPA at two pints per acre for the, mainly, nettles. All this time we were getting RMC and laying the base for the bins.

At the end of the month we had Agricon Engineers here for the first time, sorting out the base panels for the bins and air-sweep floor, and got a start putting them together in the afternoon. By the second day we had virtually got all the base panels and air-sweep floor assembled. By the beginning of June John Sleight was doing a very good trade getting manure out for all the various neighbours at Arram, Lockington, Scorborough, Maltas at Roos, etc. AIS came again with the helicopter to spray 20 acres of barley for mildew. The same day Millers Aerial Sprayers spread 12 tonnes of 34.5 per cent nitrogen on all the winter wheats—240 acres at 1cwt per acre at a cost of £5 per acre.

June 3: all the six of us went to the circus at the Kelleythorpe corner showfield, Driffield. There were lions and tigers, acrobats, horses, clowns, performing dogs and elephants, which had paraded through the town in the afternoon. A circus in those days WAS a circus, and a very big attraction.

June 6: the erection of the bins was going apace, with every spare minute that we ourselves had, plus the two from Agricon, Rex Harland and assistant, spent working. We put trailers down the stackyard side of the bins, and then put Howard bales on to lift as necessary. It was a hive of industry.

June 13: the whole of the bins area was up to eaves height; we had hired a compressor to tighten all the thousands of bolts as there were two people tightening bolts virtually all day. Obviously all this work going on was a big attraction for all the neighbours and representatives alike. We had had seven representatives up on June 6 alone.

At the same time we had quite a bit of surplus straw under cover—Neville Merrington was buying all this all the way up to harvest. The Howard bales averaged 337kg each. By the end of the month the work area and penthouse was nearly complete. Sissons made three windows to go into three panels in the penthouse as well as the wooden stepladder to get up to the catwalk above the bins and into the penthouse.

We went to Elgey and Libby Byass's to a wine and cheese and Von won a large box of fruit.

June 26: RMC brought five loads of concrete for bridging between the air-sweep floors: they brought a pump to pump it through a side panel of each bin. All of us were working like—well, hard. We paid £583.20 for the concrete plus £135 for the pump. The building was more or less complete with the roof on; just guttering and finials to put on and the bit round the penthouse to finish off. The inside work was then to start: elevators, conveyors, drier, furnace, grain ducting, etc.

Von and I went to Queen Margaret's speech day on June 30, and the following day was open day; we took George and Christine Walker to the ball in the evening.

By the beginning of July the calves we were getting from Malcolm Ashley had gone up to an average of £79 a head and this was becoming non-viable.

July 7: we had finished all the internal works, penthouse, roof and all the complications that involved getting the elevators in before the penthouse roof could be put on. After this it was a case of us getting the two sliding doors made and hung. Peter Fisher made the doors and we sheeted them in situ after hanging them. Peter Burnell's gang of six began pulling wild oats at Lickham.

We took Andrew and Helen to one of their first YFC events—a wine and cheese evening at Turtons at Tibthorpe Lodge. The next day it was the garden fete at Lund; it made a record £596.

July 16: we had a good clean up, and had 40 in for lunch. Mostly this was on the lawn at the side of the house. As it was a really hot day people were sitting on the grass and had their glasses nearby on the ground. Robin, the Jack Russell of the moment, had been socialising and cleaned out some of the glasses; at the end of the party he was laid out dead drunk. Two days later Thorngumbald YFC brought a bus-load of Young Farmers for a farm walk: we visited all three farms and then they had supper in the newly-whitewashed garage at the front. Eddie had been busy during the day.

Later that week Helen, Von and I went to the national Red Poll Field day at Rosemary Phillipson Stow and Adrian Darby's in Worcestershire.

John had a week's holiday and after that we five went off in the caravan to Scotland. We had wet and cold weather at the beginning of the week but then it came out very hot. We had got as far as Perth on the way back when I rang Mother to see how all was and she told me a tale of woe ending with the fact that Robin (the said Jack Russell) was lost for a day already: they had searched all over. Well, that was it, we had to pack up and head for home the following morning. Needless to say we arrived home at the same time that Bob Hall brought him back—he had been caught in a sheep net.

By the end of the month Lancaster's had finished wiring all the lights and motors in the drier. At the beginning of August the pea viners started vining peas in Chalk Road and averaged 53cwt per acre at 100.9 TR.

August 6: Von and I went to lunch at Blooms at Decoy. It must have been a nuisance to them because every time you went in or out you had to get the gatekeeper to open and shut the railway gates. Two days later all of us went to Allan's at Harrogate to get Angus's uniform for Cundall Manor and I got a new suit as well. I had just received an invitation to judge at the 1979 Royal Show so now was prepared.

We had our staff outing—they all came to the farm for a buffet tea, then the 21 of us: the five of us, Mother and Mrs Farnaby, Lil and Grandad, John and Margaret Sleight, Mr and Mrs Sleight, Chris and Christine, Eddie and Pauline, Mrs Ellis, Mrs Hesletine and Peter and Jeanette Fisher, went to Scarborough to see the Danny La Rue Show. These 'dos' always seemed to go well and, fortunately, they all appeared to get on well.

By the middle of August the pea viners had vined the peas at Lickham, and MAFF drainage advisor Paul Staniforth came to inspect our drainage proposal for Railway Side at Lickham. He subsequently approved of the plans. Lancasters were working getting all the motors going the right way on the new drier and got the furnace going. Garry Hyde started cutting all the hedges around the pea fields and grasses at Wold House and Vicarage Farm and Sissons started to paint at Wold House. Unfortunately the tax man had to be paid again, this time £4,400.

August 17: we started combining the Espe winter barley in 20-acre, and got about 45 tonnes. We pushed up all the thorns into heaps, dragged twice round the hedge side and then burned all the straw. At the same time I rotavated Queen's Mead again for the umpteenth time.

August 24: Andrew, Ian Whorley, Helen and Angus started putting polystyrene shedders in the bins to make it easier for cleaning down and stop corn resting on the bottom ledges of the panels.

Mr Wilson, our bank manager at the Midland Bank, came out to lunch and to see what we were spending his money on. He had a look round the farm as well, as the bank managers did in those days: they were far more hands-on and agreeable and had authority to give loans as they thought fit.

The following day Sue Whorley and I went to Kirkstall in Leeds for the last of the polystyrene shedders and adhesive. We got the same for Gordon Kendal, who also had Agricon engineers helping him with a similar Bentall set-up to ours, and some for Richard Henley at Market Weighton, who was just putting up some bins.

The same day we started combining Hobbit wheat in 52-acre across the road: Jack Ingle was there most of the day, showing us how to work the drier. Arnott's also started draining on Railway Side at Lickham. The 52 acre and Wood Flat Hobbit wheat together did approximately 230 tonnes from 70 acres, about three and a quarter tonnes per acre. Grandad Carr was now in full-time occupation for harvest and sowing time—driving corncarts or rolling corn or whatever. Andrew, Ian, Helen and Angus finished putting shedders on the drier bins just in time.

September 1: we sold Maurice Robson 36 tonnes of feed wheat at £80 a tonne plus £1.80 delivery to Fridaythorpe. In those days Maurice would bring you a cheque at the end of the first week. I think he also wanted to have a look round the drier. MAFF completed a check weighing on the Kinsman pea land wheat in 50-acre: it was estimated to be doing 3.6 tonnes per acre. Von and Mother went to Mr Steele's memorial service in Locking-ton Church; Mr Copeland, from Bracken, died the same day.

Later on that same week Peter Jackson, from Fishers, came and bought 220 tonnes of feed wheat, at £81 per tonne, and 45 tonnes of Espe barley at £85 per tonne to go immediately. Dry corn was in demand.

September 9: eight of us—Eddie and Pauline, Chris and Christine, George and Christine Walker and we two went to Scarborough to see Ken Dodd. Von took our Mercedes and I took John Beaumont's Jaguar back to Doncaster, as he was now back in England. Whilst we were doing this a cow died with staggers; Wiles came to collect it and paid us £22. Nowadays we have to pay them to collect.

The next day Angus started at Cundall Manor School. He had been go-ing there for the last five years when picking up Andrew so it was not such a shock for him. I paid JV £480 for the term. Five years previously, when Andrew started, it was £190 per term. We dropped Andrew at St Peter's on the way back. By the middle of September we were beginning to dry quite a bit of corn for Fishers of Cranswick; we charged £3.75 per tonne up to 20 per cent moisture, and then 50p for every per cent over, and had a handling charge of 40p per tonne, in and out. Jim Beales came up and I paid him £2,174 for the Barclay, Ross and Hutchinson cleaner/grader in the new dri-er.

September 17: we finished combining—it had been a very wet harvest. We still hadn't sufficient storage for all the grain, hence the need having to sell so much corn in harvest. A nice position to be in. Arnott's finished draining all the Railway Side at Lickham after we had burned the 30 acres of wheat straw at the road end of the field.

September 25: Martin Clarke was installed as priest-in-charge of Lund with Lockington; he was already in charge at Leconfield and Scorborough. This was the first of the amalgamations. He followed our good friend Arthur Lawes, who went to Leavening-with-Acklam.

The following day Fred Arnott brought his bill for draining work at Lickham. I paid him £5,943—this was excluding the pots and John Binning-ton's fee for surveying, etc. They connected in to the original main drain that Richardson's had put in previously. The entire field was now drained at 11-yard intervals. John had to go over with the drag to level up the tops of the drains. Simon H Ogram brought a straw boiler to put into a shed which became the boiler house, ready for installing central heating for the house at Lickham. Mother went to Bournemouth with Molly for a holiday that day.

September 29: I went into Richardson's and bought a new four furrow reversible plough for £2,150 and spool valves for the 7000 tractor. The next day was the first of the harvest festivals, this one at Scorborough Church with another at Lund the following evening; they were packed to the gunnels as usual. Two days later we started to plough the fields and scatter, sowing Hobbit wheat on the pea-land in the field next to Paddock.

October 8: all the three children returned to school on the same day—for the first time ever. Von, Helen and I went to church at Cundall before travelling on to Queen Margaret's. The following day Von and I went down to Bournemouth to fetch Mother back, leaving Grandad and Aunty Lil at home as caretakers. We stayed the night with Molly and came back the following day. Whilst we were away Grandad had pulled basketfuls of damsons, of which Mother sold 48lbs for £7. The following day he pulled another 80lbs. Bert Cheetham came over and he bought six heifers paying £340 each for them. I paid him £90 for two calves.

In the evening I took Bill Pinkney, our solicitor and president of the ER Federation of YFCs, to Holme-upon-Spalding Moor to a meeting. On return it was always obligatory to go in at Tibthorpe for a very stiff drink and to be licked to death by Charles, his boxer dog, a big, powerful animal, named after Lord Halifax, who had given it to Bill. They were both masters of the Middleton Hunt.

October 13: Received a cheque for £3,492.63 from Fishers for 41 tonnes of Espe winter barley seed; we had already had three tonnes (which Chris Atkinson had dressed at home for us) out for ourselves and others. This was the total yield from 20-acre and equalled £187 per acre. Not bad for a cereal crop.

The following day we collected Angus from Cundall Manor and then went to Glovers of Ripon to see about a Land Rover, for which there was a year's wait—so no joy. A week later we went to Cundall for parents' evening, brought him home and then went to Pocklington School for a supper dance with George and Christine Walker.

We had finished drilling wheat that day at Lickham—there was 127 acres of Hobbit wheat there in total. That was the end of drilling for that season. Then Andrew was back for half-term. The following morning he brought John Sleight's tractor and plough up from Lickham. Aged 16, Andrew now had his provisional tractor driving licence.

October 24: I went to see Mr Wilson at the Midland Bank in Beverley regarding Bernard Shaw's land at Wilfholme: he gave us the OK to go ahead and bid for it. At the end of the month I brought Helen and Samps (Miss Simpson, housemistress) home. She lived in Beverley and had already informed me that she had a black belt for judo—should I have had any wayward thoughts. That night Andrew, Grandad and I went rabbiting and shot 18 rabbits and three hares. On the last day of October I took Von, Mother, now 83, and Mrs Farnaby to London with me, while I went to the Red Poll Cattle Society Council meeting at the Farmers Club in Whitehall they went off round the shops. I parked outside the Ministry of Defence and Von fed the meter. No problems.

November 1: I took the seat from the church entrance up to Cundall Manor and JV took it on to Carters at Swinderby—for what purpose I cannot remember. Angus was home for half term. The day after at the Beverley Pea Growers meeting we ordered two new self-propelled Food Machinery Company pea viners at £80,000 each. The group would now operate these viners and be paid harvesting costs by Birds Eye. Before this the pea viners were tractor drawn with pea-cutters going in front to winrow. We had to forgo our usual celebration of my birthday as both Helen and Andrew were back at school that night. St Peter's never acknowledge bonfire night as Guy Fawkes had been a pupil there.

From **November 6** I sold Feedex 12 tonnes of wheat per week up to Christmas at £88.50 per tonne for November and £89.50 per tonne for December. This was to be a contra on our feed bill, as we were getting our beef nuts and calf rearing nuts from the company. Garry Hyde finished cutting all the hedges and limbed up the lime tree down the paddock, which had blown down. Angus went back to school in the evening.

A couple of days later I went to Bridlington, saw Bill Atkin and gave him a limit of £57,000 for Lot One of 54 acres and £103,000 for Lot Two of 73 acres, for the land at Wilfholme. A couple of days later he went to the Beverley Arms Hotel for the sale: lot one made £73,500 and lot two made £110,000. He was runner-up for us.

Bob Rodgers, plumber from Driffield, started to install central heating at Lickham, using a Farm 2000 straw burner, which would take ordinary small pick-up bales of straw for fuel. Eddie and I, although he was on holiday, went to Holmfirth Market where I bought 14 calves for £833 (£60 each). Mother and I collected Angus from Cundall Manor and then went to Swinderby to pick up the church seat before collecting Andrew in York on the way back.

Grandad and I stripped out the old fireplace in the Wold House dining room, which we were having decorated, and Bernard Sissons built an arch and shelving on which to put the television. The following night all three children were home for the weekend, so that was good. Sheila and Tony Riby came and bought Helen's Hercules Jeep bike for £15.

At the end of the month I went to the estate office and saw the agent, Mr Wilson, regarding Mr Thompson's land at Lund as he was retiring. I agreed to swap our 52 acres at Road Ends, which we had bought previously from Alwyn Middleton, for Watergarth, Short Lands and Bramble Butts—50 acres in all, which Mr Thompson had been farming, I believe Lord Hotham had to pay capital gains tax because he was getting better value per acre than we were. We retained the tenancy of 52-acre, but we would have to surrender the tenancy of the 18-acre grass at Dalton, which was now arable, on April 5 1980.

We would also farm the Wold land that Mr Thompson had been farming for that summer only. It was five fields, which were 119 acres in total. Bulmers gave up land at Lair Grange and would take the 119 acres over in the autumn. The same day Rodgers got the central heating finished at Lickham and lit the boiler, which was appropriate, as it snowed heavily in the afternoon.

December 1: Von and I took Uncle Tommy and Aunty Betty Carr to Norman Winstanley's funeral at Thornaby-on-Tees. Norman was husband to Edie, Lil's sister. At the same time Bernard and Geoffrey Sissons finished all the alterations and decorations in the old dining room. Mr Mayfield came and re-laid all the carpet tiles in the kitchen and passageway and the carpet in the old dining room and then cleaned both.

Von and I took John and Margaret Sleight to Smithfield Show at Earls Court: we left home at 6am and were back home by 11pm. The next day Grandad and I went to Holmfirth mart and bought another seven calves at an average price of £49. We also bought two calves from Cheethams. Eddie took Chris and Peter down to Smithfield for the day.

December 12: Andrew passed his tractor driving test. I bought six calves at Haltwhistle Market, which averaged £40 each.

We now started the end of term carol services. No wonder we know O Come All Ye Faithful, etc, off by heart: we had Queen Margaret's and Cundall Manor on the same day. We also went to Hull to the NFU annual general meeting at the City Hall to hear Sir Henry Plumb, our NFU national president, speak. He was very good.

Von fetched Andrew from school whilst I took Helen and Angus to collect the Christmas trees from Keith Simpson's at Cranswick, and so Christmas was here again.

December 30: Diana Thomas and Phillip Evans came from Anglesey, Wales, and bought five in-calf heifers and one cow—ex Adrian Darby—at £375 each. The Maltas family came for the evening. It started to snow quite heavily as they left and the next morning Andrew was out with the forklift clearing the road with the Sanderson.

January 8 found us going down into Holderness, to Roos, to the funeral of Mr Maltas senior, David's father. John had started ploughing Long Field on Thompson's land, next to 50-acre.

Later that month Eddie went to Holmfirth Market and bought three calves for £128. While there he met Alan Cheetham, who had brought two calves, and paid him a cheque for £90. When we first met Eddie said he never stayed anywhere for more than four years. He had now been with us for six years and, hopefully, felt more than just an employee. After all he did ask Mother to be Teresa's godmother, which we felt was a big honour.

It was about now that the lorry drivers went on a nationwide strike over rates of pay. We were selling our corn to be delivered immediately to various mills and compounders together with corn from other local farms. The biggest problem this caused was taking heavy loads of corn—heavy for our trailers—from four tonnes up to 14 tonnes. It was heavy on punctures and also wheel rims on the trailers, but we had up to four tractors and trailers per day going into Hull and other mills.

We paid Bob Rodgers £1,627.67 for the installation of central heating at Lickham and paid separately for the chimney for the burner from Arco. We also paid Brian Lancaster £595.64 for the balance of the drier's electrical installations and repairs to date. At the beginning of February, while I was drying beans for various people, the restricted tariff electric meter in the saddle room caught fire and burnt the fuse board meter and fuse box out. The YEB were quickly requested to replace same.

At this time calves were becoming expensive: I went to York Market and bought seven calves for £419.

John Sleight went to the funeral of Tom Taylor, of Hall Garth, Lockington: he had been getting manure out for Taylors and several more locals since we had had the Sanderson.

February 15: it started to snow really hard and was blowing. At 11am Peter Fisher escorted Chris Towse home to Goodmanham with the Sanderson, via Kiplingcotes and Grannies Attic, as a lorry had got stuck at the bottom of Wood Flat hill. When he came back via the same route the road was blocked at Pit corner by a car, so he had to go round by Lair Hill and Middleton to get back to Wold House. He arrived back at 2.30 pm. Eddie couldn't get through for snow; it really was bad. The council had based a bladed snowplough with us to be used in such circumstances, but there was too much for it to cope with so we used the Sanderson with the bucket. The snow lasted nearly a week before roads were reasonably passable.

February 19: I went to the estate office at South Dalton with Tom Helm and agreed with the agent, Tony Wilson, to pay £30 per acre for 23 acres of Mr Thompson's following crop winter wheat at Wold plus £27 per acre rent for the 119 acres of land at Wold until October 1 1979, when we should relinquish it and Bulmers would take it over on a regular tenancy. We would also pay Mr Thompson £110 per acre for six acres of following crop winter wheat in Bramble Butts.

We were again doing the YFC Club of the Year competition and were visiting most of the clubs in the county in the winter period. Each club had to produce a complete programme of weekly meetings for the winter and another later on for the summer session. These were most interesting; a mixture of speakers, demonstrations, stock judging, county quiz, rally entries and events. Each club was completely run by its members. They ranged from 10 or a dozen members in the smaller, more remote clubs, to 60-odd in the larger ones. Each club had an advisory committee, usually made up of parents or local farmers, who often went along to meetings out of pure interest but seldom needed to interfere.

February was turning into a busy month: Alf had a heart attack and was in hospital, Andrew and Grandad lost a ferret in 20-acre park hedge bottom and Mother, Von and I went to Mr Abbott's funeral: he had the smallholding, Ivy Cottage, opposite the playing fields at Middleton. Jessie, his daughter, grew flowers and arranged them and did bouquets, wreaths, etc for many years afterwards and lived with her mother.

March brought Millers Aerial Sprayers, and they spread 303 acres of wheat and winter barley at Wold House and at Lickham, with 1.5cwt per acre of 34.5 per cent nitrogen. Blooms, Hunters and Lambs brought their nitrogen to be spread from our airstrip on Middleton Tops. Later that day Von and I went to Elgey and Libby Byass's for a meal. In those days we had a very friendly and co-operative community, particularly in and around the village.

The following day R D Webster, of Kilham, brought a 14-foot Cousins Dutch harrow with straight teeth and a crumbler bar. It cost £685 and made a good job of levelling the ground before drilling.

We went to Harry Fenton's funeral: he had had Vicarage Farm until we took over in 1958.

I put in an application form to MAFF for a grant for four more 75 tonne Bentall Goldhanger bins with air-sweep floors, etc. We received a £6,220 cheque from J Bibby and Sons for the barley we had delivered into Hull; 71.5 tonnes of Lofa Abed at £87 per tonne. John finished spreading 22.11.11 fertilizer on all grasses at Wold House and Lickham. Watergarth was sown later, when the deed of exchange was completed.

March 9—Helen's birthday: We went to see her at Escrick at 5pm by special arrangement; girls' schools are much more restrictive than boys'. She seemed pleased with her presents and introduced us to her friend, Pauline, who was a day girl; they seemed to be good friends. We then went to see Andrew at St Peter's regarding having an interview at Lackham College.

I had a parish council meeting later in the evening. Our clerk, Percy Wharram, the hunt tailor in the village (his shop was next to the Wellington Pub and is now known as Lotties), had died and had to be replaced. Alec Snowden and I had approached Joan Helm. We told her that there would only be about four meetings a year and persuaded her to take on the job. She was to remind us of this for the rest of her life. The first year she had eight meetings as we were just beginning to get involved with the Best Kept Village and Britain in Bloom competitions and this involved a lot of paperwork, meetings and working round the village.

During the previous autumn we had tried a new experiment: we had quite an amount of Ark Royal dressed spring barley left over at spring, so we sowed all 18 acres of Wood Flat with this. It looked very well until Christmas but, with there being so much snow and frost during the winter it had completely died off by the beginning of March so we had to start again.

Von and I went to lunch with Bill Pinkney and the rest of the judges for the YFC public speaking competition. Von was judging with Bill and Alec Snowden—she had to give the judges' reasons at the end. She always enjoyed those competitions. We went to Snowdens for a meal in the evening. Whilst she was doing all this, I took Mother, Grandad and Aunty Lil to Cundall to collect Angus for the weekend.

On the Monday following we discovered that two bullocks had gone missing from Vicarage Farm. We had the policeman, Peter Hardwick, taking statements from everybody and we were checking all ear tag numbers to ascertain which ones were missing. The following day CID officers came; they told me I had to go to Beverley Cattle Market the following Wednesday to see if I could identify either of the animals, but no such luck. We never did discover what had happened to the bullocks.

We went to Muston, in a snowstorm, to judge their club, and Mitch came for lunch to discuss the competition. We went to Curtis Travel in Beverley to book our ferry crossing to France at a cost of £116 return from Dover to Calais.

It started to snow very hard and there was a blizzard for about three days. The road was blocked from the air station down to Clarks. Eddie was going to and fro to work on the Fergie tractor. Chris took the Sanderson home to Goodmanham and cleared the road from the racecourse to the Road Ends while coming back to work the following day. He then continued clearing snow from Jerusalem to Beswick Heads. The council was paying us for this work at £10 per hour. I paid Mr Sissons £2,640 for the painting and repairs at Wold House the previous autumn and Eastwood's £950 for building the cesspit in the paddock and elevator shaft and pits for the drier.

Von, Andrew and I went to Lackham College, at Chippenham, Wiltshire, where we had a look around the farm and the college. We stayed the night with the principal and his wife, Peter and Jan Morris. Peter had been vice-principal at Bishop Burton under Denis Hurst and we had been friends from his arrival in the East Riding. Previously he had been working for Arthur Austin, a Red Poll breeder in Wiltshire, and owner of the Seven Springs herd. Peter, in turn, introduced us to Howard Petch, who, in turn, became principal of Bishop Burton and is a good friend to this day. The following day we went to London via the M4. I went to the Red Poll Council meeting at the Farmers' Club while Von and Andrew did some sightseeing.

The following day I met Bert Cheetham at Garland Farm, North Newbald, where his son, Mark, was on a year's work experience prior to going to Bishop Burton. He brought two calves for me.

Andrew and I went to Briggs in Middleton to see the new Land Rover, which had arrived. However, on the journey the engine had blown up and a sleeve had gone through the side of the engine block; therefore we had to wait until a new engine came. This vehicle had already been converted from left hand drive to right hand drive and had been exported to Belgium under Harold Wilson's export drive. When it was eventually delivered Eddie was on his back underneath it examining it when he pulled out a card from under the chassis with all its history—when it was manufactured, exported, etc.

March 29—the end of term: Von, Mother and I went in the van to fetch Angus—with his trunk—from Cundall and then went to Bettys in Harrogate for lunch before coming back to Queen Margaret's at Escrick to collect Helen and her trunk. We three sat in the front of the Commer van with Helen and Angus perched on their trunks in the back. Health and Safety—no seat belts or such then. After tea I went to the parish council meeting: Joan Helm would take over as parish clerk at the beginning of April.

April 1: we took Helen and Fenella to York to catch the train to Kings Cross: they were going to stay with Ankar, a friend of theirs in Germany and flying from Heathrow. At lunchtime Von and I went to Mr John Wilson's retirement party. He had taken over as manager of the Midland Bank on January 1 1968, just after Father died, at a time when he could have made or broken us. Fortunately he had faith in us and we became very good friends. We were very sorry to see him go and, as it turned out, he was the last of the 'proper' bank managers the Midland Bank ever had. Subsequently responsibility for farming finances was taken over by York or Leeds area offices. Cyril Barker of the National Westminster, who was county treasurer to the YFC, was another such manager; they were the end of an era.

April 6: Bentall's sent all the panels and air ducting for the next four bins, which we were going to connect onto the end of the bins, making 10 75-tonne bins and two 55-tonne bins next to the holding bin; a total storage of 900 tonnes of corn.

Von, Andrew, Angus and I went down to Dover in the Mercedes and caught the 1.35pm ferry for Calais. We got to Rheims by 9pm French Energy Saving Time (FEST). We had had the car serviced in Pickering by the Mercedes agents prior to leaving home, but they had put the wrong oil in the brake fluid. By the time we got to Rheims the brake cylinders were going on automatically, as the oil had perished the seals in the cylinders. By the time we got to Cavalaire, near San Tropez, the brake drums were red hot and using a tremendous amount of fuel in the process. Fortunately we were meeting George and Joan Thompson, Sarah and Ruth, who were there already in their caravan. We arrived at midnight and had to knock up the guardier and his wife to guide us to our apartment.

We had left the farm in the hands of the men; Chris, Eddie and John Sleight and whilst we were away they were getting on working and drilling land for corn and peas when the weather would allow, but it was quite a wet time.

For the four or five days we were in the south of France, George was taking us back and forth to Marseille to where the car was being repaired—interpreting was a bit of a problem. We enjoyed looking round the beautiful south of France: it was good that the Thompsons were there.

After we got the car out of dock, paying £52 for repairs, Von and I went to Nice to meet Helen and Fenella, who were coming in on a Lufthansa plane from Frankfurt. It was a beautiful afternoon; we had been sitting on the airport rooftop watching the peaceful scene below us, when suddenly everything changed. As soon as the Lufthansa plane's arrival was announced, there was a flurry of activity. French armed guards appeared and formed an avenue through which the passengers had to pass. We couldn't understand it as we had not read the newspapers whilst away, so didn't know that there had been a terrorist attack in Germany. The two girls were quite unfazed by it all, even though they and their luggage had been searched. We met the Thompsons at the airport; they had taken Sarah, Ruth and our boys to Monaco and seen the famous Monte Carlo rally area.

We spent a bit of time on the beach nearby—Sarah and Angus were running up and down the beach, counting all the nudes and comparing notes. Von got too much sun on her leg, ended up with phlebitis and had to go to the doctor immediately on our return.

April 19: We left Cavalaire at 8.30am and got to Rheims, 681 miles away, at 10pm. Von was the only one to be sick on the journey. The following day we went to Epernay and saw the Rapeneaus and Alain and Florence Drusellier. They were cousins and both had champagne cellars. Their son Christophe had been to stay with us as a student. When Christophe married three years later he invited us to his wedding but, unfortunately, we had to refuse because Tim and Caroline Maltas were getting married at Howden on the same day and we were invited there first. The cousins took us out for a seven-course lunch and Angus got drunk on the wine.

We left Rheims late in the afternoon and went to stay in the Novotel Hotel, in Lille, so that we were reasonably close to Calais as the car was still not quite right. The following day we got the 11.15am ferry from Calais, had an excellent meal on board and then the car decided to stop on the way down the ramp from the boat in Dover. We called in at Canterbury and went around the cathedral: how different from the churches we had seen in France. We had a puncture on the M1 at 60 mph; the boot had to be unloaded to get at the spare wheel. We arrived home at 6.45pm—shattered.

The following Wednesday, Chris Waite took 58 store calves from Lickham into Beverley Market. Dee and Atkinson sold them, making £12,064, an average of £208 each. Tom Helm came in the evening with the cheque and gave us £10 back for luck money. While we were away 14 fat bullocks had gone from Lickham and had averaged £317.

At the end of the month, Pauls' new representative, David Cornwell, who formerly worked for Barkers & Lee Smith, came. Eventually he was headhunted by Kenneth Wilson and became our agronomist, with whom we would spend a lot of money. But that's yet to come... The same day the Feedex representative arrived and I paid him £5,100—the feed account to the end of March. We took Grandad and Aunty Lil to Manchester Airport for their Wallace Arnold holiday to Rome and Sorrento. We called on the Cheethams on the way back. Unfortunately, Von fell down the stairs and went head-first through their hall table and it just shattered into pieces. However, they were very good about it. When we got home Mother was sitting looking very dejected so I took her with me to take Andrew back to school.

Richard Briggs brought the new Land Rover (FAT 906T) and I paid him £5,924. I took Angus back to school in it the following day.

At the beginning of May we had to fence all around the perimeter of Watergarth field in Lund because the fencing was abysmal. We pig-wired and barbed-wired all next to Lambs' field, right round to Short Lands corner at Guest Pits, and then we post-and-railed a fence from Alwyn's hedge at the back of the pond round to the road and along the road side. This was after

Richard Hall had brought his digger and loaded all the bricks and rubble from the Shaw barn base into trailers and pulled up the hedge on the roadside from the pond. It was all taken down to the pit on the Beverley Road.

May 3—Election Day: it snowed hard all the afternoon. Mrs Thatcher's Conservative Party won with a 42-seat overall majority. This was after seven years of the Labour Government headed by Harold Wilson and then Jim Callaghan. I had been buying calves in York Market, as we were rearing a tremendous lot of calves because every cow that calved had two or three foster calves put to her, dependent on the amount of milk she had, which, after being milked, was quite considerable. In the end we started buying calves from Albert Hall at York; he brought nine black Hereford calves that averaged £70 each.

The following day we took Andrew back to school and went onto Manchester to collect Grandad and Aunty Lil from the airport; she was ill and looked quite dreadful

Richard Hall came again with his digger, and dug out several largish trees, which we planted down the side of the drive in the front paddock at the end of the drier. This was to make room for the next four Bentall bins. Three days later we had a tremendous gale, which blew several of these trees over so we had to pull them back upright and secure them.

May 13: I took five youngsters back to school, Helen and friend Jane to Queen Margaret's, Andrew to St Peter's and Angus and Mark Leonard to Cundall. We received a cheque from Humberside County Council for £672 for the snow clearing. Chris finished sowing 70 acres of peas on Thompson's land at Wold.

After Richard Hall had removed the trees and the loose soil from the end of the drier, we fetched about 20 trailer loads of chalk from Horn Hill Top to use as a base, and then approximately 40 tonnes of face gravel from Watts to level up and make solid. Then we had it all to roll down. Von had arranged a coach to take the WI to the Chelsea Flower Show—even Margaret Maltas went. Frank Watts came about Nickerson's crop competition, for which he said he would enter us. Andrew and I went into Hull and collected the go-kart and Helen's motor bike after repairs and in the evening I took Jonathan Walker for cattle judging.

A few days later I fetched Angus, Helen and Samps from school, dropping Samps at her home in Beverley. In the afternoon I took Andrew, Helen and Ian Beaumont to the YFC County Rally at Low Caythorpe and then to the rally dance in the evening, collecting them, plus Fenella Thompson, to bring home with us at midnight. A good time had been had by all.

June 1: Chris sprayed all grasses for docks and thistles with MCPA and Peter was making gates for Watergarth and also a calf creep. AIS were here as well and sprayed all the wheats with Cycocel, Bayleton and Suffix. We received a cheque for £291from MAFF for sub-soiling at Lickham.

I took Helen a letter and a parcel before collecting Andrew and then Angus from school. A couple of days later John spring tine harrowed Clark Field at Lickham and then sowed it with Perfection peas—the last sowing of the season. I took Von, Mother and Mrs Farnaby to Mrs Lamb's funeral at the Driffield Methodist Church. It was very sad.

Millers spread all 333 acres of wheat at Lund and Lickham with 1cwt per acre of 34.5 per cent nitrogen. We received a £10,206 cheque from MAFF for the grant for last year's installation work on the drier. Alan Eastwood's man was here, drilling kale in Little Field and Little Wold. At the same time we were letting 41 South Street for holiday lets. Humberside County Council delivered three Hull City Council street lights, with swan necks, for us to put in at the front of the farm, outside the kerb. Mike Lazenby managed to find the lost ferret and we met the new bank manager, Mr Ringrose, so it was all happening. Jim Beale came and I paid him £9,745 for the four new Bentall storage bins. Sadly two men died in a head-on crash at the top of Etton dykes on that day.

June 13: we collected Angus and Mark Leonard from school, and then called and saw Andrew at St Peter's; he had taken his GCE O-level in maths that day. I thought he was getting ready to leave school: he would have liked a motorbike like Beaumont's but we said: 'No' and that they were too dangerous and we would buy him a car as soon as he passed his driving test. So he was fed up—with revision, exams, school: the lot.

June 14: Angus and I were in charge of the farm as Eddie, Peter, John and Chris went off to Basildon for two days to Ford, and then to Ransome's in Ipswich. Grandad came over in the afternoon as Von and I were invited to Beverley Races by RBM as a thank-you for the trade we have given them. We had a very good afternoon. Von said: 'We must do this again,' to which I answered: 'Yes, next time we get some free tickets.' She did a cookery demonstration in the evening for South Dalton WI.

June 15: I took Mother to Ces Waites' funeral. Ces, 82, had been the fellmonger in the village, and he used to train greyhounds. Additionally he was a staunch member of the church choir—even though he only had one ear. When I was at school in Lund he had the field, Cherry Garth, next to the school playground. There were several fruit trees on the perimeter and when the fruit was ripe we boys would all jump over the wall at playtime to scrump, etc. One day several of us were up the trees when he appeared from nowhere and threatened to give us a good leathering.

Next day Mother and I went to the funeral of Les Norton, who had died aged 78. He had been our butcher in Beverley for many years; he used to come out and kill a pig and dress it for us and then cut it up later for curing. Even after he retired, and had had a leg amputated, he still came out to cut up a bullock's carcase after the vet and I had slaughtered it at midnight and hung it in the foldyard roof.

Three days later Mother went to the funeral of Mrs Barr, who had died aged 95. Mrs Barr had been a staunch member of the WI for many years and lived next to Mrs Calvert on The Green, opposite the Market Cross.

June 18: Suzy, the Jack Russell, had three puppies by Robin, two dogs and a bitch, all nicely marked brown and white. Ready Mix Concrete brought two loads of concrete, for which I paid the driver £260. All of us laid it at the end of the new drier for the four bin bases.

Arthur Prescott (cousin Eddie's son) came to stay from Johannesburg, South Africa, where he lived and worked as a sales manager, selling precision instruments. We had just booked with Curtis's to go on the Red Poll Second World Congress in Australia, in October; we paid £1,159 for two of us to travel to Sydney return with Singapore Airlines. Ullyotts booked at the same time: little did we know that it would lead to them emigrating a year later.

We then had to begin erecting the four Bentall bins; it was a matter of getting the base panels and the air-sweep floor all put together, before we could start to go up at all. Putting the floor together was the most time-consuming job. This was more or less a fill in job between the regular work, mainly amongst stock and hay making, etc.

Von took a coach load of WI members to Sandringham for a day trip— for £3.50 each. The following day I followed roughly the same route to Cambridge for a sprays and sprayer demonstration. As from April 1 we had been able to achieve a more realistic rent from our three houses in Middleton. Mrs Horne and Miss Norman were in numbers eight and six respectively and their rent went up to £4 per week each. Therefore, by the end of June, we had 13 weeks' rent to come from the two, a total of £52 each. This made the investment look a little sweeter after all the expense of the alterations. By the end of June we had the base of the drier extension to the state where we could install the conveyor in the trench for the air-sweep floors. As soon as we got the first lift on, the outlets were to connect into the conveyor itself, which was quite a time-consuming job.

Bert Cheetham came over and bought eight in-calf heifers for £2,900. He had Walter Watson with him, from whom we had bought several cows when he was reducing numbers before he retired. One of these was Barnsfold Primrose, which was the mother of Woldsman Adam, one of our best bulls ever. She was also mother to a lot of our best breeding cows. We finished leading a first cut of hay from Thompson's Low Field next to Lambs, by the end of the month. Andrew and Chris had baled it all and we stored it in the lean-to of the old drier. Chris then sowed 100kg per acre of 34.5 per cent nitrogen on the field.

At the beginning of **July** Mother and Von went to Ripon Cathedral to see Jeremy Valentine ordained as a deacon.

The following day Von and I went down to the Royal Show where I judged the Red Poll classes on the Tuesday. We left John and Chris at home, scruffling kale in Little Field and Little Wold. It was the beginning of the 'silly season'—garden fetes and parties, sports days: they all happen in July. Lund Garden Fete made £740, a record. Mother had baked a fruit cake for a 'guess the weight' competition and she made £10. Andrew went to the garden fete on a tractor as we were at Angus's sports day at Cundall.

By that time we had the second lift completed on the bins and secured the tunnel for the air-sweep. All the outlets were joined in. We paid £120 for a new impact drill and angle grinder from Waddington's as we had worn the others out. AIS had to spray Metasystox on all the peas at Lund for pea midge.

The day after the Royal Show closed we had a great shock: Tony Mowforth, who farmed at Spaldington, had shot his wife, Anne, and their two sons, who were in bed, and then himself. He had just returned from the Royal Show where he had been presented with a £12,000 Massey Ferguson tractor for winning a competition. It really knocked the farming community sideways; we had all been in Young Farmers at a similar time. What drove him to such a desperate state of mind, no-one will ever know. He farmed with his family, whose main farm was at High Hunsley.

July 10: Peter Fisher started working with the pea viners that afternoon; he was in the portable workshop. Then the school holidays began. Helen broke up on July 12: the first one home.

Bainton YFC held a wine and cheese evening at Tibthorpe Lodge. Cousin Arthur had returned from his travels to get his clothes washed and the next day he, Von, Helen and I went to Andrew's regatta at St Peter's: we arrived just in time to see Andrew and Megginson win the pairs. He got the sculls, pairs, and house cups for rowing, so that was a good day. Mr Dawson told me that Andrew had achieved an 'A' for class work, so we were very pleased.

July 15: Arthur went off to Murton to one of his vintage tractor and steam engine rallies: that was the object of his visits at that time of the year—going round all the different steam rallies. Then in the evening he, Von and I took Mother, now aged 84, into the Nuffield Hospital for a hip replacement. We then went on to check on the building of the Humber Bridge: they had completed the main suspension towers after great difficulty with the base of the tower at the south side, where they could not get down to solid rock. They had to go down approximately 60 feet in the mud. They were now stringing the wires across. Chris and Mr Sleight scruffled the kale again that day.

July 19: Angus broke up from Cundall. We collected him, his trunk and bags in the Land Rover. Poor lad, he was full up as we had got lost on the way across country and were three quarters of an hour late. However, he soon cheered up when we got going. We started putting up purlins on the drier roof. A couple of days later we had all the asbestos on and everything except the barge boards completed.

It was about now that Sir Emrys Jones came to judge the Nickerson's cereal competition, telling us that we were in the first 11, which was quite an achievement. We didn't win, but were pleased to be in the final first half dozen. Sir Emrys was a most interesting and charming man: he was an ex-head of ADAS, the then principal of Cirencester College of Agriculture and had been an agriculture advisor to Fred Peart, ex-Minister of Agriculture.

We decided to burn our boats completely and we sold the remainder of our grain sides to a Mr Burniston for £650. David Hastings, my godson from Oxford, arrived in York and Von and Helen collected him; he usually came up at that time to give a hand. Steve Stephenson, our agronomist from AIS, called and I paid him £6,465 for summer chemicals we had had so far. The drainage board started to clean out weed in the beck at Lickham. It had been a very wet summer and the weed growth had been tremendous so it was a relief to get it cleaned out as early in the season as that. The same evening we had 22 Beverley and Sherburn NFU members looking round the Bentall Goldhanger setup and drier. They then took me to dinner at the Pipe and Glass, at South Dalton.

Von and I had a day out, calling in to have lunch with Liz and Jack Wells at Ossington, Newark, to where they had moved from Burton Fleming. Liz is Angus's godmother. We went on to see Cockayne's herd at Plumtree, Nottingham, before visiting John and Anita Wass at Lowdham, Nottingham, with whom we had a nice meal. We ended the day by visiting cousin Brian Prescott and Margaret—Helen's godparents—who also live at Lowdham. A good day.

At the end of July RMC brought three loads of concrete for putting between the air-sweep ducts in the bottom of the four bins, which we put through the centre panel of each bin. Unfortunately, these were all to shovel in by hand and it was a problem getting all the concrete out of the air-sweep ducts before it set. The following day we had them all to point up with sand and cement to get the apex between the laterals smooth. I paid Mr Tutty, of A1 Fuels, £1,208 for 500 gallons of petrol and 1,000 gallons of diesel. I received a cheque for £800 from Neville Merrington for straw, which he got the previous year.

August 1: the pea viners started vining in the 35-acre field next to Park and vined 85 tonnes at 93 TR 2.42tpa. Two days later black group vined one of our crops in Thompson's field, with their two podders; it was not vined very well, but did 4.8 tonnes per hectare (tph) at 105 TR. We received the £6,854 grant for drainage done on Railway Side at Lickham. This was part of the FHD Scheme (Farm and Horticultural Development Scheme), which was part of the EU membership package. Anyone who had not taken advantage of this scheme had sadly missed out. It proved to be a godsend to us; we got work done which would never otherwise have been attempted.

The 60 per cent grant on the drainage scheme was the top priority.

David went home just before we started combining winter barley in 20-acre on **August 12**; we got the whole field done in the day. I received a cheque from MAFF for £870.

August 22: they finished vining Perfection peas in Clark Field at Lickham with the blue group podders; they did 33cwt per acre in 12 weeks.

Peter finished with the pea viners the day we started combining, so that was convenient. Andrew was baling with the Howard baler, which was proving to be quite a problem.

I took Grandad, Mother and Angus to see Giant Haystack and company wrestling at the Spa in Bridlington—we and 3,000 others. With Mother having a disabled sticker we were able to park outside the front door of the Spa, near the sea. As I parked, Big Daddy, Giant Haystacks and two other wrestlers got out of the Jaguar parked next to us, went in together and then proceeded to knock seven bells out of each other in the ring. Andrew and Helen went round the amusements and Von visited her friend, Phyllis, at Bempton. We ended the night all having fish and chips at Grandad and Aunty Lil's. The next day Pauline Darcey came with her parents from Selby; she was a very nice girl, who ended up working for Air Traffic Control at Heathrow and then at Ayr in Scotland.

Betty Gray, a cousin of Pat Bentley and a friend of Von's, sold us their blue Aga, in perfect condition, for £350, Sam Archer came and installed it. It seemed a very good buy.

We started combining wheat at Lickham on the Railway Side on August 29. We had a wagon train of corncarts, driven by Peter, Eddie, Mr Sleight and Grandad, leading the corn up home to dry. At the same time Garry Hyde started cutting hedges at Lund. I went to a standing corn sale at Ces Waites' in the village—his spring barley made £101 per acre—and then to another at Holme Dale—Lord Hotham's spring barley. One field made £105 per acre and two fields made £122 per acre. These were all to be harvested by the purchaser. Needless to say I didn't buy any. Ces Waites had died and George Foster at Holme Dale had retired; hence the need for a sale which Tom Helm conducted for Dee and Atkinson.

Railway Side wheat at Lickham did approximately 220 tonnes off the 60 acres. Two days later we took it all back to Lickham, dried, to store. Andrew accepted a place at Lackham College the same day. That day he baled the second crop of hay in Thompson's Low Field, and we took it down to Lickham and stored it in the Dutch barn. We received a £28,710 cheque from the pea group for our 63.8 hectares peas that year; this worked out at £450 per hectare. The same day Von went to Mr Thurlow's funeral. He was the father of Mrs Ellis, who was a wonderful help to Von in the house. He had been ill most of the year and Mrs Ellis and her sister, Mrs Hesletine, had been looking after him.

September 1: we finished combining all the wheat at Lickham, taking approximately 390 tonnes off 128 acres, ie 61cwt (3.05 tonnes) per acre. The next day I paid 25 bills totalling £8,125, which had been queuing up waiting for the pea cheque.

We had intended going to the Red Poll Conference in Australia at the beginning of September. In the spring we had sown mainly Zephyr barley, which would be the earliest ripening but it had been such a wet summer that the crops had not ripened at all. By August 25 we started harvest proper in the spring barleys; by the end of August we had completely filled all the old drier bins, one small bin of barley in the new drier, one bin of barley in the barn and the new drier itself was full—12 tonnes.

We were having problems with the Dalton Estate at this time, as they had no deeds for their land, ie Watergarth, Short Lands and Bramble Butts and could not supply a good root to title. Bill Pinkney was reluctant for me to accept their assurance as we had a very good root to title of our 52-acre, which we were swapping. Bill made me sign a declaration that I would not hold him responsible if anything went wrong; I am thankful to say that nothing has happened. The estate was threatening to renege on the deal if we didn't complete forthwith, so the exchange went through—after all we had known the family and estate a long time—almost 100 years.

September 5: Von and I should have been going to Australia to the second Red Poll congress, but it was not to be. The weather had been atrocious, making harvest so late that it was impossible for us to go. But I had other ideas in mind. We were very fortunate that Curtis's refunded all we had paid them for our flights, which we thought was exceptionally generous.

The same day we received our 10 per cent grant from MAFF for the 14-tonne Warwick trailer that we bought for £322. We also learned from Nickerson's that we were not in the first three awards that year. The first prize was £5,000, second £1,000 and the third £500. Not to be sneezed at.

We eventually finished combining on September 8 in what was Mr Thompson's Low Field, which was sown with Atou wheat, and in Bramble Butts; the 29 acres did approximately 80 tonnes. Malcolm Ashley brought eight black Hereford bull calves at £88 each: they were getting very pricy. Bert Cheetham came over, brought a calf, and bought five in-calf heifers at £400 each. Helen back to school that day, Angus would return the day after so there was much activity in the house, packing trunks and tuck boxes.

September 13: we took Andrew to Lackham College at Chippenham, in Wiltshire, to start an agricultural engineering course. We stayed the night at Tewkesbury on the way back.

Andrew had finished baling all the straw before he went so it was now a case of going round all the stubbles, burning any loose straw and generally tidying up the fields in preparation for autumn drilling.

We had a confrontation at Lickham with Geoff Eastwood, of the Ramblers Association. He had brought a group of Ramblers across the field in front of the house at Lickham and then proceeded to exit down the farm road. Frank Taylor had seen them approaching down the road and had gone across to them with a pitchfork, looking very menacing. Much to our amusement he threatened Mr Eastwood and told him, in words of one syllable, what he could do: turn round and go back the way he had come. He also threw doubts on Mr Eastwood's parentage. One path was a public footpath and the other a bridleway but they did not join for the whole length of the garden and farmstead. A year later we had a two-day tribunal at The Hall, Lairgate, Beverley, where an independent inspector decided to make no decision until the next review. What we called a 'cop out'. The footpath sign clearly states: 'Terminal footpath' and the bridleway sign at the end of the drive states: 'Terminal bridleway'. To our knowledge no-one has attempted to walk this footpath since. Good old Frank.

Burton and Sissons started to strip the granary and loose-box roof facing the foldyard, as the rock lathes were in a very poor state. This was a very big roof to contemplate felting and re-lathing. Albright and Wilson brought 15 tonnes of 0.20.20 fertilizer and AIS brought Roundup, Prebane and Chandor sprays. The rent officer came to 39 South Street, where Alf and Mrs Dowson were living, and suggested that £7.50 per week was a fair rent for the property. Prior to this they had not paid any rent, but Alf was no longer working at all so we felt it was time to put things on a proper footing—to help pay for maintenance if nothing else.

We were now into autumn drilling; it was our practice to put fertilizer into the seedbed prior to drilling. We sowed 160kg per acre of 0.20.20 on land that had previously grown peas and approximately 170kg of 9.24.24 on second crop cereals. Seed rates would be 65kg per acre. We started drilling Hustler wheat on the pea land next to Park on September 21. I bought five 40-gallon drums of molasses at United Molasses in Hull for £113. Roundup was one of the best chemicals to come onto the market and I sprayed quite a bit at Lickham, Bramble Butts and Little Field.

September 24: David Neave, a local historian, was at the Oddfellows Hall, Lund to give a series of lectures on the local history of the area in and around Lund, pre and post enclosure. Von had arranged this via the WEA (Workers Education Association): it was very well attended with 54 going on the first evening. This continued until Christmas. Over the next five years classes on various similar topics were held.

I received a cheque from the pea group for £2,895 for Peter's labour, mileage and spraying. John Sleight sowed Clark Field pea land with Hustler wheat, mixing slug pellets with the seed in the drill. I started spraying Prebane when Eddie had rolled down the wheat after Chris drilling. Tractor licences were now £8.50 each.

Burton and Sissons eventually finished re-felting and lathing the granary, mill house, barn shed and loose-box roofs. They also rebuilt the pillar at the foldyard doors into the stackyard and re-leaded the guttering between 39 and 41 South Street, Middleton. On our 18th wedding anniversary we took Angus and Helen back to school and then went to the newly-opened Plainsville Hotel, Wiggington. It was owned and run by one of the Rowbottom brothers along with whom we had been members of the YFC. There were four boys and four girls in the family; they used to farm at Low Mowthorpe.

The day after I took Woldsman Randy Boy—named by Eddie—one of our home-bred stock bulls, which had been at the Royal Show previously, to Shouler's abattoir at Carnaby. This is now run by Dawn Foods; Edward Shouler originally built the abattoir but when the big supermarkets were springing up they wrote to him and said that instead of taking one month's credit they were going to take three months' credit. He was paying his suppliers 10 days after slaughter, so he sold out.

We had Garry Hyde cutting the hedges; we had to rake up the thorns and burn them as they were too big to plough in. Jim Cox and Horace Marshall raked the thorns up in Thompson's Wold land on the roadside and threw them into the field as well as down Lambs' hedge side and the boundary hedge at the bottom next to Bulmers. It was our responsibility to cut the hedges at the end of the licence period. The Dalton Estate agreed that we need not do all the internal hedges as Bulmers were going to pull up the hedges between the five fields and put a centre hedge down the middle making two equal fields. I pushed up the thorns into heaps and they burned them. They did the same in Watergarth, Short Lands, and Bramble Butts.

Mortimer's sent a 20-tonne load of wheat to be dried and cleaned, as it was full of short straw and chaff, etc. Unfortunately, when I got the drier full and started the furnace, the drier caught fire at the end of the heated section. We quickly sent for the fire brigade and two fire engines attended. We had to empty the drier into the holding bin. Fortunately there was not too much damage done, but we had to get Agricon engineers to come and replace the melted gauze in the burned places. The drier being out of commission convinced us that we needed to take out extra cover for loss of income.

Aunty Ethel at Scarborough was in hospital; I took Mother to see her. We fetched Angus and Busby from school and took them to Hull Fair. Then Von and I went to Lambs for a meal in the evening. The following day we had the three Ullyott boys to Sunday lunch, as Peter and Betty were away on the Australian trip. We took the boys back to school in the evening and then visited Helen for half an hour; we took her a boiler suit—and it was still too small. It had been thick fog all the way.

I had been considering, with Adrian Sherriff at St Albans, importing a bull from the USA, but in those days with blue tongue restrictions on importing cattle from America it was not possible. Marshall Mohler, at Pinney Perdue University farm, near Chicago, Illinois, had sold an in-calf cow to Joe Marshall at Red Deer, in Canada, and it had had a bull calf. This bull was now 18 months old. Import restrictions in those days only allowed us to import a bull during the month of February. Time was of the essence to get the bull tested for all the necessary diseases that it may have. I decided to go over and have a look at the bull so, as we had missed out on our Australian tour, on October 15 we booked our flight to Canada at Curtis's: we could not fly direct into Calgary or Vancouver, as we had to give at least three weeks' notice for a visa, so we would fly to Seattle and then go by Greyhound coach to Vancouver and fly from there to Calgary.

The following day it was rent day at the estate office at South Dalton. I paid £1,202.50 for half year's rent for 138 acres at the old rate, £707.50 for a half year's new rent of £27 per acre on the 52-acre Road Ends piece, and £3,205 for cropping licence on Thompson's Wold land—118 and a half acres at £27 per acre. I also paid £690 for seed and labour on Mr Thompson's Low Field Atou wheat, following crop. A total of £5,804.05—quite an expensive rent day. The same night we went to David and Barbara Brumfield's silver wedding celebration at Dunken Hill, Cherry Burton.

October 17: Andrew celebrated his 17th birthday: he had already applied for his provisional driving licence, which was waiting for him at home. The following day it was Angus's 11th birthday: he got a sonic car, which worked by remote control and was well pleased. Helen and Pauline came for half-term on the Friday. On the Saturday Von went to York railway station to meet Andrew, handed him the car keys and said: 'Right, over to you.' He drove through the middle of York and home. In the evening he drove Von, Helen, Pauline and I to Bridlington to the fair on High Green. Angus telephoned—he had got his 800-metre badge for swimming and his bronze badge for life saving; very good.

I sold 220 tonnes of wheat to Maurice Robson, of Mortimer's, to go into RHM, Hull, for November/December delivery at £102 per tonne and took a fat cow into Shouler's in Driffield: she made £186.

October 25: We had a shock when Eric Smith, with whom I had gone to Askham Bryan, died in a car smash on the York/Malton road, near Kirkham. Eric was married to Beryl Wharram, the village tailor's daughter; they lived at Kilnwick and Eric, who was a St Peter's old boy, was a representative for Kenneth Wilson. Paul Byass and I went to his funeral at Kilnwick.

I paid David Cornwell £624 for four tonnes of linseed meal. Andrew drove me to Cundall and we collected Angus and a friend called Andrew Hill, who came from Diss, in Norfolk. Later in the day we went to see some trees at Ellerker for planting on Queen's Mead for the parish council and returned via the Humber Bridge. They had just one road section in place.

As chairman of the parish council I seemed to spend a lot of time in the village. I took the Sanderson, with Andrew, down to the middle of the village and we lopped the three cockpit trees (there used to be five). All the rest stood and watched. Later that day Von, and I took Andrew to catch the train at York to go to Wiltshire, Helen to school at Escrick and Angus and Hill out for a meal, after we had walked round the walls and before taking them back to school at Cundall.

On the Monday morning Von and I went into Hull to get my international driving licence at the AA centre and travellers' cheques for our trip to Canada and the USA. We got $2.40 to the £1 in US dollars, and $2.85 to the £1 in Canadian dollars. The same night I went to Bainton YFC give a talk entitled My Farming System—and the following night gave the same one at Fimber Discussion Group. Von and Mother went into Driffield to buy a fireplace for the Dowsons at 39 South Street.

I went to a Red Poll Council meeting with the Shorthorn Society regarding a possible amalgamation of our secretary-ship as they too were without a secretary. Ours—Walter Dunnaway had separated from his wife and apparently abandoned his position as secretary. He and his son, a travel agent, had organised the first International Red Poll Congress and tour in England three years previously.

A typical day for us… Paul Byass arrived and I paid him £3,400 for seed corn from Dawson's: he stayed until 3pm; John and Margaret Wilson (ex-bank manager and wife) came for coffee and to deliver tickets for their amateur operatic show; Paul and I went to Eric Smith's funeral; George Cotterill came and I paid him; John Sleight came—he was on a week's holiday; I fetched Angus and Mark Leonard for half-term; Rosalind, Ian and Claire Harrison came to stay; Rita Leonard came to collect Mark; Von and I went to the Yorkshire Countrywomen's meeting at Bishop Burton to hear Phil Drabble's talk entitled One Man And His Dog. Bed.

Von paid YEB £510 for the three farms' electricity bills and £32 to John Watt from the NFU for insurance for the five houses in Middleton.

November 5: Nurse Ingleby came to stay with Mother whilst we had a couple of weeks in the USA and Canada. The following morning she took us to York to catch the train. We flew from Heathrow in a Pan Am Boeing 747 over Iceland, Greenland and the North Pole, arriving in Seattle at tea-time. This was the first big flight we had ever done. We stayed in Seattle overnight, had a look round the next morning and bought a camera in the process.

We caught the Greyhound coach, well, the second one: the first one was full, so they put on a second one for us and another couple who were waiting. On the journey the four of us had the two front seats and it was one of the most wonderful journeys we have ever done. It was the fall and the colours were magnificent—the tall trees all golden and green and yellow: something we will never forget.

I was talking to Von about the farming we were passing when the gentleman next to me leaned over and asked 'What part of the East Yorkshire do you come from?' A little bit disconcerting, as we didn't think we had such a distinct accent. We got chatting, and something at the back of my mind was niggling away throughout the conversation. I told him who we were, but he was a bit reticent. Suddenly I said to him: 'I know who you are. You work for Velcourt Farms.' I told him we had had Sir Emrys Jones a couple of months previously to judge the crop competition and I was waiting for some crop record forms, which he had promised to send me. He had already said he was a manager in Herefordshire and with this he was flabbergasted. By this time we were drawing into Vancouver; as soon as the coach stopped he and his young lady companion shot off the coach never to be seen again. The Morfords told us on our return home that he was a confirmed bachelor.

We stayed overnight at the Grosvenor Hotel and hailed a taxi early the following morning. We had an excellent driver, who had lived in Vancouver for 19 years and had never done a tour of the city for anyone. He took us round all the sights, including the Capilano Suspension Bridge, some 300 feet over the canyon. We persuaded him to wait for us and suggested he came to see the bridge. He was a very big man and as we were coming back across the bridge he came to the edge and jumped up and down. Not funny when you are in the middle.

We flew in a Canadian Pacific Boeing 737 to Calgary, where Joe Marshall met us and took us back to his place: it was snowing quite hard when we got there. This was on November 8 and there was still straw lying in swaths on the ground. That evening they entertained us to supper and then took us down into the basement, which was an Aladdin's cave of Red Poll memorabilia. Joe's wife, Pearl, was secretary to the Canadian Red Poll Association.

The following day Joe took us into Innisfail, where we booked our flights to Chicago for the following day. They then took us to Harold and Grace Howe's for lunch and a look round his snow-covered farm, where a railway sleeper formed the front door step. Grace gave us roast beef and Yorkshire pudding to make us feel at home, which was very kind. Then she said: 'Do have some jelly.' Von was looking desperately at Joe, who winked and pushed the gravy on his plate to one side. Von did the same, and the jelly was put on her plate. She's never forgotten it.

I shall never forget seeing two young bulls, semi-housed in an outside yard, with icicles hanging from their nostrils. I asked Joe: 'Why do your cows have such short ears?' He replied that they lost about a quarter of an inch of ear with frostbite every year: the older cows had very short ears indeed. Three years previously, when they were on the first congress, they had bought a Capps bull from Adrian Sherriff.

In the evening they took us to the Motor Lodge in Innisfail for a meal. On the pavement outside the motel there were power plugs, into which you plugged your engine heater to keep the engine warm and to stop it freezing up: these were commonplace. We went back to their place where they showed us the slides they had taken of the Australian congress which we had missed—we got to bed at 2am.

After breakfast we left the Marshall's house for Calgary airport at 6.45am, in a snowstorm. The snow was very dry and blew about. The road had a central dyke, which prevented traffic crossing from one carriageway to the other and, in winter, filled with snow blown from the road: a very good preventative. Apparently the snow got so deep that boys having fun riding snowmobiles were prone to be decapitated by telephone wires, which they could not see in the snow when going across country. When we got to the airport there were eight snowblowers in tandem going up and down the runway, keeping it clear for the planes to land and take off. We were very relieved when we were airborne and on our way to Chicago. We went from the airport to the Holiday Inn at Merryville by tri-state bus, which was an experience in itself—16 lanes of traffic, eight each way, and dual railway lines down one side of the highway. This was on the Chicago loop.

The following morning it was 'Wakey, wakey!' by Marshall Mohler, who telephoned at 8.30am when we were still in bed to tell us: 'I will pick you up in half an hour.' Marshall took us to Pinney Purdue University farm where Von went with Peg, Marshall's wife, to do a cookery demonstration in a mall. Peg was surprised that Von knew how to demonstrate. Marshall and I had a look round, sat down to lunch, said grace and then had our food.

In the evening we went to a steak house for our meal before looking at their slides of the Australian tour as well as those they took in England in 1976.

Next morning Marshall took me to see a carcase in the local abattoir, which he had had slaughtered: he checked every carcase they sent and measured the rib eye area of each carcase with tracing paper. This bull was 13 months-old and its carcase weight was 300kgs: it had been finished on a maize and soya ration. We had a quick look round Wanatah with Peg, and also round the campus. Then, after lunch, they packed Von and I off in their Granada car to see John and Carrie Ragor, some 88 miles away. As soon as we got onto the interstate highway there, coming down the road towards us, on the wrong carriageway, was another car. Marshall told us later it was not unusual: they had too much to drink at lunchtime and that was what hap-pened. The purpose of visiting the Ragors was to see Pinpur Baron, the sire of the bull we were importing, Pinpur Intercontinental.

The next morning, at 6.30am, John Ragor brought his cattle ready to go to the national show and sale in Montgomery, near Birmingham, Alabama. Kevin and George, who worked for Marshall, left at 9am with all the cattle. Marshall said: 'You are welcome to come with us so long as you don't mind riding in the back of the truck.' The truck was a four-seater luxury (to us) car with a pickup body attached. We quickly agreed and off we set. We stopped for lunch at The Hen House, where we were supposed to meet Kevin and George, but they had been and gone. We went on to Tennessee and stayed the night with Gerald and Sue Kirksey.

Breakfast was 6.30am and we were out and looking round at 7am. Marvellous weather, but they had had 82 inches of rain since the beginning of January. We moved on to Nashville, mainly to see Pinpur Walkin' Tall, half-brother to Intercontinental, and lunched with Bard and Sherrye Young. At 2.30pm we headed for Montgomery, Alabama, where we arrived about 7pm, unloaded the truck at the Coliseum, had supper with a bottle of wine from Gerald Kirksey (except Marshall, who didn't drink) and went to bed exhausted.

We were up 7am and Marshall introduced us to some of the Red Poll breeders at 7.50am in the reception area in the hotel. We met the Speagles: their children wore t-shirts on the back of which was written: Fighting Irish. We immediately got the wrong impression and didn't know until years later that the Fighting Irish was their local baseball team.

We then met Dorothy and Emery Parks, who was the auctioneer at the sale. Their son was the man in the ring whipping up bids for the animal up for sale, which could take up to 10 minutes to sell. After breakfast Von and I went for a walk down the street, which was overgrown with weeds. Obviously the streets were not walked or cleaned regularly. We were stopped by a large policeman, guns on both hips, who asked us what we were doing. We replied we were out for a walk, much to his puzzlement. It was a black area: we did not realise for another 10 years that, at that very time, there were massive uprisings within the black community. He advised us that it was not safe to walk about and suggested we return to our hotel. We did this and decided we would hire a car for a couple of days, as Marshall was tied up at the show and sale and we didn't want to be a liability.

November 16: we went on a tour round Montgomery, the Alabama state capital, which, in 1861, was briefly the first capital of the Confederate States of America. In the afternoon we went to the American Red Poll Association annual general meeting, which was followed by a banquet at the Cattlemen's Association of Alabama. They had an auction during the evening for the endowment fund—phew. Everything but the kitchen sink, bids taken from unwary people for either scratching their heads or blowing their noses. We managed to escape.

The following morning, it was breakfast at McDonalds again, and then to the airport for our tickets to fly back to Chicago. We were back at the sale just in time to see Marshall receive the reserve championship sash before going on to win the female champion. The sale was very drawn-out and protracted; we left about 4.30pm and made our way back to the airport for the flight on a DC9. We had to change planes at Memphis; there was something wrong with the plane—apparently it was falling apart. On arrival at O'Hare Airport we returned to the hotel we'd stayed in previously.

Next day we had a tour of Chicago, the windy city. And it was. We ascended the Sear's Tower, which is 1,450 feet tall with 103 floors, in less than one minute.

We caught the TWA Boeing 747 flight bound for Heathrow and the following morning we were over London by 8.30am: it was very foggy. We circled for an hour before trying to land but nearly came down on the house roofs near the runway, so the pilot had to pull it up sharply and take us to Prestwick as we were short of fuel. After re-fuelling there we had to wait until 1pm before we could get a 2pm slot to land at Heathrow. We caught the next train to Kings Cross and arrived in York at 7.45pm where Von's friend, Freda Downes, met us. It had been very foggy all day.

Back home

Whilst we had been away John Sleight was leading corn into Hull and Fridaythorpe for Mortimer's.

December 6: Eddie, Peter and Chris had a day off and went down to Smithfield Show, then to Heathrow, and then to Soho—all off their own bat. We had Mr Fletcher, the NFU county secretary, to visit: he was featuring us in the January issue of the East Riding NFU Journal and contacted all our suppliers asking them to support by having an advertisement in the journal.

John finished leading his 200 tonnes of wheat into RHM and 100 tonnes to Fridaythorpe. Halder's took 100 tonnes of Atou wheat to Selby and John took 50 tonnes of barley from Walkers into Mortimer's.

From the time we returned from America until the middle of December, Taylors Timber Merchants, Driffield, had been felling all the elm trees at South Avenue in Lund, adjacent to Queen's Mead, as these trees were either diseased or at the end of their lives. However, it was still useful timber and their sale paid for the bulldozing of the roots. They felled the last tree into Watergarth at the corner of South Avenue—as this was leaning over the road they had two tractors with winches to prevent it falling onto the road. Unfortunately, when they got to the critical stage one winch pulled faster than the other, spun the tree round and it landed on our fenceline, dragging all the electric cables down with it. The south end of the village was blacked-out for several hours. After Taylors had cleared all the good timber away, Clifford Watts dug out the roots on the roadside; their low-loader carted them down to the tip on Beverley Road. Richard Hall was there with his digger, pushing them off the low-loader. Chris and Eddie were engaged cleaning the road up—at our expense.

Christmas Eve: after I had rotavated it all, Chris, Eddie, Angus, Wayne and I were picking up bits of roots on Queens Mead and tidying up. The same day I received a cheque from the MAFF for £250 for the brucellosis incentive scheme after testing and inspection for same. Ken Walker, of Manor Farm, died that evening.

Back to Midnight Service and the festivities of Christmas: Molly Course, Grandad and Aunty Lil were here.

December 27: Maurice Robson brought us a cheque for £9,402 for the 98 tonnes of Atou wheat that went to Selby. Andrew took the load of small tree roots that we had picked up from Queen's Mead to Lickham for John to burn in his boiler. The next day Von, Mother and I went to Ken Walker's funeral in Lund. He and his wife had come to live at Manor House in 1930, when the Binningtons retired. William Binnington carried on as foreman for the Walkers.

John and Mary Beaumont brought Ian to stay and Andrew had a driving lesson in Bridlington at 9am with Sinnett Jones.

New Year's Day: we had a parish council meeting on Queen's Mead about planting the variety of trees we were getting from Green's at Ellerker to replace the avenue of elms, which had been felled because of Dutch elm disease.

We went into Beverley to buy some travellers' cheque for Helen to take to Austria the following day: the rate of exchange was 4.72 German Deutschmarks to the £1. The following morning we ferried Helen to York to catch the 7.45am school coach to Luton for her school trip to Birgitz, Austria. Then we took Ian Beaumont back to Wetherby. We then went on to Leeds and Bradford to a couple of Mercedes garages to see what they would give us for our car, but no joy.

We took Molly Course down to see the cottage that Anne Wildsmith subsequently bought from Bruce Marr. He wanted £32,500 for it, but Molly felt it was too much. She came up regularly and thought she might like a retreat of her own.

Maurice came again with a cheque for £10,250 for the 104 tonnes of wheat which John had taken to Fridaythorpe Feeds.

January 6: Molly took Andrew back to Lackham on her way back to Bournemouth and arrived home by 2.30pm. Von and I went to Joan Hardy's joint 40th birthday party with Mike White, from Garton-on-the-Wolds, at the Manor House Restaurant, Fridaythorpe. They had each invited 40 guests.

The following day William Lamb, Mike Lazenby and I measured out and dug holes for the trees on Queen's Mead. I fetched 30 trees and paid £246 of parish council money. I also bought 400 hawthorn plants for £70 for us for gapping hedges.

The next day Northern Chimney Linings came to start re-lining the west end chimney stack at Vicarage Farm. They took the chimney stack down and told us we would have to rebuild it ourselves. We had a long and involved argument about who was going to pay for the rebuild, after which they agreed not to charge us the £500 contracted to line the chimney, in lieu of us replacing the chimney stack.

Helen came back from her school ski-ing trip covered in bruises but, fortunately, no broken bones. The following day we took her back to school.

January 11: Von and Mother fetched Pam Roberts from York Station, in order that she could go and see Aunty Ethel at Scarborough. Aunty Ethel had brought her into the world somewhere abroad and she and Pam's parents had remained firm friends. Pam, a single lady, had continued the friendship. They took her to the Green Gables Hotel, Scarborough, where Aunty Ethel was living, and took her back to York two days later.

Edward Duggleby, my cousin, and his wife Margaret, who lived at High Farm, North Frodingham, came for a meal. His mother, Hilda Prescott, was born at Lickham and was Uncle Alan's sister. She was the last bride to get married from Lickham until Andrea and Charlie Young in 2007.

Edward and Margaret had two daughters, Gillian and Rosemary. Gill married Tom Julian, our local NFU secretary, when Gill was YFC county organiser. Tom died after they had a daughter, Catherine, when Gill was pregnant with Tom junior. Catherine died a year after her father with cot death. A few years later Gill married Paul Butler—after Von had arranged a 'blind date' for them at a county ball. Rosemary married David Ashbridge and had three children. Unfortunately, she had a tumour on the brain and died quite young. Frank, Edward's brother, had also died quite young with a similar condition. He and his wife, Kay, had two children, Alan and Jane. Unfortunately Jane also died with a tumour on the brain. Alan Duggleby married Dorothy Kirkwood and they live at Pinder Hill Farm, Beeford.

It started to snow hard on January 14 and a blizzard blew most of the day: fortunately, the snow turned to rain. The following day Von and I took Angus back to Cundall.

Dave and Sue Greaves came to see the kitchen at Wold House to give us an idea of what we could do and how much it would cost, etc. We had already bought the Aga from the Grays, and wanted to recess it into the chimney breast, as the present Aga was standing out into the kitchen.

During this time Chris and I were fencing in Watergarth, from the old council houses on South Avenue right round to Damson Garth, where we had regular interruptions from locals. We were setting posts and rails opposite Damson Garth when John Horsley stopped for a talk; we were joined by Willie Woodall, who was going to Beverley to bank the church carol singing money. We started to talk about the local history lectures David Neave was giving in the church hall. I said to John Horsley: 'You ought to come, they are so interesting.' Willie Woodall said: 'Why, no! He wouldn't be interested, as he's not a Lund lad.' Quick as a flash John said: 'Why, no! I've only lived here 67 years.' He died a few years later aged 101: he was a real gentleman. He lived in what is now called John's Lodge and I have a feeling he could be a distant relative, as he was born at Tickton, and my paternal grandmother's brother, John Horsley, went to farm at Tickton after his father died suddenly, aged 66, in the harvest field at Bishop Burton.

Maurice Robson brought another cheque—for £10,616—for the November/December wheat that went into Rank Hovis McDougall (RHM) in Hull. The same day I sold Feedex 50 tonnes of barley for £96.50 for February delivery. On January 24 Wykeham Estates sent 70 semi-mature trees, and showed us how to plant them. We planted them in the holes in Watergarth that John had previously dug out, round the perimeter and dotted across the field. There were 10 or a dozen different varieties of trees.

Von had been attending evening classes and had learned how to use a 'Banda' spirit duplicator, which could be most useful for the village news sheet we sent out round the village. By the end of January we had all the trees planted in Watergarth and protective fences round them. I think that all these trees, bar an odd one, survived the first few years. Unfortunately, sheep in the field did them a lot of damage.

January 29: Andrew went to Bridlington to take his driving test. Audrey took him for an hour's lesson before he took his test, which he passed. Sinnett was well pleased. It was very foggy and we quite thought his test would be cancelled. The lessons were £3.50 an hour so with the test his full licence cost £5. Grandad and Aunty Lil took us to lunch at the Star Inn in High Street to celebrate. The next day Andrew returned to Lackham from York.

We collected our new 702D Mercedes van on February 1 (LKH 532V) for £5,666, from Humberside Motors at North Cave. On the way back we left it at Masseys at Market Weighton, for them to put a fibreglass lining in it. The following week Massey's gave us a price of £133 including VAT, so they would be doing this within the following couple of weeks.

Mother and I went to Denis Eastwood's funeral; he was father to Judith, Alan and Mavis. He originally farmed at Staveley Wold, Middleton, and had retired to a new house opposite 41 South Street, Middleton.

Von and I went to Peter and Betty Ullyott's at Kelk for supper: they showed us their pictures of their visit to Australia, and informed us that John and Mike Burdass, who were their landlords, were having to buy their farm at Dotterill Park, near Rudston, and had asked Peter if he was prepared to give them vacant possession of the farm at Kelk. They had also had a letter from Geoff Webster in Australia, telling them that the 500-acre farm next door to him was coming up for sale. The coincidence of the two situations coming together, plus their liking for Australia and the possibility of a golden handshake to come out of dairying, brought them to the conclusion that they were meant to emigrate. This came as quite a surprise to us as Geoffrey had just got engaged, Nicholas was with the Scottish Ballet and Robin had just left school.

We were having problems within the Red Poll Cattle Society, as Walter Dunnaway, who was the secretary to the society, had parted from his wife and all the Red Poll office documents and equipment were in a lock-up garage in the middle of a wood at Riseholme in Lincolnshire.

We had just managed to get the services of Phillip Ryder-Davies, a practising vet in Woodbridge, Suffolk, to take over the position on a voluntary basis, assisted by his wife Mary. At the time I was the only council member living remotely near Lincoln so I volunteered to take the contents of the garage to Woodbridge. Grandad Carr and I did this delivering everything to offices at 6 Church Street, Woodbridge, which Phillip had rented on a short-term basis. We later moved it all to Market Hill in Woodbridge. Ten years later this was turned into a museum for the Suffolk Horse and Red Poll Cattle societies, which were two of the Suffolk trinity. The third was the Suffolk Sheep, but it was under the umbrella of the Sheep Breeders Association.

We had to meet Walter Dunnaway at 10am on February 6 at the Eastgate Hotel in Lincoln, and he would take us out to the garage. We got all the basic office equipment, and filled the van with as much as we could get in, leaving behind about 20 tea-chests full of old herd books and other paperwork. We arrived in Woodbridge at approximately 6pm and we then proceeded to dump the load in the upstairs office at 6 Church Street. After Phillip had given us supper at his home, Grandad and I returned home, arriving about 11pm. There was still another load of herd books and Red Poll reviews, all enveloped up and ready be sent out, but which had never been posted.

February 9: Mother, Von and I went to Lincoln to retrieve the rest of the stuff from the garage. Everything was very wet and so a lot had to be discarded. After a wash-and-brush-up we lunched at the Eastgate Hotel and then we went round the cathedral. After that we called at the Veitches at Linwood, to see Bill and Sheila and the family. Over the next couple of months I had to sort through all the tea-chests that we had stored in our granary.

We had been trying for a long time to have the bull, Pinpur Intercontinental, which we had seen in Alberta, imported into this country. The Ministry vet came and approved the shed in Moat Field at Scorborough for isolation quarters for a period of six months. We later fenced round the moat and those were his summer quarters for the six-month period.

Friday February 15: In the evening Andrew and I went into Richardson's in Driffield, where John Spencer showed us a car which Biddy, Richard Ullyott's wife, wanted to trade in. It was an emerald green 1.3 Ford Capri, which I think Andrew believed would give him a lot of 'street cred'. We went to see Biddy and agreed to buy it. On the Monday morning, Andrew and I went into NFU in Beverley and negotiated the insurance for Andrew's car from John Watt at £243, fully comprehensive, for the year. We then went back to Driffield and collected the car, registration LKH 284P, which had almost 50,000 miles on the clock. We came home, dined and then he made his way back to Lackham—a five-hour journey: He telephoned at 7.30pm to say he had arrived.

The same weekend we had all the men and their wives to Wold House for supper; we showed them our slides of Canada and America when we went to see the bull. A couple of days later Von and I went to the funeral of Miss Norman, our tenant at 6 South Street. Eddie came with us as she was a close neighbour.

Chris started sowing 22.11.11 fertilizer on all the grasses, at 180kg per acre. The last day of the month, Leap Year Day, Andrew came home from Lackham and brought Hugh Rodgers with him. That evening we went rabbiting round the grasses and got a couple of hares and four rabbits.

March 1: Von went off with Bill Pinkney to judge the senior YFC public speaking debating competition; Shirley Coleman, who had taught Von public speaking at Bridlington YFC, was also a judge. Bill took them all to the West Bulls Pub in Bricknell Avenue for lunch and it was 8.30pm when she got back.

The following week we started working land for spring corn—putting fertilizer on and working it into the seed bed before drilling. We sold the 250-gallon bulk milk tank for £500: we had to take down the wall at the front sliding door to get the tank out. Chris and I re-built same and re-hung the door. Hambleton Aviation came taking photographs of all three farms, as well as infra-red pictures of land at Lickham and Watergarth, Lund. We paid them £316.

Peter and Betty Ullyott had made up their minds to emigrate to Kojonup, Western Australia, We went for lunch and agreed to buy 29 of his young bulls, plus his stock bull Notton Supreme Duke, bred by Charlie Kidson of Wakefield, and also a couple of in-calf heifers.

March 9—Helen's 16th birthday: We, accompanied by Angus, took her a cake and presents to school. We delivered Angus back to Cundall and went to the church where they were having a communion service: it was a lovely little church.

March 11—Tuesday: Millers were spreading 80kg per acre of 34.5 per cent nitrogen on all our wheats, plus 21 tonnes of the same for David Brotherton at Wold Dyke and 5.3 tonnes for Lord Hotham. Audrey Jacobs' bungalow caught fire, so they moved into 6 South Street, where Miss Norman had lived, until they had their house repaired and re-decorated.

Next day Von and I went to Betty Gray's and agreed to buy her blue Aga, which is still in the kitchen at Wold House; we paid £350 for it plus £60 for 75 gallons of paraffin and the tank. We took the forklift to put it onto the low loader and brought it home. I fetched the Mercedes van, in which they had put in the fibreglass lining, back from Massey's.

Andrew was home for the weekend; the following morning he brought us a cup of tea in bed and went to fetch Angus from Cundall, calling to see Helen at Escrick on the way home—and had a family committee meeting. Angus and I went rabbiting and then Andrew fetched us all fish and chips. Very pleased with his car.

I received a cheque from Humberside County Council for the grant on planting the trees in Watergarth and round the fence line: it was for £749, which helped considerably. Francis Jackson of ACC came up and I paid him £5,490 for 50 tonnes of 34.5 per cent nitrogen (£109.80 per tonne including VAT).

March 21: we left home at 5.45am with the Land Rover and cattle trailer to fetch Pinpur from Prestwick Airport, Scotland. It was a terrible journey as there was a lot of snow and ice on the roads. The plane was diverted from Prestwick to Glasgow, so the four Holstein bulls and Pinpur had to be transported back to Prestwick to the official import layerage, where all these bulls would have to be inspected for any visible health problems.

They had to have a two-hour rest period before we could load our bull for the return journey. One of the Holstein bulls was one of the top Holstein bulls of the day; he cost £54,000. I paid £51 import duty for inspection, etc. We arrived home at 3am the following day after we had left him in the shed in Moat Field. The day after Adrian and Pen Sherriff came up from St Albans to see the bull. We were going into partnership with this venture (we collected semen from him at the Avoncroft Cattle Breeding Centre at the end of the quarantine period).

The following day we took them to see Peter Ullyott's stock, then all returned to Wold House for lunch. Later we all went to see the Humber Bridge being built—one of the road sections had fallen into the Humber. On the Monday morning Adrian and I went into Beverley to the Midland Bank where we opened a joint account for the bull venture. We initially put in £2,000 each. We then went to see John Watt about insurance.

We received a cheque for £31 from Jack Wiles for a dead bullock and three calves. In those days we got paid for dead animals by the fellmonger—not like today when we have to pay for animals to be taken away. You put a bag on a stick in the hedge at the bottom gate and the fellmonger, who went round daily, would see it and come to collect whatever had died: £2 for a calf and £25 for a bullock or cow. The animals would be skinned at the yard and the carcases were sold on for dog meat, etc. The hides went for tanning. There were several tanneries in Beverley at one time; latterly there was just Hodgeon's, which employed quite a lot of people—some people from Lund worked there. We renewed the Mercedes (NVN 700M) road fund licence for £50. Again, a big difference from today.

North County Breweries gave Lund five ornamental trees for winning the Best Kept Village competition—a cherry tree was planted on the village green (it was removed in 2015). We also had a tree commemorating Prince William's birth on the roadside at the new graveyard. Unfortunately, it did not survive so the Helms donated a tree which Keith, their son, had grown from a seedling planted in the year of Prince William's birth.

March 28: it was the Clark brothers' farm sale of livestock, machinery and implements at Corporation Farm: I bought half a bay of straw and hay for £75. Ullyotts were the auctioneers. That same evening Jill Flint rang and invited Helen to go with Maria, their daughter, to a disco at Holme-upon-Spalding Moor; they arrived home at 1.30am. This was the start of their career in Young Farmers. On the following Monday, Helen and Andrew went to their first YFC meeting at Bainton. Helen came back doing junior beef judging at the YFC Rally.

Von and I went to Ullyotts for lunch and I bought 11 in-calf heifers for £2,000, two of which had calved already. Andrew and I then went to the Thompsons furniture sale at Hotham House, where I bought Von a dish for £2. The following day Helen and I fetched the last five heifers from Ullyotts—Eddie said they were a load of 'screws'. It was that day that Dave Greaves, from Homecharm in Bridlington, came to give us an idea as to how much the units would cost for the kitchen.

Mother and Von went to Mrs Abbott's funeral in Middleton: she was Jessie's mother from Ivy House, the smallholding opposite the playing fields at Middleton. Jessie did all the floristry for this area: she was very good at arranging flowers and did most of the weddings, funerals etc. Von got a new TV licence—£12 for a black and white set.

On the third Thursday of March the Kiplingcotes Derby is always run, starting from an old stone post on the verge on the road from Etton to Warter. The course goes across the Lair Hill to Kiplingcotes Road, then across the Goodmanham Road, over the old railway bridge and up the side of Ash Slack plantation (a very rough grass road), across the A163 and down the Warter Road to the winning post.

We used to go to take Bill Pinkney, who was one of the trustees for the race. It is invariably cold, wet, snowing or raining, with a beastly wind. The joy of it was that Bill invited several of us back to lunch at Eastlands at Tibthorpe, and that was something not to be missed. In those days Keith

Dalby, of the Westgate Practice, was the honorary vet; he did the job for quite a few years.

The Kiplingcotes Derby is the oldest race course in the country, having started in 1519; it has to be run or walked with a horse every year or the race stops. The winner gets the interest from the original investment and the runner-up gets £4 of the £4.25 entry fee paid by all competitors. Sometimes, if there are a lot of entries, the runner-up gets more money than the winner. The clerk receives 25p from each entry, but has to pay 50p to the starter out of this. Needless to say, nowadays the entry fee is £5 per horse.

The jockey has to be a minimum weight of 10 stones and if the rider doesn't come up to this they have to carry weights on their body, not in weighted saddle. The current prize money is £50 and a trophy to the winner and £4 from each entry for the second. The current trustees are Guy Stephenson, William Bethell, both of whose families have had a long association with the race, and Phillip Guest, the Beverley jeweller. Nowadays the race is well sponsored and up to 1,000 people attend: it is a logistical nightmare for the organisers.

Von had been delegated to type out Ullyotts' application giving their reasons for wanting to emigrate to Australia. A total of eight A4 sheets—quite an epistle. Anyway, it was successful.

After a very wet March, we started to work land for spring corn on April 3, starting in 20-acre where we sowed 200kg of 22.11.11 per acre. After spring tine and Dutch harrowing, Chris sowed Georgie barley and John sowed grass seed after it had been rolled down. At the same time we had AIS here with their Snowcat, spraying the 35 acres of Hustler wheat next to Park with Rogor and Dimethoate for wheat bulb fly. Andrew and Helen went off to fetch Angus from Cundall for the Easter break.

Von and I went up to Bill Pinkney's at Tibthorpe and signed the forms for the completion of the exchange of land between ourselves and Lord Hotham for the 52 acres which we had bought from Alwyn Middleton 11 years previously. We were exchanging it for Watergarth, Short Lands and Bramble Butts, a total of 50 acres. We retained the tenancy of the 52 acres.

Von and Angus walked round to Middleton, by Lair Hill and back via Lund, and then she and I walked all round Lickham in the evening. At least the dogs had no complaints. Andrew took Helen and Angus to Bridlington to see Grandad and Aunty Lil and, no doubt, to explore the amusements.

April 5: Von and I went to Kelk and paid Peter Ullyott £4,000 for 30 young bulls to fatten, and then went on to Bridlington to 6 Portland Place, to see Aunty Nelly and Uncle Sun and take them a cake for their golden wedding. Aunty Nelly was not at all well; she was suffering from Parkinson's disease.

John sprayed the wheat on Railway Side at Lickham with three pints per acre of CMPP for cleavers. All of us at Wold House started working the Clark's field next to Wood Flat, as they had sold all their equipment at their sale. We were drilling their following crop of Keg barley. I sowed 110kg per acre of 20:5:10 fertilizer. Chris then started to spread 125kg of 34.5 per cent nitrogen on all the winter wheats. On the 88 acres of arable land at Road Ends I spread 50kg of 0.20.20 and 50kg per acre of 60 per cent muriate of potash. This was all for peas.

During the Easter break we had been trying to get work experience for Andrew with some of the local agricultural machinery firms for his year out. I think we went round at least 10 dealerships and large farms but no-one was prepared to give him a chance. No-one wanted apprentices for just a year. He returned to Lackham on April 13.

After we had finished the main of our spring sowing I set to and rotavated all of Queen's Mead after sub-soiling and collecting up all the roots that had been buried with felling the trees. Then I fiddle-drilled the whole area with grass seed and Peter rolled it all down; it looked very neat and tidy.

We received a cheque from MAFF for £479, which was the 10 per cent grant via the FHD Scheme for the purchase of the Mercedes van. On the same day I received a cheque for £11,522 for the steers and heifers that went on April 9.

April 24: I went to Driffield Town Hall to the sale of Peter Ullyott's farm at Kelk. It made £302,000 for the 185 acres and was bought by Bob Jagger: it was a very wet farm.

The following day we had the Northern Counties Red Poll Breeders Association (NCRPBA) annual general meeting at the Chase Hotel at York, and, as Peter was emigrating to Australia, I took over the secretaryship of the association (with the aid of my trusty other half). Again, as a follow-up from our trip to Tennessee the previous year, Gerald Kirksey, the Red Poll breeder with whom we stayed, telephoned to ask us to buy him a tea set for his wife for their 10th wedding anniversary. Von had to go to Mulberry Hall in York, choose a suitable set—including tea pot, he was most insistent on that—and get them to ship it over.

April 29: in the evening we took Angus back to school: he was in Cormorant Dormitory, right at the top of the house.

May 1: Alan Eastwood's was man here, drilling three acres of kale in Little Field and the same in Little Wold, next to Middleton Woods. They had a precision root drill to drill at 24inch rows, with precise seed placing. We no longer had a root drill since we had stopped growing turnips for sheep several years previously. I ordered a Niemeyer grass cutter from RBM for £1,400, less 15 per cent, and went on to York Market, where I purchased two calves for £99. I then went into Hull and bought six 40-gallon barrels of molasses for £163. The molasses was for mixing with the cattle food to bind the cubes together.

May 2: Andrew went to Erdington, near Birmingham, to collect Sister Mary Mildred, Von's ex-headmistress. He amused us telling us how he had gone to the convent and knocked on the door to collect a nun in full Dominican habit. He didn't know it, but her sense of direction was nil and she directed him up the motorway to Manchester before Andrew realised that he was going a long way round. He stopped at a filling station to get some fuel, where the attendant said: 'You have a good travelling companion' or some such. They arrived home at 11.15pm. They were always the best of friends. He took her back to the convent—his way—after the weekend. After that she came for two weeks every year until she died. The whole family liked her enormously.

May 3: we had the first letting of 41 South Street as self-catering holiday accommodation.

May 5—Spring Bank holiday: Tom Helm, of Dee & Atkinson, making the most use of a day off, came to do the annual valuation for the year end, which was on April 5. Two days later we took 28 Hereford cross yearling steers into Beverley market for him to sell. They made £6,673, averaging £238 each, nearly as much as we were getting for fat cattle at least six months older. The following night I was re-elected chairman of the parish council for the second year running; Joan Helm was our parish clerk and I could always work well with her.

The following weekend, Helen, Angus and Mark Leonard were home: we took them back on the Sunday night. On the Tuesday the Ullyotts and we went to the Farmers Club, London, for the Red Poll Society's annual general meeting where I had to give my president's report. We used to park the car on a meter, which Von had to keep feeding during the day, outside the Farmers Club in Whitehall Court. Von and Betty went off shopping to the Army and Navy Stores just round the corner.

Malcolm Ashley brought five black Hereford bull calves. I paid him £440—£88 each, different from the previous week when I had bought two in York Market for £99—but they were red. Fashion!

May 15: Chris started drilling Perfection peas in Road Ends, after we had spring tine harrowed and Dutch harrowed it in front of him. Peter rolled all down after he had finished drilling the peas two days later. I paid Francis Jackson, of ACC Fertilizers, £1,208 for spring fertilizers.

Horstine Farmery's men were here, with their tracked trencher, digging a trench for us to put in 110mm poly pipe. This would incorporate three core electric cable and draw string, from the front door and across the front of the buildings, to feed the three new street lights, and to the bottom gate, where we put two more lamp posts with a power point and a magic eye for a warning alarm in the new wall, which we had recently built. We had widened the gateway and inset it in order to give a better turning circle for the larger lorries, which were getting more than 40 feet long and carrying up to 40 tonnes gross. Two days later, after we had concreted the lamp posts into position and wired them in, Horstine Farmery workers pushed all the soil into the trench. This all came about because the Red Poll sign which was on the roadside had blown down during the previous winter's gales.

On the Saturday night, as usual, Von and I were going round the cows and calves in Far Field and found a cow laid out with milk fever. I had to shoot back for a bottle of calcium and get it into the vein for a rapid recovery. The following night we were up again at 3am calving a heifer in the front paddock; it had a big bull calf. We had Mr Lamb and his near neighbour Mrs Blackett, the widow of our former vicar, to tea that night. Chris drilled nine acres at Short Lands with Puget peas—or petit pois. I had to go into Hull to Humberside CC lighting department for three 'chokes' and resistors for the street lights, and got them all working properly.

May 23: Von, Mother and I went to William (Bill) Clubley's funeral at South Dalton church. He had farmed at Lair Hill since about 1945, after Mr Towse had retired. Leonard Clubley took over the farm. Mr Clubley had been a very well-known sheep dealer, buying sheep from the Northumberland area for breeding and selling on to farmers all over Yorkshire and Lincolnshire: he was very observant and would ring us up to say our sheep were out in Wood Flat. When we got there, there would be one sheep with its head through the wire. However, he once had some sheep stolen from opposite Lair Grange, but didn't see them go.

May 24—YFC rally day: I was judging static classes; Von was judging active craft demonstrations, and Helen doing junior beef judging. Poor lass was landed with doing 'oratory' at the last moment with five minutes to prepare, as the girl who was doing it had laryngitis. She had to talk for five minutes on: Why I Want To Be A YF Member.

Andrew had gone to fetch Angus from Cundall at lunchtime, and then they came on to the rally. We brought Angus home, collected Mother and went into Hull to see Chipperfields Circus at 5pm. The lions all got mixed up; they all had to go back in and come out again and they were very ruffled. Andrew and Helen arrived home for tea and then went off to the rally dance. When we eventually arrived home we found a letter wrongly delivered to us for Maltases, so Von and I walked down with it: it was from Trent College, saying that Martyn had got an Exhibition, which gave them a 10 per cent discount. By the time we got back home it was 11pm. The following day it was Hugh (Tom) and Joan Helm's silver wedding anniversary, which was a very happy occasion.

Andrew took Mother to stay with Molly in Bournemouth on his way back to Lackham in Wiltshire—a somewhat roundabout trip. At 17 that wasn't bad.

We took 20 tonnes of 34.5 per cent nitrogen down to Cranswick air strip for Millers to spread 50kg per acre on all our wheats. At the same time we had AIS spraying wheat with Baleton and manganese and folia feed. We sent 10 steers and seven heifers to FMC (five steers to Sheffield, the rest to Chesterfield). Von and I went to the wedding of Heather Dunning and Paul Heywood at Bishop Burton the same day—Paul came from Shropshire. We went back to the farm for a reception in a marquee. All very nice.

May 31: we fetched Angus and his pal, Mark Day, for the weekend and then went on to the Cheethams in Cheshire, to collect three calves; Margaret took Von to Ashton-under-Lyne market where they both bought a suit. I paid Bert £270 for three calves, 15 pairs of FMC overalls and some towels.

Margaret got all sorts of things from the various factories over there.

Grandad and I started to pull out the Aga and boiler in the kitchen at Wold House; Von and Mrs Ellis had spent a couple of days clearing out the kitchen, always a big job. After we had removed the Aga and disconnected the piping, we proceeded to take out all the bricks from the old chimney breast so that we could recess the new Aga into the place where the old Yorkshire range had been, many years before. The Aga we removed had been installed in 1952; it went to Snowdens eventually. After we had the entire chimney breast cleaned out, we proceeded to take down the ceiling— it covered the beams, which were hung with wires and pipes. We put a false ceiling in between the beams, which was a terrible job to do.

In the meantime Chris sprayed all the spring barley, plus Clarks field, next to Wood Flat, with three pints per acre of MCPA; 20-acre had Trifolex extra as it was undersown with a new ley.

I went to a sale at North Dalton of Naverac bankrupt stock, and bought a lawn mower and various bits and pieces. Andrew came home on the Friday night, and fetched Angus from school the following day. I went into Taylor's wood yard in Driffield, and got a green oak beam for making a mantle shelf in the kitchen. I took it down to Sissons at Beswick for Percy Sissons to make it look distressed. It took six of us to lift it into place. The only unfortunate part was that being so green it dried out from the underneath side, and with the heat from the Aga it warped leaving it tilting forward slightly. Never mind, it was distressed in the end.

I paid RBM £1,828 for the Niemeyer mower, paid Bentall for repairs for the drier where it caught fire, and Steve Stephenson (AIS) £711 for April chemicals. Alec Snowden brought a stone of sausages in the evening. They cost £7.70 and were home-made: this was the forerunner of their butchery enterprise.

June 17: we had 18 bullocks away to FMC. Grandad and I took the sink unit out of the kitchen and installed it in the cooler house where the milk tank had been. In the evening we had 25 members of Bainton YFC come for a farm walk. Von had a gutted kitchen so had to feed them in the garage, which Eddie had white-washed out specially. This was the first time a certain Miss Dorothy Hunter came to Wold House. She was never going to marry a farmer. Right.

Andrew came home the following weekend and brought with him Hugh

Rodgers, who lived in Wiltshire. Molly brought Mother back at the same time. The first thing she said when she saw the kitchen was: 'I can't bear bare beams.' Tough. Andrew had to take his car into Barrett's on the Saturday morning as it was using a lot of oil and rattling; they put in new pistons and rings and he fetched it out the same night. Andrew, Hugh and I put all the plasterboard up in the kitchen between the beams.

June 27—a big weekend: Helen left Queen Margaret's School at Escrick: everyone was very complimentary and sorry to see her go. We stayed for the speeches and then had to beat a hasty retreat before it all became too much for Helen. She had been very popular at school.

The following day Von, Helen and I went down to Lackham College for Andrew's open day; he had enjoyed his time on the engineering course and made some good friends, one of whom was Hugh Rodgers. Leslie and Joan Rodgers, Hugh's parents, insisted that we stay the night with them, which was very kind, as we were going straight on to the Royal Show at Stoneleigh.

The day after Von, Helen and I went to Stratford and visited Shakespeare's birthplace, the waxworks and Anne Hathaway's cottage before heading off to the showground. Eddie arrived with the cattle at 5.30pm followed by Grandad and Jack Gregory, his long-time friend from Bridlington. They came in the Land Rover, towing the caravan, in which they and Eddie lived for the duration of the show. We stayed with a Mrs Timms, at Wheathill Farm, Shearsby. She had been recommended to us by our former vicar and his wife, the Rev and Mrs Foster, who lived nearby. We called to see them the next day; a lovely couple.

July 1: the first day of the show proper. Von, Helen and I were going to the showground and arrived at the final corner when the alternator on the car went. The battery was completely flat and was not getting a proper ignition. A policeman stopped to assist us and he managed to start the car using jump leads from his motorbike battery to the car: I was surprised the battery on his bike was strong enough to get the car going. It was a case of keeping plenty of revs on the engine to keep me going until I got into the car park. In the meantime, Von and Helen set off at a run to get across the field and into the showground. They arrived just as Eddie was exhibiting Notton Supreme Duke, which came third.

The next class was the dry cow class, so Eddie took that as soon as he got back with the bull, and got third, whilst Von and co prepared the four heifers for the next class—with Grandad, Jack, Helen and Von leading them. Jack somehow lost his way and the heifer he was leading upended him in the Charolais lines. Von called to Peter Ullyott, who was watching the judging, and he raced across to rescue Jack. I was still fighting with the car at this time. They ended up with Grandad winning first with his heifer, Eddie second and Peter fifth. Von ended up with a reserve, and then discovered she had put the halter on her heifer upside down. What a circus!

We won first for the group by the same sire, reserve to the grand champion with N 36 Woldsman Denzil a good heifer, and second for the group bred by the owner. We also won first for three heifers sired by the same sire. The heifer, Denzil, was in the team entered for the Burke Trophy. It was Eddie's first foray into showing and very good actually: usually he stayed home and I did the showing. When the showing was over Grandad towed me to a garage and I managed to get a new, fully-charged battery and this got us home that evening—Eddie, Grandad and Jack stayed on.

Sam Archer came and installed Gray's Aga in the kitchen. Harrisons of Nottingham, the Victorian centre, sent the new kitchen units ready to be installed. I took the car into Barrett of Bainton and had a new alternator fitted. The car had 107,000 miles on the clock. Peter started with the pea viners and took the van to use as staff carrier to and from shifts. John Sleight was helping out for a couple of days working with the pea viners.

Von fetched two New Zealanders, Don and Judy Davy-Martin, from York Station, to stay for a couple of days. Six years later we visited them when we were on the Red Poll tour. The vet came the same day and blood-tested Pinpur Intercontinental, the bull we had imported from Canada. After this we moved him into a field with some heifers as he was now officially out of quarantine. Eddie, Grandad and Jack returned from the Royal Show; I think they had thoroughly enjoyed themselves.

July 5: Angus's open day at Cundall. Von, Helen and I attended: he was beginning to work harder and was sixth out of 14 in the class. He was in various races, had to run a mile, then half-a-mile, and then he was in the tug -of-war, which his team won. No wonder he had a headache. He came home with us for the weekend and then had to stay home as he had a virus; he was off for a few days.

July 7: Andrew started working with the pea viners; he was driving the high-lift cart, which was used for collecting the peas from the two or three mobile viners as they worked the field. He would then take the peas to the road transport, which would be waiting at the gateway to take them to the factory in Hull. The high-lift cart had a scissor-lift mechanism, which elevated the body of the trailer above the side of the transport; it would then tip into the lorry. In the early days anything up to a maximum of four tonnes would be in the trailer. However, even if there was only half a tonne it would still be taken to the factory as there was always a 90-minute rule: that the first pea that went into the viner tank had to be in the factory and being processed within 90 minutes, otherwise they would be no use for freezing. Peter was working in the field workshop so he and Andrew travelled together. They worked 12-hour shifts for six and a half days a week, alternating one week on nights—8pm to 8am—and vice-versa.

Dave Greaves and Phil fitted the kitchen units and tiles and the Aga was lit.

July 9: Andrew was stood off peas so he and Helen took Angus back to school: Angus still wasn't quite well but had exams.

July 14: Von, Mother and Helen went to York to meet Molly Course, who was coming to stay. We had a bit of a shock as John Stephenson, of Wandale Farm, Bridlington, died suddenly, aged 51. He farmed on Woldgate, and had land on Easton Road, which his son Brian and Joan his wife, later developed into a garden centre. Now, many years later, it has a restaurant, coffee shop, delicatessen, plants and shop and is one of the best in the area. We had Peter Burnell and his gang pulling wild oats at Lickham, and I paid him £716. Raymond, Yvonne and Marianna Cogswell came to stay for a couple of days, whilst Raymond, Mother's nephew from South America, who was working on one of the big estancia there for Vestey Meats, was on leave. We all went to Cheethams the next day for the Red Poll Field Day; it was very good.

John sprayed the peas in Bramble Butts with MCPB plus a quarter of a pint of MCPA per acre for charlock. We took all the guests to Cammidge and Robson of Flower Hill at Newbald to see the shire horses; it was a most enjoyable afternoon. It was sunny and the horses looked wonderful in the fields. Flower Hill is the North of England Shire Horse Centre. They hold demonstrations there, using all the old horse-drawn implements. In the evening Von, Helen and I went to Turtons, of Tibthorpe, for a wine and cheese event for Bainton YFC and we went to Snowdens for supper afterwards.

All this time we were struggling to make and bale hay on Middleton Tops as the Howard baler was not working properly. Howards came to look at it, with Jim Bcal from RBM, and they decided it was scrap, so we bought a new baler for £5,600: Howards would stand £2,000 of this as they accepted part responsibility. They brought the new baler and all the hay on Middleton Tops was baled by night with 150 bales led home and stacked in the Dutch barn.

Malcolm Ashley brought five bull calves the same night; I paid him £265. Andrew and Peter were vining at Peter Blacker's at Cherry Burton. Andrew was fed up with being stood off for various pea reasons. All this time Homecharm men were working on the kitchen; it was almost finished and looked good. Bernard was wall-papering.

Von and I walked over the peas at Road Ends, across Bramble Butts, through all the new trees in Watergarth and back home. Mother and Molly had gone to tea with Mrs Farnaby. I cut the newly-sown grass on Queen's Mead for the first time as well as the thistles and nettles in Watergarth.

Von and Mrs Reffold were judging produce at the Driffield Show, always one of the big events of the year, to which we all always go. In the evening Betty and Peter Ullyott took Von and I to the Pipe and Glass for a meal.

July 24: Mother and I went to the Rev L W Foster's funeral at Leicester. We had only been to see them when we were down at the Royal Show at the beginning of the month. He had been vicar at Lund and Lockington for quite a number of years from the early 1950s: they retired from Lund, and were, in fact, the last vicar and family to live in Lund vicarage. When they left the vicarage was sold and Col and Lady Catherine Phillips bought it, in approximately 1960. Von and Helen fetched Angus from school, as it was the end of term.

A couple of days later Von judged at Bishop Wilton Show and then she, Mother and I went to Angela Ellis's wedding to John Rutty followed by a reception at the Bell Hotel. Mrs Ellis had been working in the house for Von for quite a few years and we thought most highly of her. Her father was foreman at Holme Wold for many years, and she, her sister and two brothers lived in the hind house—the children going to South Dalton School. Just to finish the day off Von and I went to Bishop Burton College to a wine and cheese event to support the Voluntary Services Overseas, for which Freda Downes was the organiser. On the same day the pea group requested our VWF 5000 tractor to pull one of the trailed viners as one of their tractors had broken down.

By the end of July Chris had finished taking all the previous year's barley into Feedex, a total of 101.5 tonnes at £99 per tonne. This was all offset against our feed account, with the balance being paid to us in the middle of the following month. Andrew and Peter were working nights, pea vining from 8pm to 8am; John Sleight started a week's holiday and Chris took the following week— getting a rest before harvest began.

Party time— 1980.

Chris finished fetching 105 bales of barley straw from Flints of Cawkeld, and I bought seven acres of barley straw from Sam Walton, to bale in the field, for which I paid him £70. Von bought a whole freezer-ready lamb from Dewhursts in Beverley for £33.

We had Brian Prescott from Lowdham (not to be confused with Brian Prescott from Middleton) for the evening. He travelled for J J Blow, the dairy appliance company, and came to this area every three months, staying at the Bell Hotel, Driffield. He always visited us when he was over here.

Von and I, with Mother and Mrs Farnaby, collected Aunty Ethel in Scarborough, and we all went to see the Black and White Minstrel Show at the

Futurist Theatre on the sea front; a brilliant show.

Andrew and Peter swapped nights for days that week, doing a 12-hour daily shift on peas. It is very tiring, doing an 18-hour shift at the weekend when they are on changeover. It was good money but hard work.

August 9: Von and Joan Gurney were at Wold Newton Show judging produce and preserves: this was the time of year when she was in great demand for all these village shows.

August 12: Von and Helen collected my niece, Susan Whorley, who had travelled from her Winchester home, from York Station. She was suffering from leukaemia and had, two days later, to take a matter of 20 tablets as part of her chemotherapy treatment. This put her in bed for two or three days and we had to get Dr Rose to come from Beverley to see her; he gave her some anti-sickness tablets. It was wretched to see her suffering so. By August 19 she had decided that she ought to go home and see her specialist; we didn't like to send her on her own, so Helen volunteered to go with her down to Winchester. Susan's father met her off the train and Helen carried on to Bournemouth to stay a few days with Molly Course. Ted telephoned in the evening to say that Susan was in hospital, prior to having more treatment.

Malcolm Ashley brought another seven calves and I paid him £884 for a total of 11 calves (£80.36 each). Peter Payne, from Holme-upon-Spalding Moor, brought 44 point-of-lay pullets for Eddie and I to put in cages in the old coal house, for which I paid him £80.

August 14: Mother was 85-years-old and was still going very strong. Avery's representative came about installing a 50-tonne weighbridge and gave us several ideas on prices, etc. At this time Richard Morford was working for John Dunning at Bishop Burton and came to us every evening for tea. Subsequently he left John Dunning and came to work for us—this was prior to going to university at Newcastle with his brother, David, and Ian and Nicholas Snowden.

At the end of the week eight of us—Mother, Von, Mrs Farnaby, Aunty Ethel, Grandad and Aunty Lil, Bernard Sissons, his friend Rose and I went to see Max Bygraves in Scarborough. The same time Chris baled the straw at Sam Walton's and had it all baled and brought back to Wold House by night. Sam Walton's men were bringing Sam's barley up to Wold House for me to dry.

August 20: we started harvest with John and Chris driving the combines and did Chalk Road and about half of Air Station field in the day. The following day I sold Feedex 100 tonnes of wheat at £98 a tonne—dry corn was very much in demand as it had been a very wet time. The following day Feedex fetched three loads of wheat. The viners were here and did all of Road Ends and started in Bramble Butts and Short Lands: Puget peas were the last peas to be vined in the group—they did 35cwt per acre which, for these high grade peas, was a very good yield.

August 26: Andrew and Peter had finished with the viners after cleaning all down and taking tractors back to their owners and viners into store. They brought the van back. Homecharm finished all the tiling and fittings in the kitchen and Bernard Sissons was doing a bit of decorating.

At the end of the month we had Brian Grainger, from Richardson's of Driffield, out and agreed to buy a new Ford 7600 for £12,500. He allowed us £3,250 for our 5000 tractor, JWF 783E.

September 2: The new tractor, registration PAT 745W, was delivered. Andrew, using it, baled barley straw in Little Wold and half of 20-acre the same day. One of the advantages of growing peas for vining was that we were paid for our crop much earlier than we would have had it been grain. That year our cheque for peas vined was £13,500.

September 7: Von and I went to Roger and Joyce Parkin's at Wansford, where they were hosting a farewell party for Peter and Betty Ullyott, before they left for Australia. The same day we finished combining at Lickham. Angus and I burned Clark Field straw at Lickham a few days later. David Hastings went home and Betty and Peter came to stay until they left the country.

There seemed to be a few people quite ill at that time: Aunty Farnaby was suffering from shingles; Betty Bentley had a tumour on the base of her neck; Christine Walker had developed breast cancer and had an operation. It was all very depressing for Von and Mother.

Andrew Taylor had baled a couple of hundred bales of wheat straw for John Sleight to use in his straw boiler at Lickham, and John and Mr Sleight were stacking them in the foldyard near the boiler house door.

Monday **September 15**—a busy day: Helen went off to Beverley College on the 8am bus and Von and I took the Ullyotts to York for the start of their big adventure in Australia. It was funny really as, quite coincidentally, we met Mary Burdass, who was the wife of the joint owner of Whitehall

Farm, Kelk, where Peter and Betty farmed. She was out with Libby Byass, a good friend of ours from Lund. Not just that, an aunt of Peter's from Helmsley turned up on the platform as well. On our return we found Helen at home—they had a half day on Mondays. She went back in the evening for a class and Andrew went to Driffield for his first welding class, where he was instructed by Don Newlove. Angus 'Booey' went back to school the next day—the last one of our children to be at school.

September 16: Chris started drilling Igri winter barley in 50-acre across the road, after he had spread 150kg per acre of 9.24.24 fertilizer. The same day Freda Downes took her dog, Topsy, to the vet because it had been sick. She then went into the bank in Beverley, leaving the dog fastened in the car. When she returned it was to find that the dog was dead: it had hanged itself with its lead. Awful.

On a more cheerful note, Grandad won at the Bridlington Chrysanthemum Show with his gladioli and chrysanthemums. He did well with his showing. The next day was the family service: Von got us all there—it was good to see all the families in church, six Snowdens, six Peter Walkers, four George Walkers, and we six, including Mother. This was the village they said was dying.

Mrs Farnaby came to stay—Julia brought her as she had to return to barracks: she worked for the WRVS and was based at Ouston, in Northumberland. Poor Aunty was really poorly with the shingles.

I sowed 110kgs per acre of 0.20.20 fertilizer on all pea land, Andrew spring tine harrowing after me and Chris following, drilling Virtue wheat in Short Lands and Bramble Butts and Brigand wheat in 52-acre; Peter was rolling afterwards. John was drilling Hustler wheat in Clark Field at Lickham. Mr Sleight rolled after the drill. Eddie started to halter train the steers we were taking to Smithfield Show after the vet had injected them with Feenaplix, a growth promoter. He de-horned all the bought-in calves whilst he was here. The same night we started David Neave's class in the Oddfellows Hall in the village. Von had arranged for him to come via the Workers Educational Association to give a series of local history talks. To our pleasure there was a full house, with more than 50 people in attendance. The courses were always well-attended and ran for several winters, with visits to places of interest in the summer.

Mother and Von were visiting Betty Bentley, who was still in hospital, and in a very bad way. It was Middleton Show and Grandad won the cup for the vegetable section. The same day he cut the privet hedge; he really was most useful. We had Shippey's of Bridlington working at the same time, they rebuilt the chimney stack at Vicarage Farm, replaced the chimney stack of pots and plastered inside the false roof of the gable end. I received a cheque from the Ministry for £238—a 10 per cent grant for the purchase of the grass cutter. Garry Hyde started cutting the hedges up at Lund Wold.

October 8: Von and I went up to North Riding Garages at Pickering where we viewed a very nice marine blue Mercedes 250, which we agreed to buy for £10,250, plus our own Mercedes (NVN 700M). We collected the car (KDC 350W) a week later. Steve Stephenson, the AIS representative, came and I paid him £2,565 for Prebane and Roundup, to the end of August. Bob Webster senior and I did a deal to buy a new Ivor Williams cattle trailer for £1,072 net.

October 16: Mr Ringrose, the manager of the Midland Bank in Beverley, came to lunch. He was quite happy with the current financial arrangements and agreed to extend the overdraft a little further. At the same time Turner's from Leven were here cleaning out the dyke at the bottom of Road Ends in Harold Wood's field for Beverley Borough Council, as it was the sewage outfall for Holme-on-the-Wolds. They had agreed to do this as it was always cleaned out previously by the Beverley Borough Council. Later on that week we had the man from the Milk Marketing Board (MMB) to collect semen from Pinpur Intercontinental. This was for home-use only in the UK. We collected semen from Pinpur, not because he was of a better conformation but to get a new bloodline into the gene pool. In any case his breeding went back to the Knepp herd in the fourth generation.

October 17—Andrew's 18th birthday: he was full of cold and not in very good form. He and I went to FMC at Seamer to see the carcases of the four bulls, which had gone the previous day. In the evening all of us went to Scorborough Church harvest festival and back to the Ellison's at the Hall for supper. Andrew went to Nick Snowden's do, but was back in bed before we got home at 11pm. The following day it was Angus's 12th birthday: we went to fetch him from Cundall in the new car and his eyes nearly popped out of his head when he realised it was us. As it was to be his birthday he brought another boy, William Terry, home with him.

I went into Jopling's in Hull to see about getting a tow bar fitted on the new Mercedes car—it would be £90. In addition I ordered a new low-loader, which would be £1,036 net, for which I paid £100 deposit. They would fit the tow bar there and then and I would collect the low loader a month later. Halder's collected five loads of wheat; 105 tonnes, at £101 per tonne for a Feedex order.

October 24: John Sleight had a day's holiday. Little did we realise that a month later he would hand in his notice, as he was going into partnership with his brother-in-law, Derek Starkey, at Laburnum Farm, Etton.

Andrew and I went to Marrs at Bainton Balk for the farm live and dead stock sale conducted by Leonard's. I bought some front-end tractor weights for £57.50. We received a cheque from MAFF for the 10 per cent grant for the tractor and baler under the FHD scheme.

On the following Sunday, Von and I went to Corwen, North Wales, to collect the Ivor Williams cattle trailer, which was on order from Webster's. We called to see Bert and Margaret Cheetham, at Hyde, and collected six bull calves. I paid him £450 for nine calves, three of which we had got previously. The following day Malcolm Ashley brought 10 Hereford-cross calves and I paid him £760. The four bulls which went to Seamer came to £1,302.

At the beginning of November, Warwick Chinn, the vet from Market Weighton, came to TB blood test 150 cows, in-calf heifers and maiden heifers and three bulls for brucellosis. He returned three days later to check the animals for TB; fortunately they were all clear.

November 10: things were beginning to brighten up on the grain sales, we sold Feedex 200 tonnes of wheat at £102 per tonne, to go as soon as possible—it started going the following day. Chris and I were making a show box, and I bought all the aluminium one-inch angle iron for the corners at Elthringhtons in Hull. Andrew and I went into Jobling's, where we collected the new low loader and paid £1,091.

PC Hardwick came up and I paid him £37 for Andrew's shotgun and firearms certificate. Andrew Marr and Tony Todd came in the afternoon; they wanted to increase the rent to £32 per acre as from April. As we planned to go to Canada early in December, I thought we ought to pay a few outstanding bills before we went. I paid 16 bills—a total of £4,886. Maurice Robson came, and we sold him 100 tonnes of wheat at £103 per tonne. I paid Mr Tutty, of British Fuels, £1,080 for gas oil.

November 27: I collected Molly Course from York Station; she was staying with Mother whilst we were in Canada and the USA. Mother was nervous of being left on her own, even if the children were there, so it was kind of Molly to fill the breach. Andrew and Eddie were going down to Smithfield the following day; they went in the van and Chris Waite took the nine steers we had entered for three different classes. I collected the new show box at Hallum Signs at Tickton and, whilst in that direction, went in to see John Watt the NFU representative in Beverley as we are transferring all our insurances from the Eagle Star Company to the NFU as from December 1. I also cancelled the standing order at the Midland Bank to Eagle Star.

On the last day of the month Molly took Von and I to York Station to catch the London train; we stayed two nights near Earls Court. The following day was judging day at Smithfield, and we won three firsts, three seconds, two thirds and a fourth as well as the breed championship and the reserve champion. Little did we know then that would be the end of the Red Poll classes at Smithfield, as no-one else entered in subsequent years. We sold all the steers to a butcher at £1 a kilo live-weight, so we had no further transport costs.

The day after judging, Von and I left Heathrow at 11am for Toronto. We were met by Geoff Pilmoor, Von's cousin; we were the first relatives he had welcomed into Canada in the 33 years he had been there. He had booked us into a flash hotel in the middle of the city—he had said to the management that I was Mr Prescott, Minister of Agriculture or some such. We had never slept in such a huge bed in such opulent surroundings. The following day he took us round Toronto, up the CN tower and to see the Niagara Falls, which were wonderful as they were frozen over; there was no-one else there except a group of Japanese tourists. There were huge icicles hanging down from the tops of the viewing 'windows' as we walked beneath the falls. It was an amazing experience.

The following day he took us to the airport to get the plane to Regina, where I was judging the Red Poll classes at the Agribition. This was a tremendous indoor arena and very well heated. On departure we were warned over the loudspeaker that naked skin would freeze in three minutes. It was minus 35 degrees outside. It was like entering a Wild West town—everyone was wearing Stetsons and boots. There was a bucking bronco for anyone to take a challenge; that was absolutely fascinating. I was assured by one breeder that however I judged the animals no-one would bear any grudges. He didn't win, and he never spoke to us again. It was at this show that I first saw a Chianina—an Italian breed of beef/draught cattle. This beast was a year old and stood six feet high at the withers, on tremendously long legs. I had 19 classes to judge—there were up to a dozen in each class, some of which were excellent animals.

In the evening many of the animals were sold at an international show and sale. Some of the animals for sale came up from the Pinney Perdue herd near Chicago, Illinois. Even in those days a bull was bought by a syndicate for $4,500.

We met Joe and Pearl Marshall, friends from Innisfail, Alberta, who insisted we return with them for the weekend—we had already booked our tickets to go to Los Angeles to have a bit of 'sun time' but they would accept no refusal. Pearl insisted that I had long johns on, as it was dangerous to travel all that way and not have any protection. She gave me some of Joe's. So we set off in the back of their car, with views of snow in every direction. It was a dual carriageway most of the way, with a big central reservation which was steeply 'dished' to prevent traffic going from one carriageway to another. As it was full of snow, the road surface from one side to another resembled the top of a marble. Their snow is very dry. It blows across the plains and polishes the roads so they look very smooth, but can be very dangerous. We travelled some 600 miles, leaving Regina just after 6am and arriving at their home in Red Deer by 7pm. The windscreen and back window of the car were heated and clear, but Von and I in the back had to scrape the ice from our side windows. We occasionally saw a herd of buffalo on the horizon, but that was all. A journey never to be forgotten.

We spent the weekend with Pearl and Joe, where he showed us his herd in their winter quarters. They had snowmobiles to get about on cross country. Many teenagers lost their lives on these machines, flying along and decapitating themselves on telegraph wires, which they could not see as they were covered in ice. He also showed us how their water supply and all their services came in at nine feet deep below ground level to prevent freezing up in the winter.

Joe had more or less retired from farming but had a few cows which calved in the spring. I asked him why his cows had such short ears, and he replied that they lose a quarter of an inch of ear every year with frostbite.

We also saw two young bulls at another farm, with icicles hanging from their nose ends. It is seriously cold in the winter.

At that time Joe spent most of his time as arbitrator between the farmers and the oil companies regarding compensation for disruption of the land where they had brought the oil pipeline down from Alaska. Piles of sulphur, which was extracted from the oil to allow it to flow more readily, were heaped up at the side of the pipeline workings. These heaps of sulphur had no use at that time and could not be disposed of: now we have to buy sulphur to put on crops as there are not the sulphur emissions from power stations and domestic chimneys.

On the Monday morning he took us down to Calgary airport to catch the Los Angeles flight; we really thought we would never get to the airport there was so much snow, but when we arrived, there were eight snowploughs working in tandem on the runways, blowing snow into lorries to keep them clear and the plane took off, no bother at all. The first full day we had in Los Angeles we visited the world-famous Disneyland. Uncle Tommy had told us we had to go there, as it catered for children of all ages—and he was right. The entrance was fantastic, with a toy town band playing in front of a huge bed of poinsettias. Von was in tears as, at that time, Andrew and Helen were attending the funeral of Christine Walker in Lund. A very sobering thought to die at the age of 41. We had a wonderful day—everything was as Uncle Tommy had promised, but it was tinged with sadness.

The next days we did the Hollywood tour, visited Chinatown, the Hollywood Bowl, the Farmers' Market and Universal Studios. We went to Santa Monica and Tijuana in Mexico, which was an experience in itself: we saw all the caves in the hillsides where people were living in poverty. The main aim of the Mexican was to cross into the USA, so the border posts were guarded day and night. However, many of the migrants crossed during the night under the wire, well away from the border posts.

We flew back to Toronto on December 13, had two nights there and saw Geoff again. We left on the evening of December 15 and arrived at Heathrow early the following day. Andrew met us in York in the late afternoon. It was straight back into the usual routine. Angus broke up the following day, and the day after it was Von's birthday, which she shares with Tony Morford, so we went out for a meal with them. On the Saturday evening it was the Brumfields' Christmas party and after that it was, as usual, carol singers to supper—church, chapel and young farmers. Grandad and Aunty Lil, Molly Course and so on joined us for Christmas. There was the Lambs' Christmas party, Christmas carol services. It all happens in a village.

I sold Maurice Robson all the wheat left in the new drier, approximately 250 tonnes at £108 a tonne, which had to be dried down to 14 per cent as it was going for export. We also had to dry 50 tonnes of wheat for Alec Snowden to go on the same shipment.

W ith the Christmas festivities behind us, Von took Molly Course into the Nuffield Hospital in Hull to have a toe removed. It was just day surgery so Von collected her later.

The following day we had a nice surprise; we had a cheque for £281 from the FMC for bonus on 127 animals that had graded Q or AA—£2.20 a head, which was worth having. This was for animals supplied during the previous 12 months.

The straight grade A did not qualify for this bonus.

Chris and I had started a big fencing programme; we erected a post-and-rail fence in the Park bottom, next to Middleton Wood, from the hedge next to Little Wold to the bottom of Park Hill. Mike Payne brought a Karcher steam cleaner and I paid him £1,293. This was what Andrew wanted for Christmas. At the same time John had been ploughing for his brother-in-law, Derek Starkey, at Etton, with whom he was going into partnership, and finished ploughing a total of 34 acres. Unfortunately, Andrew ran over a bullock at Vicarage Farm with the forklift so Wiles, the fellmonger, had to come and collect it.

January 18: Von took William Lamb, John Duggleby and me into Hull to catch the London train—we were going with Barrett's to the Fendt factory in Germany. We had a very interesting time amongst the snow; it was a great deal colder there than at home. We spent a whole day looking round the tractor factory, seeing the production of the many different specifications of tractors that they produce, and all the implements, including the snow ploughs that would go with them. We also saw some of the local sights and visited a night club, which opened our eyes somewhat—never having been served by topless barmaids before. We certainly drank plenty of German beer—in steins. We felt it was less intoxicating than the beer at home. We also visited a couple of farms where they were intensively fattening cattle and pigs. We got back home on January 23, and the following morning Von and I went up to Cundall to watch Angus play in his first rugby match; it was a good game, which they lost by two points. We brought Angus and his friend, Mark Bedford, back with us for the weekend and took them back the next night.

The following day Andrew and I went to Green's at Ellerker and collected 400 hedging plants, 50 beech hedging plants and eight trees to replace those on Queen's Mead which had not taken. John and Mr Sleight planted the beech hedge from the dugout to the wood at the top of far garden. They then started filling in gaps, many of which had been caused by tanks during the war, on the roadsides with the hedging plants. We tried to fill up a few gaps every year: it was almost 200 years since the hedges had been planted over a 10-year or so period after the enclosure system's introduction in 1798. We also seemed to have quite a few people taking their cars through the hedge on the Malton Road. Some gaps were caused by self-seeded elderberry bushes that had killed the hedge round them and then died off themselves after about 30 years.

Von took Molly to York to catch the 9.13am train to Bournemouth; she was now recovered from the operation on her toe, so was able to go home. Maurice Robson came up with a cheque for £26,795 for the 245 tonnes of export wheat which had gone earlier in the month. I sold him another 100 tonnes at £109.50 a tonne, which John would deliver to Fridaythorpe the following week. Francis Jackson came and I ordered another 10 tonnes of 34.5 per cent nitrogen at £99 a tonne and 27 tonnes of 22.11.11 at £135 a tonne.

At the end of the month John, Chris and I set new gateposts into the Park and hung the new gate which Andrew had made. We then started what turned out to be a major fencing programme of post and rail fencing, with posts every two yards, four rails high, from the end of the new drier up to the Park gate and from the Dutch barn end up to Park gate. In other words, making a secure area where we could keep some bulling heifers in the winter. We then continued fencing in the Park from the hand gate right across to 20-acre hedge, re-aligning the non-existent fence line. We also made a gateway into Little Field in the opposite corner to the wood. Andrew then started making a cab for the old Claas Giant Matador combine; this, hopefully, would eliminate the weather elements and dust at harvest time. He even put a tinted red Perspex roof on it.

We had obtained three redundant Hull City Corporation cast street light columns, with swan necks, from their lighting department. Andrew cleaned and re-painted them and I took them down to the village where Mike Lazenby, Bernard Calvert and I erected them; one at the bottom of Queen's Mead on South Avenue, one at the end of Eastgate near Levitt Lane and the third one at the top end of North Road, opposite Manor View. Unfortunately, when we were erecting this one it fell over and broke in the middle; we took it to Norman Colley, at Holme-on-the-Wolds, and he welded it back together. The following day William Lamb, Mike and I finished erecting it and put the swan-necked fittings onto the top of the posts, ready for wiring into the main street lighting supply. I sent a cheque off to the DVLA for Helen's provisional driving licence.

February 3: George Gowthorpe, from Aike, came up and bought 22 Hereford-cross steers from Vicarage Farm and paid me £4,224—£192 each. These were nine months to a year old and ready to turn out to grass. The same day we received a cheque from the FMC for the five fat steers that had gone to Sheffield two weeks previously and made £368 each. Von got the annual road fund licence for the Mercedes van—it was £52.

We were now coming up to the time of the year when it was the Kiplingcotes Derby, which was run on the third Thursday in March.

One Sunday afternoon Andrew tried to go down the racecourse with the Land Rover from the main A614 to the Goodmanham Road; he got as far as Ash Slack and then became stuck and could not move. After walking home, which took him about two hours, he enlisted Helen to help drive the Land Rover whilst he pulled with the tractor. The tractor then became stuck fast. During this time Von and I saw no sign of them when we went for a walk to meet them, so we went home for the car and eventually found them, with the tractor up to its axles in mud. I went to John Morley, who lived in the farmhouse at Enthorpe and was married to Mary Sellars, to ask him if we could borrow a tractor to pull everything out. It was beginning to get dark by this time, but we managed to have everything out and home by 6.30pm—all soaking wet. I don't think Andrew has taken a vehicle down there since.

February 9: Millers Aerial Sprayers spread 48cwt of 34.5 per cent nitrogen on 50 acre barley across the road from Wold House, Andrew went down to AIS to get au-fait with the sprayers so that he could help demonstrate them later in the week at Bishop Burton. Chris and I finished setting the post-and-rail fence in the Park across the top end of Little Field at Wold House, and then we did from Little Wold ash tree to the hedge in the Park bottom. This field was now fairly stock-proof and secure. Alec Snowden paid us £386 for drying his wheat that went on the boat at Christmas.

The following week I set the two cast iron posts and hung the little hand gate at the petrol tank that was originally in the well yard, at the front of the house at Wold House. Chris and I then started to set a three rail post-and-rail fence from the petrol tank down either side of the ramp, across the front of the buildings and down to the bottom gate. Von was doing cookery demonstrations for various WIs and went to Garton; there were about 50 in the audience, so that was quite good.

February 17: Andrew Marr and his agent, Anthony Todd, acting for his sister, Mrs Caroline Brown, who owned Vicarage Farm, came to discuss a rent increase and we agreed to pay £4,400 a year—£30.50 per acre—as from April 6.

Mike Lazenby came up with Lambs' digger to dig holes for the gateposts in front of the foldyard doors and at the bottom gate, where the gateways were. On the Saturday morning Andrew was at the Memorial Hall in Beverley preparing for the YFC entertainments competition; Von, Mother, Helen and I went at night to watch. Each club did something different: short plays, singing, comedy sketches and it was all very good. The clubs put a lot of effort into these competitions.

I went to Freemans at North Newbald where I met a Mr Watson and gave them the order to erect and cover a new shed over the top of the wagon shed. This would involve putting a row of stanchions down the stable side, a lean-to over the stable, loose boxes to the foldyard shed and making a valley gutter in between. I have never liked this gutter; it proved to be a nuisance and was always blocked with leaves, etc. After I had got him to adjust his price somewhat they would do this for £10,500, for completion by July 31.

Andrew started to make cab for the Senator combine; he was quite pleased with his first effort—a cab for the Giant Matador. A heifer (F6) had calved that night; her calf was deformed: it had its heart in its neck and was most strange. It died the following day.

Ron Downes, from Mortimer's, brought a cheque for £11,100, for the last 101 tonne lot of wheat we had delivered to Fridaythorpe in January.

On the last day of the month we visited Aunty Ethel at Scarborough and went on to Grandad and Aunty Lil's; it was snowing hard for most of the day. That evening we had Stella and Peter Harvey up for supper, I kept looking out of the window and saying: 'It's snowing quite heavily', but they sat on. Eventually, at about 11pm, they would leave but once outside they found that they could not get down the paddock for snow. Stella could not believe it—they ended up staying the night.

Chris and John both fetching fertilizer 22.11.11 and 34.5 per cent nitrogen from Hull Bridge—by this time Stephenson's had been taken over by Albright and Wilson. They, in turn, were taken over by ACC. Chris had a puncture in Wylies Road, Beverley, and had to call out National Tyre Service (NTS) to fit two new tyres and tubes.

March 4: Eddie, Chris and I were freeze-branding all the heifers on their back ends with the year letter and their number; it certainly was the easiest way of identifying cattle, as they were always moving away from you when you wanted to identify them, particularly when they are all red and fairly similar to each other. We sold Maurice Robson 80 tonnes of barley out of the old drier and barn to go to intervention at Driffield, for £100 a tonne. I went to York Market and bought 10 calves for £462.

March 5: John and Mr Sleight were both at Lickham having a final tidy up as John was leaving the following day, which he was having off to go to Greathead's sale at Lockington. John, Margaret, Catherine and Jennifer were moving to Laburnum Farm, Etton, to farm with Margaret's brother and father. We were sorry to see them go after 10 years. The Sleights were certainly leaving a farm vastly different to what it was when they came.

It is interesting to note here that since Andrew had come home we had effectively halved the employed labour force. Employees were only Eddie Jowsey and Chris Towse. A lot of that was due to the fact that we had fork-lifts and were coming into the telescopic handler stage. These are much more versatile and efficient than the fore-end loaders, especially when they have a grab on the muck loaders and four-wheel steer and crab steer as well as the two wheel steer.

I took the plans for the new shed into St Mary's Manor and saw Mr Wilkinson but permission was not needed, as it was included in the FHD scheme, drawn up some three years previously.

That evening Angus was confirmed at York Minster by Morris Maddocks, the Bishop of Selby. Everyone turned up to support him: Margaret Shipley and her mother, Mrs Thompson, John Richardson, Ben and Christine Goodwin, who were his godparents, and of course Grandad, Aunty Lil, Mother, Aunty Farnaby, Andrew, Helen, Von and me. The Bishop had confirmed Andrew. At that service we sat in the main body of the church, this time we were in the choir stalls. Afterwards we had a warm cup of coffee and a hard bun in St William's College next door. Von had been in York the whole day anyway, helping Christine Mudge from Bishop Burton set up for a day school for WI judges.

Von was judging at the Young Farmers public speaking competitions in Hull with Bill Pinkney. The following evening we took Angus back to school and went to church where he had his first communion.

March 9—Helen's 17th birthday: She had her first driving lesson with Audrey at Sinnett Jones. She drove Von to Bridlington in the Maxi car. Von was exhausted when they got there and Helen could not bend her legs. She then had an hour-long lesson. They visited Grandad and Lil and then Helen drove home—and went to bed exhausted. Chris spread 200kg per acre of 22.11.11 on all the grasses.

Maurice Robson brought a cheque for £13,360 for the last lot of wheat. I put this into the bank before going on to Lord Hotham's grass lets: they went for between £59 and £88 an acre. Chris took one and a half tonnes of 22.11.11 onto Middleton Tops—the 34.5 per cent nitrogen was already there. Millers, using their fixed-wing light plane, spread the former on the hillside grasses, Park, 20-acre, Hut Field and Far Field and then the nitrogen on the wheat at Lickham and at Wold.

A Mr Ownsworth, from Barnsley, came to see the milk parlour and agreed to buy it for £500. He gave me £100 in cash and they took all the milk jars, milk pump, clusters and quite a lot of piping. I paid Millers Aerial Sprayers £165.60 for the first lot of spreading and £2,872 to Pauls and Whites for the previous month's feed. Andrew took seven steers to FMC at Seamer with the Land Rover. It broke a half shaft at Seamer so I had to take it into Barrett's the following day to get a new one fitted.

I did a deal with Barry Watson (J Wood and Son) for a new Massey Ferguson 30 grain only drill: 31-row narrow spacing disc coulters—overall width 14 feet seven inches with hydraulic markers, wheel eradicators and grain agitator for £5,244, less 15 per cent discount—£4,457.40 net.

March 29—Mothering Sunday: The children bought Von a cake plate to match our dinner service; she was delighted with it. At 1am the following day we had a call from Geoffrey Maltas: 'All your heifers are out on the road near Lair Hill.' Up Von and I got, dressed, and went out with flashlights, which we needed because the heifers were red and all you could see was their eyes.

We got the heifers back fairly easily but the bull decided differently; he was in Little Wold and I had to walk him across to the middle gate, across 20-acre and back into Hut Field. All this took us just an hour; we arrived back at the house to find that Andrew had come in, locked up and put all the lights out. I had to climb in through the back kitchen top window.

At the end of March, Von arranged a visit to the Humber Bridge for WI members and husbands. Denis Peacock, who lived in Holme-on-the-Wolds and was working on the project, gave us a most interesting tour on top and underneath the roadway and inside the road sections and columns.

April 1: we received a cheque from Mortimer's for 86.5 tonnes of barley for £8,308.70 after deducting £340 for 1.4 tonnes of Triumph seed barley. A couple of days later I took out life insurance policies for Andrew and Helen with the Life Association of Scotland and paid the first premium.

April 4: Grand National Day: Andrew and Mother both backed the winner, Aldaniti, and won £20 each. Von, Helen and Angus won £5 each for a placing. Oxford won the Boat Race.

April 5: I went to Watton Abbey and paid Peter Brown £780 for a half year's grazing rent for the two grass fields on the roadside there. Chris was top dressing 140 acres of wheat at Vicarage Farm, and got 310 x 50kg bags of 34.5 nitrogen and then continued with the remainder of winter wheat and barley at just over 100kgs per acre.

The following day we took 30 steers and heifers down to the grasses at Watton. I paid C A Wood and Co £1,693.83p for auditing the previous year's accounts.

April 8: Alec Snowden and I went to Brandesburton to see the Voases' trenchless draining machine working inserting plastic perforated pipe for land drainage.

During this time the plumbers were at Vicarage Farm, finishing off the electrics and installations and fitting the boiler. Bernard Sissons was working at 39 and 41 South Street, painting both cottages; we were preparing 41 South Street ready to let as self-catering holiday accommodation. I paid David Cornwell £839 for Pauls' feeds account to the end of March.

The following day, Saturday, was a very wet day. Tom Helm, from Dee and Atkinson, came to do the end-of-year valuation. He lived in the village and it was handy for him to fit us in. Richard Morris took Helen to a clay pigeon shoot at the Humber Bridge.

April 12: Four Bentleys, Mrs Bentley, Harold Duke, Grandad and Lil come for lunch and Helen brought home her first boyfriend—Richard Morris, from North Frodingham. Dorothy Hunter came too and they all went off to the Pipe and Glass to play Bridlington YFC at darts—and lost. Angus had been outside all day on his go-kart and was covered in mud when he finally came in.

Rodgers, of Driffield, had installed central heating at Vicarage Farm, making a tremendous difference. Bernard Sissons had done some decorating and Mrs Ellis's sister, Mrs Hesletine, gave it a good clean, so we felt we had done as much as we could in preparation for Chris and Christine Towse, who were to move in. Andrew went off ice-skating with Dorothy and Longcroft sixth form to Billingham Forum.

April 14: the half yearly rent day at Dalton Estate office. I paid £2,327. 50 for the previous half year's rent, then went to Page Office Equipment, Hull, and bought the new chairs for the village hall for £275. I left the chairs in the village hall.

J Wood and Son brought the new Massey Ferguson 30 drill, and, after they had set it up, Chris drilled Wood Flat and then drilled Pit Field—1.5 acres—with barley by 4 pm.

April 17—Good Friday: Helen and I went to AIS at Selby for Hytane, Tilt and CMPP chemicals. Eddie and Pauline went to Cheethams at Hyde for six calves and I gave him a cheque for £270. Andrew was spraying Railway Side and all in front of the house at Lickham, and then did Short Lands at Lund with CMPP and Tilt.

Mother, Von, Helen, Angus and I went to Grandad's for tea and then for a walk on the sea front: it was blowing a gale. Angus went into the amusements. For a while we lost him but, fortunately, managed to track him down.

We called at Edward and Margaret Duggleby's at High Farm, North

Frodingham, on the way home and saw where Richard Morris lived. When we got home he had rung up and came to see Helen in the evening.

The following day, the phone was red hot: the three Rs were ringing Helen up: Richard Walgate, Richard Morris and Richard Delany, from North Cave, all wanting to take her out. It was all happening for Helen. Aunty Ethel from Scarborough came to stay.

Easter Sunday: Beverley NFU had arranged a visit for some German farmers, and we had one to stay. I collected a Frederick Pape from the Memorial Hall in Beverley in the morning: he could not speak a word of English. I brought him home, we had lunch and then he retired to bed. Morris and Sue Clarkson, from Kiplingcotes, had two staying with them. A Wilfred Stock, who spoke English, agreed to swap with Frederick. (Wilfred, who had been at Leconfield Camp as a prisoner-of-war, kept in touch for very many years afterwards.) Morris and I took them down to Leconfield Camp where they had a brief look round. We took them to a service in Beverley Minster in the evening: it was extremely long and boring and I dread to think what they thought of it. There was a reception afterwards in the art gallery.

The following day, the Monday, I took Wilfred and Ernst to see the Humber Bridge, which was under construction, and met Fred Woodall and his guests at the Hull Crest Hotel for lunch. In the afternoon Sam Walton, who was hosting Ernst, took us over the North York Moors and onto Castle Howard, then all back to Wold for tea.

Alan and Dorothy Duggleby had arrived with Kay, Alan's mother, and Andrew had Paul, Ian and Jonathan here too. Von could run an army kitchen. The next day Sister Mary Mildred came to stay. Von took Wilfred and they went on to the York Railway Museum after collecting Sister.

April 22: Christine Towse gave birth to Cheryl, a sister for Clare and Craig. For the time being they were still living in Goodmanham.

Grasbys came for four steers, three young bulls and two heifers to go to FMC at Sheffield. Sam Walton and I took Wilfred and Ernst to David Stephenson, at Skelfrey Park, to look round his pig unit. We then went down into Holderness to see John and Edward Hinchliffe at Otteringham, returning by Sunk Island and Burton Constable. We had a party that night for about 30 of us. Then the dishwasher packed up and pumped out water onto the kitchen floor.

April 24: it snowed hard all day: I took Wilfred into Beverley to meet Glen Sotherby, with whom he had corresponded ever since he returned home from the war, at Beverley Minster. In the afternoon I took four of the Germans up to Manor Farm at Warter Estate, where Tony Morford showed us their Masstock unit. Tony was one of the two managers on the Warter Estate.

The following day I took Wilfred to see Glen Sotherby at home in Tickton before taking him back to the Memorial Hall, from where they all left to return home. I got home to find that a school friend of Von's, Susan Witty, and family had called in, mainly to see Sister. In the evening Von and I went to Janice Eastwood's 18th birthday party.

On the Sunday, Mo Westoby took Sister to the Catholic church in Beverley. We all went to Lund Church, except Helen, who was still asleep. I read a lesson. When we returned she had gone to a clay pigeon shoot with Richard. We had Len and Barbara Robinson up in the evening to see the kitchen as they were hoping to have theirs done. Len was a huge man, a policeman in Hull. When we got to know them better we found them to be a nice couple: he was a 'proper' policeman.

Phillip Ryder Davies, the secretary for our Red Poll Cattle Society, persuaded us to show at the Suffolk Show at Ipswich, as it was their centenary year, and he wanted a good showing of Red Poll cattle. Chris, Andrew, Eddie and I had to start halter training the animals we were taking there.

On the Tuesday it was the implement sale at Driffield: we had entered quite a few obsolete items, so I went there, and Von took Booey (Angus) back to Cundall School. She took Mother and Sister too and returned via Malton—a nice ride. Freda Downes was waiting for them. In the evening I took Andrew and Helen to Lambs for cattle judging for YFC.

April 30: Mr Tutty (British Fuels) came and I paid him our fuel bill to the end of March—£1,495. Von and I went to Scarborough to see Aunty Ethel and we bought a new Colston dishwasher at Goods for £199.90. Chris fetched Christine and Cheryl out of hospital that day.

It was the day of the Northern Counties Red Poll dinner at The Chase in York, where we had an excellent meal for £6. The head of ADAS, Colvin Williams, was our speaker. I was re-elected honorary secretary; Benny Bradshaw was chairman, with Charlie Kidson, from Royston, near Wakefield, as honorary treasurer.

The next day we took Sister Mary Mildred for a ride across the moors to Whitby, calling on the way back in Lealholme to see Nick and Charlotte Wykes. Nick was a Red Poll council member for many years and worked for the Vestey organisation in Argentina and Brazil organizing the estancias where the cattle were being reared prior to slaughter, after which the carcases were sent to England.

Mother, Sister and Von went to Bridlington with Helen for her driving lesson. Von and Sister went round the St Dominic's Convent where Von went to school and Sister was headmistress: they were full of it. It had been Spartan under the Dominicans, but now, under the Sisters of Mercy, it was sumptuous. Von even went up the main staircase, which they were never allowed to do, and could not get over how small the school was in comparison with her memories of it.

Andrew, Dorothy, Helen and Richard Morris went to a YFC dance at North Newbald: Richard was told off for getting in late—3am and then up for milking for 5.30 am. He went back to bed in the afternoon to recover.

Margaret Shipley and son, Ian, came over, and also David Maltas, so all was very lively.

The next day we took Sister back to the convent in Erdington, Birmingham. She always seemed to enjoy coming, even though she had to have a special dispensation for staying in a non-Catholic household—and we certainly enjoyed her company.

After dropping her off we went along to Avoncroft Cattle Breeding Centre to see Pinpur Intercontinental, our bull, which we had imported from Canada. He was there in quarantine for three months before semen could be collected for UK use; it is six months' quarantine for international use. We had a good discussion with Dr Mark Philpott and Mr Maurice Elliot regarding the collection and advertising, etc. We then went on to the RASE showground at Stoneleigh to take in our entries for the Royal Show and paid £246.55 entry fee.

May 7: Eddie and I went to Bridges' paddock in Lund, and sowed 200kgs of 34.5 per cent nitrogen on the grass with the fiddle drill. We then set the barbed wire next to Don White's paddock at Poplars before taking three cows and four calves there—one cow had twins. We received a cheque for £3,620 from FMC for nine beasts that went a fortnight ago.

May 9: Tottenham Hotspur and Manchester City drew one all in the FA

Cup final at Wembley. The rents for six and eight South Street, Middleton-on-the-Wolds, went up from £4 a week to £4.50 a week from April 6.

The following day was the Young Farmers' sponsored pram push from Market Weighton to Beverley. Andrew made a pram with car wheels and steering wheel, etc, and he, Ian Snowden and Stuart Lazenby pushed Charles Lamb in the pilot position. They managed to get to Beverley in the time allowed

I gave the parish clerk, Joan Helm, a £20 cheque for the rent of the pit on Wold Road, approximately one acre. I sowed 112 x 50kgs bags of 0.20.20 on 52 acre, which was for vining peas.

Joe Huxtable and I went down to the Farmers Club in London the next day for the Red Poll Cattle Society annual general meeting. When I returned it was to find Andrew making rhubarb wine. He had sprayed both the grasses at Watton with CMPP and then in the Park at Wold. That evening I retired after my two-year stint as chairman of Lund Parish Council and William Lamb took over.

May 15: I went to Tom Young's funeral at North Dalton. Tom, who had been a bachelor all his life, ran the livestock haulage business from Mill Farm, on the right hand side of the road from Middleton. It has all been knocked down now. On the left hand side there are still some of the farm buildings and the granary, which has been converted into living accommodation. He lived with a brother and sister called Rawson. Both, like him, were unmarried. They retired to the old keeper's house at the top of South Street in Middleton. His business was taken over by Chris Waite transport.

Tom Young did all our transportation of livestock until the mid-1960s when he retired. He took me to many of the shows in the early days and he would stay at the show all day giving a helping hand if needed. It was his pleasure as well as his work and he was very reliable. Sam Walton came up the same day and drilled approximately four acres of kale in the field next to the front paddock for strip grazing for the cows in the winter.

Von took Andrew into Hull and they bought him a new suit at John Collier for £49.95. In the evening Von, Andrew, Helen and I all went to Caroline Snowden's 21st party at the Cottage Grill in Bridlington. A very good do except that Andrew must have leaned on the bar or somewhere and got all black on the front and sleeve of his new jacket, which had to be dry cleaned.

The Greaves, from Homecharm, who installed our new kitchen, brought Mrs Urquart from Walkington to view it—we must have been their exhibition kitchen of the moment.

May 23: I went to judge North Riding YFC cow judging competition at Sinnington and then on to pick Angus up from school, whilst Von, Andrew and Helen were at the YFC Rally at the Baystons, at Gilberdyke. Von was judging sedan chairs, but as Andrew had an entry she swapped with Shirley Coleman. She then helped Margaret Snowden and Mrs Mudge judge the crack an egg competition—19 clubs had entered, with six items in each entry.

The following days Chris was drilling Waverax peas (petit pois) in Little Wold, Little Field and 52 acre, opposite the farm. These were the last peas for Beverley Pea Growers to be drilled this year. Andrew was rolling down all the peas after Chris. Eddie and I were getting the show box and the cows ready to go down to Suffolk Show the following day. We had hired Sam Walton's 7.5 tonne Renault cattle wagon.

Andrew and Eddie took the cattle down the following morning and Von, Helen and I followed with the car and caravan. We left Andrew and Eddie in the caravan and we three stayed at the Marlborough Hotel in Felixstowe. In the evening we went to see Mrs Reynolds and her son, Rowland. Her late husband, Angus Reynolds, used to be the agent for Stuart Paul of the Kirton herd, and was a most well-respected man. Our Angus was named after him.

We won third with the young bull (in a class of eight), fourth with Primrose (in a class of 14) and second and third with heifer in-calf class. They were all excellent classes and a very good exhibit for the breed, which gained lot of good publicity. Andrew and Eddie left the show on Thursday evening and were home by 11.30pm—a total of 238 miles home.

Von and I went with Alec and Margaret Snowden to Shipley to have a lunch on a boat cruise: we met up with the Cookes and the Mowforths, etc and cruised to Bingley on the Leeds Liverpool Canal, through five locks: it was all very interesting, but quite expensive at £6.50 each.

That same day we got the news that Eddie's brother Michael, had been blown up in Northern Ireland whilst defusing a bomb.

The same evening when we got home we went down to the Reffolds at Cranswick to take a clematis plant to Mr Reffold for his 80th birthday. Von and Mrs Reffold did a lot of judging together for the WI.

June 1: Paid Peter Brown £780 for half of the rent for the Watton grasses. Von got the annual licence—£70—for the Maxi. Dorothy Hunter was here for tea: we seemed to see quite a bit of her and she seemed a nice girl.

June 4: we received a cheque from FMC for £2,831 for two fat heifers, two young bulls and four steers that went to Sheffield. Mother and Von were down in the village—it was the annual 'blind sale' in the village hall. It rained but they still took £150 for the Blind Institute in Hull. Von gave a cookery demonstration in Beeford that evening and I had to take Mother and Molly Course to the WI in the village. Steve Stephenson, of AIS, came and I paid him £4,525 for chemicals and for spraying winter wheat and winter barley.

Eddie and Pauline went to his brother's funeral at Cowick, near Goole: it was a full military funeral with many people there, including a lot of photographers recording all the mourners. Apparently those responsible for servicemen's deaths often attend.

We went to Tom and Irene Speck's at Clay Field Farm, Middleton, for a wine and cheese evening in aid of Middleton Church: they were retiring to Driffield. This was after I had been helping to cut the grass in Lund churchyard in the afternoon. We heard that both Sue Whorley and Betty Bentley were very ill.

June 8: the vet was here first thing to dehorn about 20 of the bought-in calves and I paid him £344 for the account to the end of May. Molly Course was still looking for a property here and Von took her, Mother and Andrew to look round Mr Marsh Cox's house at West End in Lund—the Coxes were moving into Beverley.

My brother-in-law, Ted Whorley, rang to say that Susan was very ill and then rang back an hour later to say that she had passed away. She was 21 years old the previous January. She had not had a blood count for two years and they didn't know how she has lasted so long. Latterly they had just been sedating her—poor, poor girl. It was wonderful that she had managed to go to Australia with the Hampshire Youth Orchestra the previous year—that was her last big event. We will always remember her practising the Red Flag on her bassoon in the empty deep litter hut.

June 10: Von took Molly Course to York Station to return home to Bournemouth, and there on the station platform were Margaret Eastwood, Jean Creaser, Pearl Burdass, Uncle Tom Cobley and all. They were going on a trip to Holy Island. Von then went to Mulberry Hall to order a tea service to be sent to France to Christophe Rapenau who was getting married in Epernay. We were invited to the wedding on June 20 and would have dearly liked to go to see how their wedding service was celebrated but, unfortunately, it clashed with Tim and Caroline Maltas's wedding at Howden Minster on the same day and we had accepted the Maltas's invitation months earlier.

The following day father-in-law and I went to York Market, and we bought seven calves for which I paid £491. In the evening I fetched Angus from school for half-term. We arrived home to find Dorothy and Richard up to tea. Must be getting serious.

June 13: Von, Andrew and I went to Bill Pinkney's at Tibthorpe to sign a new partnership agreement, admitting Andrew into the partnership.

June 19: Angus completed the Lyke Wake Walk—it rained nearly all the day. We met them at Ravenscar in thick fog—we couldn't even see the transmitting mast. They were surprisingly good—they had done the walk in the day, leaving at 5am and arriving at 8.30pm, which was better than when Andrew did it, walking all night and arriving in the morning. We sold Feedex the last bit of the feed barley for delivery in July at £107 a tonne, plus delivery.

June 20: Tim Maltas married Caroline Whales at Howden Minster. Mother, Von and I attended—it was the same day that Christophe Rapenau was getting married. The reception was at the Viking Hotel in Goole, and we sat with old friends Colin and Pat Arminson and George and Peggy Johnson, the YFC county organiser before Margaret Mitchell (Mitch).

The following day it was the Walkington Hayride, always a spectacle to see, with all the antique horse-drawn vehicles, meticulously organised by Ernie Teal from Walkington. He used to get a different celebrity each year to start off the parade in Walkington. It made its way to Beverley, via Bishop Burton and the Westwood, and paraded in the Market Place before heading back to Walkington.

June 22: Nick Snowden started working for us as a holiday job before returning to university. Hay-making was in full swing, so he was turning hay after Chris cut it in 20 acre and Hut Field top. Bernard Sissons was painting up and repairing at Vicarage Farm, for the buildings' five yearly paint up, repairs, etc. Andrew and Eddie were getting muck out there at the same time, and I took Helen to Bridlington for her driving lesson. A couple of days later all of us were turning, baling and leading hay before stacking it in the Dutch barn at Wold. It was much easier with the Howard baler, which produced low density big bales.

In the evening Mother, Von, Helen and I went over the Humber Bridge for the first time. Not much at the other side, but a beautiful bridge.

June 25: Von had organised a bus trip to Moffat for the WI. There were 48 on the bus and they had a good day, visiting the Forge at Gretna Green and then on to Moffat. They were home by 10.15pm.

I went into York Market the same day and bought three calves for £181. Gordon Davidson and his wife came over from Cheshire, and bought eight in-calf heifers for £4,000. This with the proviso that we got eight bull calves back in due course.

On the last day of June Peter Burnell's gang came to pull wild oats at Lickham. Helen joined them and was rather taken aback at the level of the conversation, and the stripping off of clothes as the day progressed. Jim Cox was here cutting thistles and Andrew was at Bishop Burton on a first-aid course. Chris and Nick finished leading bales from 20 acre and Hut Field top, stacking them in the lean-to at Vicarage Farm.

July 3: Von took Mrs Ellis to Driffield to see the specialist, she was very fond of Mrs Ellis, who came and worked in the house three or four mornings a week, and was, as Von says, her right hand man—with all the folk that pass through our house she needs one. I paid Peter Burnell £621 for his gang pulling wild oats at Lickham.

Royal Show time again and Chris Waite took seven animals, three heifers in calf, one dry cow, one cow in milk and one bull. Eddie and Angus went with Chris, and we took Helen, Grandad and his friend, Jack Gregory, in the Mercedes, towing the caravan. Helen, Von and I stayed with Mary Casling at Stratford-upon-Avon. The rest stayed in the caravan.

Keith Simpson's man was here, with a digger, digging holes for the new shed in the wood behind wagon shed and on stable side. Chris was taking spoil away. The following day Nick and Chris tidied up the holes ready for concreting the footings.

Von, Helen and I went to the show the next day, to see all was alright at the pre-judging. Von and I went to Avoncroft Cattle Breeders at Bromsgrove, to see Pinpur Intercontinental, the bull we had imported from Canada, and we collected the handouts for semen distribution sales.

July 7: we were on the showground by 8am and all was OK. Judging commenced at 9.30am. The Brazilian judge mainly judged on the walking ability of an animal, as in his country the animals had to walk long distances to a water hole. Oh dear! We got a fourth with our bull, Capps Duke,

Angus with the cup and Woldsman Primrose after a first at the Royal Show.

third, fifth and reserve with heifers-in-calf, and first, plus a huge cup, for the cow in milk with the best udder. Von, Helen, Angus and I went home—we had to take Angus back to Cundall as exams started the following day. Angus wept all the way home as he so wanted to stay at the show. Aunty Farnaby had been staying with Mother and Dorothy was there, so all was well at home.

Andrew started pea vining with Beverley Pea Growers on the highlift cart, emptying the viners and tipping into the road transports waiting at the edge of the field. Received a cheque for £600 for Notton Supreme Duke, which weighed 977kgs liveweight, from York Livestock Centre.

July 9: I took Helen and Nick Snowden to the Royal Showground to collect the caravan and Grandad and Jack Gregory after Eddie and Chris Waite had got them loaded up.

July 10: Helen got a gang of her friends to pull wild oats, so we had Ruth Eastwood, Fiona Allan and Christine Lunn pulling wild oats in Bramble Butts and then in Road Ends. Chris, Nick and I were concreting footings on stable side and in the wood behind the wagon shed and got all finished. Peter Burnell's gang finished pulling wild oats at Lickham and I paid him £464. Andrew started on night shift at 7.15pm for Beverley Pea Group

July 11: we were now into the silly season. Mother and Von went to

Lockington Garden Fete. Richard's sister, Rachel, collected Helen; they went to North Frodingham and then to see Simon Bates from Radio 1 at a YFC do. Von and I went to Lambs for a barbecue, then on to Snowdens. Sunday saw us going to Blooms at Scorborough for lunch then taking Angus back to school before going on to Creasers at Sutton Derwent for supper. Dorothy was here—she and Helen were supposed to be going to YFC but, as Andrew was home, she didn't get any further than here.

July 14: Mother, Von and I took two in-calf heifers over to Cheetham's at Hyde in Cheshire. He paid me £1,000 less £100 for two calves. We then went over to Davidsons at Saughull for one calf and paid him £47, then went to Chester market and bought 10 more bull calves for £702. When we got home, Helen and Richard had tea ready. After that Von and I went with the Helms to Bishop Burton to see the gardens. A full day.

July 15: I had to go to the Westwood Hospital to have a sliver of steel removed from my eye and then on to Hull Royal Infirmary for three X-rays and an inspection by a specialist, who said it was OK.

July 16: John Ringrose, manager of Midland Bank in Beverley, came to lunch and to discuss overdraft facilities for the new shed. Andrew was back on days and getting tired. They were vining at Marginsons and Brumfields but knocked off at 12noon because the Queen was opening the Humber Bridge the following day and lorries were prohibited from going along Hessle Road for security reasons.

Our friend, Keith Bridge from the village, who was chief executive of Humberside, was with the Queen when she opened the bridge. We watched it on TV with Aunty Farnaby, Julia Midgley, Grandad and Aunty Lil and Bill Coughlan and his sister, Joan, who were on a visit from Australia.

July 19: they were changing shifts over on peas. Andrew was at work 8am to 4pm and then midnight to 8am: he was very tired—and he was on nights the following week as well. Von was in bed all day with a migraine. Mother and I went down to church in the morning as it was the Rev Martyn Clarke's last service in Lund Church; Mother presented him with a cheque for £83, which was a collection from the village.

The following day Helen and I took a six-month-old bull to the MLC bull testing station at Stockton-on-Forest: he would be tested over the next 120 days and get an official average daily live weight gain and food conversion rate for that period. He was considerably smaller than the other bulls which were going on test at the same time and appeared to me to be much older. However, our bull had an increasing liveweight gain right up to the end of the testing period, whilst the other bulls tailed off the growth rate three quarters of the way through the test. In those days there were no official birth dates.

The same day Ted Wright and his father from Atwick came over and bought a six-month-old bull for £300, for when he would be weaned in September. On July 21 we started combining 50 acres of winter barley, with Chris and Nick on the combines and Eddie on the corncart and myself running the drier.

Von dropped Helen in York for her to do some shopping before going on to Cundall Manor to collect Angus for the end of term. They were late out—apparently two of the senior boys, who were leaving, had let off smoke bombs in the toilets and no-one was allowed out until the two culprits confessed: they each got three strokes of the slipper.

In the evening Mother, Von, Angus and I went to Leconfield to the indoor garden fete at the Acasters' house. Richard Morris came to see Helen and she took him to watch Andrew vining the peas—Andrew sent Von a bag full of peas, which we had to wash and blanch after 10pm when we got home.

Freeman's men were here taking levels for the new shed. I went into Hull to United Molasses for seven barrels of molasses containing 45 gallons each. Coming back down the ring road, I had to stop at the Holderness Road traffic lights. When I set off up a slight incline two of the barrels shot over the chocks holding them in and broke the doors of the van open and ended up on the road. It was rush hour of course. A very kind lorry driver helped me re-load them. Fortunately, there was no harm done and no law enforcement officers around. We got the first calf by the Pinpur bull, which we had imported from Canada 18 months previously.

July 26: after three or four days of rain Chris and Nick finished combining the winter barley. Angus was on the corncart and Eddie was doing my job in the drier, as Von and I had gone to Bournemouth to stay with Molly Course for a four-day holiday. Aunty Farnaby came and stayed with Mother.

July 29: Prince Charles married Lady Diana Spencer at St Paul's Cathedral and it was made a Bank Holiday for the occasion. The following day we left Molly's and went across to the Red Poll field day at Sir Walter and Lady Burrell's at Knepp Castle, Horsham, Sussex. It was a very well-attended day, with Sir Walter and Lady Burrell showing us the herd—it was one of the best milking herds in the country for the breed.

After the field day we went to see some heifers belonging to Mr and Mrs Grant, some more Red Poll breeders from Uckfield. They were selling the cattle as they were retiring.

Meanwhile, back home Chris, Eddie and Nick finished gathering bales of barley straw. After we got home Chris and Nick were burning loose bales of straw in situ, and then Chris sprayed two loads of liquid sulphate of ammonia on the heavier land in the middle valley in the 50 acre field where there had been laid corn—this was to break down the straw. Meanwhile Nick was spreading muck at the top end of the field. The following day Chris and he did the bottom end of the field.

August 1: Von and Joan Gurney were judging at Cherry Burton Show. The following day, Sunday, was a day of rest! Andrew was laid off—no peas ready. Von and I went to David and Margaret Stephenson's at Skelfry Park for a very nice afternoon lunch with several of their and our friends. It was a beautiful sunny day and we were able to sit in the garden.

When we got home we took Mother to Scarborough to see Aunty Ethel. We all then went up to Whitby for a ride round and a meal at the Angel Hotel in Whitby—with very slow service! We returned Aunty Ethel to her apartment at the Green Gables Hotel in Scarborough.

August 3: it was Monday and all go with everyone stripping tiles off the stable block roof and getting ready for the new shed roof going over the entrance to the stackyard. This will enclose two buildings at the same time. I paid Bob Rodgers £2,900 for the installation of central heating at Vicarage Farm, Barrett's annual bill, which came to £377.79 and Avoncroft cattle breeders £1,224 for the first instalment of layerage and semen collection, which they were doing and hopefully would be distributing for us worldwide.

The following day Freeman's brought a load of steel and had the first bay erected up to the end of the new drier by night. All of us were working flat out on the stable block roof in readiness for them joining up to the fold yard roof. Andrew's car windscreen shattered on the way home from peas, so I took it into Hull and got it replaced for £48.18. Steve Stephenson (AIS) came and I paid him £1,616 for pea and wheat chemicals to date.

Von took 50 ladies on a day trip to Lincoln with Boddy's coaches. Everyone paid £2.50 and even after paying for the coach and bridge fees she still managed to make a

Helen, Andrew, Yvonne, Stephen, Angus and Mother, who was 86 on August 14 1981.

profit of £10.50 for WI funds. Richard Morford started on work experience, the same as Nick Snowden. Nick's brother Ian started Uni at the same time, and Richard's brother David was there too.

Eddie had a lump of mortar fall on his head whilst stripping the roof. I think he saw stars. Mother gave him brandy, which promptly made him sick, so Von took him to Beverley Westwood for a check-up. Fortunately, there was no damage done.

The following Saturday Von was judging at Howden Show, where it poured with rain all day and she had to be pulled out of the car park through thick mud. Next day, Sunday, we had Pat and Betty Bentley, Bruce and Alice, and Grandad and Aunty Lil to lunch. It was the first time Betty had been dressed since she came out of hospital. Margaret and Alec Snowden came up to supper—Carolyn was in California.

August 10: Sanderson's were here to our forklift as the torque convertor was playing up. They brought a new teleporter to demonstrate whilst ours was put right so we could continue demolishing the stable block roof. I did a deal with Colin Gibson of Yorkshire Handlers to change our old forklift for a new teleporter for £16,000 with our old forklift thrown in.

Freemans got all the steelwork erected and brought all the roofing sheets. I sent them a cheque for £7,875—75 per cent of the total cost, on account. I sold Maurice Robson 100 tonnes of barley to go to intervention, at £98 per tonne, ex farm. I also sold Feedex 200 tonnes of wheat at £105 per tonne, to go mid-August. We had to have a good tidy up all around, as Von was doing a demonstration for the WI Produce Guild and between 60 and 70 ladies were attending.

The following day all involved were preparing the village hall for Lund's first village show. There was a total entry of 335.

RMC brought two loads of concrete for filling in the bases of the new shed stanchions for which I paid them £207. Also paid Phil Mallet, bricklayer, £92.50 for rebuilding the front and rear pillars for fold yard doors and tidying up the gable ends.

August 15: it was an early start, being up at 6am as it was village show day. Helen was making Victoria sandwich and sausage rolls and Von was in the village hall by 9am organising the troops. Margaret and Alec Snowden and Rosalind Walker were stewards.

Von hit the roof and came down in splinters with Jack Lazenby—poor Edward Prescott from Middleton turned up with a little bunch of roses to enter, to be confronted by Jack, who said 'Thou mum tak thissen yam, it's a village show and not for thou.' Von tore into Jack, explained to Edward it was a closed show and he went home. She was in trepidation at seeing Jack again, but he was perfectly alright and didn't say a word! She had put a lot of work into this first venture, got excellent judges in Mrs Reffold, Margaret Jenkins, Colvin Williams, John Acaster, and Mrs Gabbitas, who didn't turn up. Thank goodness Mrs Reffold was there to step in. Helen was a marvellous help too. We were so pleased for her; she won with her Victoria sandwich and got third for her sausage rolls. Competition was quite fierce. Mrs Sever and Mrs Farnaby both won, so were over the moon. We had lunch at Mrs Farnaby's. A wonderful village.

Meanwhile, back on the farm, pea viners were here, and they finished vining the 52 acres of petit pois across the road. They did 1.96 tonnes per acre, at an average TR (tenderometer reading) of 111. They then did Little Field and got it done by 4pm: they did 1.5 tonnes per acre.

Chris and Eddie amongst stock first thing in the morning whilst Nick and Richard finished dragging the barley stubble over, then, after dinner, Richard started dragging the pea land next door. In the afternoon Chris and Nick combined Air Station and Chalk Road fields. Angus and Eddie on corn-carts—I was trying to keep up with everybody in the drier. A busy day!

The following day was much the same, finished the field next to the Park at the back of Vicarage Farm. The pea viners did approximately half of Little Wold, but the peas were hardly fit enough to vine. Andrew on change-over. They finished vining it on the Monday.

August 17: Grandad came to stay to help corn cart, Chris and Nick took combines to Lickham and got three quarters of Moat Field combined. Eddie, Richard and Grandad were on corncarts on the road bringing the grain back to Wold; Angus was loading corncarts in the field and swapping at the gate. David Hastings came to stay; A1 fuels brought 1,200 gallons of tractor diesel for Wold and Lickham. Chris Waite started leading barley to intervention for Mortimer's. Halder's were fetching wheat for Feedex. Freeman's men were here, roofing the second side of new shed. Massey's man was here mending the baler, and I was sort of on drier duty and Tommy Owt, running back and forth to the house to take telephone calls—get back and the drier was bunged up! Morris Clarkson gave Von some cauliflowers so she was busy freezing them. Mother was at Aunty Marjorie's at Market Weighton.

August 20: Freemans finished doing all sheeting, finials, etc, for the new shed—it really looked good and made the entrance to the farm so much more secure. Paid Mr Tutty, of British Fuels, £2,277. Borrowed Lamb's Superflow drag so as to be able to get three people on with Superflows and get all the pea land dragged over. Mr Freeman came to check that the new building was up to their specification—always encouraging to see. Eddie, Richard and David Hastings were bringing corn up from Lickham. Angus was still on corncart in the field at Lickham. Andrew was with the pea viners, washing down the viners and machinery and returning things to the various farmers from whom they were loaned. Andrew then finished with the pea group for that season—I'm sure it was quite a learning experience!

August 22: Chris and Nick were still combining opposite Park Farm at Scorborough with Eddie, Richard and Grandad on corncarts. Angus was still in the field. Andrew started baling straw in Chalk Road field. David had gone home for a rest—exhausted. I was still in the drier, loading corn in and out, and keeping the drier running at full capacity.

August 24—Monday: Chris Waite got the last loads of barley for intervention, making a total of 131.32 tonnes from 48 acres across the road. Halder's got the last load of wheat for Feedex, completing the 200 tonne lot.

Chris and Nick finished combining at Lickham and brought the combines home. I burned off all the straw at Lickham, got a good burn on the Scorborough side, adequate on the railway side. Andrew had dragged all the hedge sides off before I burned them. I took five young fat bulls into FMC at Seamer first thing.

The following day Richard was sub-soiling all day at Lickham; Andrew baled the field next to Park, and got nearly all done at the back of Vicarage Farm. Chris was off ill, so I had to go on one combine with Nick on the other one and Eddie in the drier. We got most of Stackyard Field done.

September 1: we had had a good week combining and finished off all the bits and pieces—headlands, etc, finishing harvest for the year. It is always a relief to get the combines put back in the sheds. Now we were concentrating on getting all the remaining straw baled and all gathered up. The Howard baler's low density bales make it a lot easier to collect up all the straw as they are too big and heavy to move manually, so you don't get the fatigue that we got handling the thousands of small bales that we did previously. The Howard bales are approximately eight feet long by four feet wide by four feet deep, weighing approximately 250 to 300 kilograms each, whereas the small bales would weigh 25 to 30 kilograms each. The only disadvantage to these big bales is they are a little untidy and, being low density, if they are stacked outside they get very wet. Therefore they have to be stacked under cover and the older buildings are not very handy for stacking in with the bigger forklifts or fore-end loaders.

The new teleporter was a massive step forward; it is the only machine on the farm that is used every day of the year. I always remember when I was a child the men were always saying: 'I wish they would invent a mechanical muck fork.' Now one man with a forklift, with a grab on the fork, and one man with a big dump trailer can get a yard of manure out in a day, which would have taken six men two weeks with horses and carts—and left them with very sore hands. Or else they would say: 'It's hard work carrying corn.' Now, with this forklift we can get up to two tonnes of corn in one bucketful, or, in the old terms, 20 bags. Moreover, you can put that straight into a lorry from floor level, just by pulling a lever with your hand or two fingers. Hurrah! It is more manoeuverable with the option of two or four wheel steer or crab steer, and the option of two or four wheel drive. The telescopic boom is a massive step forward—being able to extend the boom forward by more than two metres. Additionally, when loading grain into lorries the boom can be extended upwards by more than two metres when the bucket is full. However, never lift a heavy load when the boom is extended on the floor!

The next day Andrew finished baling all the fields near home and the headlands down at Lund and Wood Flat. The rest of us—Chris, Richard, Grandad, Angus, Mark Leonard and I were all gathering up bales and stacking them at Vicarage Farm. Ruston Parva Lime Company spread two tonnes per acre of lime on the old grassland on Moat Field at Lickham. Rita Leonard collected Mark that night. I took Helen to Brid for another driving lesson. The Colston area representative came with the engineer; they gave Von a new dishwasher to replace the faulty one, plus a free year's guarantee.

The next day, with all the bales gathered up, Andrew was pressure washing both combines and the baler ready to put them away until next year. Nick dragged the headlands down at Road Ends at Lund and Bramble Butts and Wood Flat, prior to burning and then all of us burned the straw in those fields. Had a marvellous burn, burning off the stubble, weeds and seeds under the swaths of straw.

All through harvest, Von—with Mother's help—was doing lunches for us all and delivering them round the fields; one at mid-morning, one at midafternoon and another about 7pm, if we were working late. This usually consisted of tea, big scones with butter and jam, baking powder cakes, sandwiches, Cornish pasties… the selection was endless. There were phone calls to be answered—no mobile phones then so I had to be fetched to the phone—that was why it was easiest if I was in the drier. I got a bicycle in the end to get from the drier to the house, otherwise something would block up.

September 4—all change: Chris and Andrew ploughing all day, Nick and Richard Superflow dragging all the stubbles that we had burned the previous night. I finished drying all the corn and put it into appropriate bins. We received a cheque from Beverley Pea Growers for the final payment of the 1980 harvest and the first payment on this year's harvest—£14,556, a very welcome injection of cash after a very expensive couple of months.

Von, Helen and Angus went into Beverley and booked a holiday for a week in Torremolinos at Curtis Travel for seven of us—we five, Dorothy Hunter and Richard Morris. The following day, a Sunday, Barkers from

Dunswell brought six loads -about 30 tonnes—of barley to dry. I got about half of it dried by 2pm and then Von, Helen and I walked across the newly-opened Humber Bridge, with what seemed like thousands of other people. Grandad took the car over and met us at the other side. It was an exhilarating experience to walk over the Humber Bridge after it had been so long in the building.

September 7—a red letter day: Helen passed her driving test in the morning—thank goodness. After we got home and had lunch she went off to Frodingham at 2pm and didn't get home until 11.30pm—so she got a flea in her ear from her mother!

Chris was sowing 150kgs per acre of 9.24.24 fertilizer on the land they ploughed last week, which Andrew had already rolled in front of him. Alan Oldfield from New Holland came, and bought a cow-in-calf for £550. Mark Cheetham brought four calves. Andrew, Eddie and I dismantled all the milking parlour equipment, and loaded it into the van, ready to take to Barnsley the following day. David Cornwell took me to see John Parson's bulk fertilizer plant at Warter, and I ordered 10 tonnes of 0.20.20 fertilizer for putting on the pea land, and 50 tonnes of 6.25:26:26 for the second crop wheats. Ruston Parva Lime Company here again and spread two tonnes per acre of lime on nine acres at the bottom of Air Station field, also on nine acres in the middle of the field next to the paddock. I sold Maurice Robson 40 tonnes of Triumph barley at £112 per tonne to go in October.

The following day Von and I took a van load of milking parlour equipment to Barnsley for Jeff Ownsworth, then went to Gordon Davidson's at Chester for six bull calves, five of which were free of charge from our heifers, and one more for which I paid him £60. I sold Feedex 160 tonnes of Brigand wheat for £108 a tonne, ex-farm.

I started sowing fertilizer on the second crop wheats at 150kgs per acre of the bulk 6.25:26:26. Received another welcome cheque from Mortimer's for £12,800 for the barley which went to intervention. Chris Atkinson here dressing seed wheat—that is taking out weed and small seeds and putting a powder dressing on for the prevention of disease and wireworm, prior to using the grain as seed corn. He dressed 10 tonnes of Brigand and 15 tonnes of Virtue wheat, Eddie stacked same in 50kg bags onto pallets with him.

I think all the reps knew that the harvest money was coming in, as they were coming one by one, arriving as the last one left. We have a saying:

'We shoot every third rep—and the second one just left.' We had had eight reps in two days. I was trying to spread 150kgs per acre of 0:20:20 on the now-cultivated pea land. Grandad Carr over the moon: he had been to Driffield Chrysanthemum Show and won the cup for a vase of six gladioli, a first for a vase of three gladioli and a first for his asters. He was a perfectionist when showing his flowers, particularly his chrysanthemums.

September 12: Chris started sowing Brigand winter wheat on Middleton tops, and then sowed Little Field with Norman winter wheat. Nurse Ingleby came over—she lived with us during the war—to see Mother, who was now universally known as Gran by everyone except Nurse, who still called her Mrs P. She took her to see Ethel Hodgkinson at Goole, another SRN, SCM nurse (as were both Mother and Nurse), who used to come to stay regularly. She was a sister at the maternity home in Hull. Andrew started spraying pre-emergence Chandor on the sown barley and wheat.

September 13—Sunday: Halder's came for seven loads of wheat for Feedex—160 tonnes. Andrew went off to lunch with the Hunters to Fridaythorpe, as it was Dorothy's last day at home before going to Liverpool on a course for dressmaking and tailoring. Whilst Andrew was at the bar waiting for drinks, a child rushed up to him, grabbed him round the leg and called: 'Daddy, Daddy.' Dorothy was rather surprised! Andrew told her there were things she didn't know about him. There were 10 of us at home for lunch that day. No change there then; usual Lund Wold hospitality.

Nick and Richard had been dragging and cultivating solidly for the last 10 days. Then Nick was rolling down after Chris drilling, before Andrew could pre-emergence spray. Richard was rotovating with the spiked rotovator on the hard clods down at Lickham. Since John and Margaret left Lickham the house had been empty, so we decided to let it to students from Bishop Burton Agricultural College: we carpeted the house through and had to get beds, furniture, etc. Five students were occupying the house.

Phil Mallet from Driffield came and started building a new wall in the new shed between the stanchions behind the wagon shed wall. Additionally he was tidying up the gable ends of the old wagon shed and pigeon cote, etc, and rebuilding the pillars hanging the doors into the fold yard.

September 17: we had a nice evening with Stella and Peter Harvey at The Anvil, Shiptonthorpe: they were going to New Zealand the following day. We were their granddaughter Catherine's guardians should anything happen to Stella and Peter.

September 18: Richard Morford finished working here in the evening —he was going off to university at Newcastle. I paid various bills in Driffield; Eddie started a week's well-deserved holiday after a fairly hectic two months solid working seven days a week at least 10 hours a day and sometimes more. Von was judging cookery at Bridlington Spa for the Garden and Allotments Association. Von always gave reasons for her placings (Young Farmer training). She was told that it was the first time any judge had left written comments.

We received a cheque from MAFF for £245 for brucellosis incentive subsidy. Thirty years earlier we were encouraged by the Ministry to vaccinate against brucellosis, which we did for a few years but, unfortunately, after they have been vaccinated against any disease it will show up for the rest of their life as a positive reactor. We also received a cheque for the first half of the 200 tonne lot of wheat that Feedex got for £10,500. I bought a Windsor chair from Mr Wright's (joiner) daughter for 50p as well as other bits and pieces for Lickham.

September 21: we went to Mrs Sleight's funeral in Driffield—she was John and Margaret Sleight's mother. We had known her for many years.
John and Margaret both married a Margaret and John. Mrs Sleight always put her children's names first when speaking of the couples so we knew which one she was talking about.

The following day Garry Hyde started to cut hedges. Instead he cut through the telephone wires which caused a slight upset. Arnott's from Leven started draining in Moat Field at Lickham. They were putting three inch lateral drains in between the others they put in five years previously, making the whole field drained at 11-yard intervals. While they were

Completion of drainage at Lickham

219

here they were going to finish off draining the land in front of the house at Lickham the same: this would complete the whole farm being drained at 11-yard intervals over the previous 10 years. I ordered a new Lely power harrow from Yates at Malton, £3,981, less 25 per cent discount. The land at Lickham is much more difficult to work down than the land at Lund, which is nearly all Wold land; Lickham is heavy clay. The power harrow broke the clods much more easily than traditional methods and left a good level seedbed with the levelling bar.

September 26: Von and Mother fetched Angus and Mark Bedford from Cundall, and we had Elgey and Libby Byass and Tony and Val Morford to supper. The following day Mother, Von and I went to Scorborough Harvest Festival on the Sunday afternoon, after which Von and I took the two boys back to school as Angus was a server at the Cundall School service at Cundall Church, which was just across the road from school. Andrew was out for lunch and tea and then took Dorothy to catch the train in York to go back to Liverpool.

October 4: Grandad and I went to Chester, to Gordon Davidson's, and got seven bull calves: I paid him £250 for four calves—the three others were in lieu of calves from our heifers, which we sold him previously. We took the rest of the milking parlour and milking machine to Mr Ownsworth at Barnsley on the way over. Meanwhile Andrew, Chris and Eddie were working land, drilling, spraying etc. for winter cereals. The vet came to implant the nine steers we were taking to Smithfield with Phenophex (growth promoter), He also saw to a cow which was down with milk fever.

October 7—our 20th wedding anniversary: I took Von to the Star at Bridlington—we drank a whole bottle of Le Flora Blanc between us! Angus rang up and was in tears when we told him that Helen and Richard Morris had split up. In the afternoon Von was teaching cookery to people with learning disabilities at Beverley Further Education College, Gallows Lane.

Received a cheque from MAFF for £103.32 being the 10 per cent grant for the accountant's bill, now received via the FHD scheme. I finished drying Gordon Hunter's peas, the second time over, which had been seeded down. I took the eight-month-old bull calf that Wrights of Atwick came to see in the summer. They paid me £300.

October 9: I paid Mr Tutty, of British Fuels, £1,654 for diesel. It was harvest festival at Lund that night, so there was a three line whip! We seem to go to a lot of harvest festivals at this time.

Von and I went down to Flints at Cawkeld, where the Bainton YFC advisory had a meeting to discuss Youth In Agriculture; it was the club annual meeting the following night. We have always been very involved in Young Farmers and really enjoy it. Trying to keep the young in the countryside involved and interested is always a challenge. Both Von and I gained such a lot through the Young Farmer movement when we were members.

Joe Huxtable and John Wass, Red Poll breeders, came to inspect two young bulls we had reared from Cheetham's, which the Red Poll cattle society had contract-mated for potential superior breeding animals. These bulls passed OK but, unfortunately, no-one wanted them. We received a cheque for £3,940 for labour supplied for the pea harvest and paid some bills—Arnott's, of Leven, £5.550; John Binnington £537; Oaklands £3,702. All these bills were for the final drainage completed at Lickham. Paid Yates', of Malton, £3,390 for the power harrow.

Steve Stephenson came and I paid him £759 for spraying off the 60 acres of wheat in front of the house at Lickham with Roundup and ammonia before harvest, as it had ripened unevenly. He then took me to their depot at Hemingbrough to see a 350-gallon Dorman sprayer, with electronic controls for £2,250, less an allowance of £750 for our Shell maxi Panto sprayer ie £1,500 net. Peter Davidson, the Yorkshire and Northern Wool Growers' rep, came and I paid him £976 for the June to September account. Also paid J Wood and Sons, Driffield, £5,340 for the new corn drill and spare parts. Later that month Barrett's brought a new Fendt 615 to demonstrate and Andrew was power harrowing with it at Lickham for most of the day. Richard Jameson, Pauls and Whites' rep, came and I sold him 100 tonnes of wheat at £110 per tonne delivered into Beverley for November.

Von, Mother and I went down to Middleton-on-the-Wolds WI to show them our slides of our visit to Canada and the USA in the reading room.

October 17—Andrew's 19th birthday: He took Dorothy, Helen and Angus to Hull Fair. We were going to a charity do at Jan and Roger Bilson's at Parklands in Middleton. We set off but had forgotten the tickets so had to return home. Then we arrived to see everyone going in dressed in evening dress, so had to return home again and get changed. Good job we didn't live far away.

Chris finished drilling Virtue wheat at Lickham—the whole farm (165 acres except the 12 acres in the bog which was newly-sown grass) sown at 55kgs per acre, plus 5lbs per acre of Draza slug pellets and 150kgs per acre of 6.25:24:24 fertilizer in the seed bed (23.5 tonnes total).

October 18—Angus's 13th birthday: all three children were teenagers. Von and I bought them a clay pigeon trap for their birthdays and Mother topped it up with 200 clays. Within an hour Andrew had made a stand and seat for it, ready for practice. William and Charles Lamb came to join in the celebrations and we had Geoff and Lynn (to be) Ullyott to lunch. Von and I took Angus back to school. He was serving in church and, of course, Von had to weep all over JV (headmaster and good friend).

During the previous week or so Mike Lazenby had been ploughing for us. Lambs had finished their planting for the year so he was here helping us to get finished ploughing the fields behind Vicarage Farm.

The following week we reversed the rolls when Andrew went down to Lambs with the Sanderson and was filling manure from the muck hills into their spreaders. Chris sowed 8:24:30 fertilizer at 150kgs per acre and I harrowed it in after him and rotavated the hedge bottoms. Chris then started sowing Brigand wheat. Andrew and Helen went to Shouler's abattoir at Carnaby with Bainton YFC to have the grading system explained to them and then to judge cattle and sheep carcases.

October 19: the glut of grain at harvest which had to be moved immediately had now passed and merchants were looking for grain for immediate movement. I sold the Feedex rep 500 tonnes of wheat at £110 a tonne for November delivery, and they would pay for it on November 27. The following morning Viv Williams, MD of Feedex, rang to ask if they could start moving it immediately, but would like to reduce the price by £1 a tonne, to which I agreed. The next day Halder's fetched seven loads, approximately 150 tonnes, and the next day another four loads.

Bert and Margaret Cheetham were here for lunch and brought five bull calves: I paid him £450 for these and four calves which Mark brought a month ago. I also paid Freemans, of Newbald, £2,814.52 for the 25 per cent balance on the new shed. The Chandor rep came up re the chemical damage on the winter barley and took samples of the damaged barley with roots and also the chemical itself. The problem was that where the previous crop of wheat had been laid badly, the straw had been ploughed down and the chemical lodged in the straw, so every time the new roots reached the impregnated straw with the chemical it temporarily killed it off. Nothing ever came of this, but other people's claims were met. Fred Lancaster was here wiring lights up in the new shed. Having retired, he was working for his son Brian, who was trading under his own name. Originally Fred, an excellent workman and a true gentleman, was working for Horstine Farmery. Andrew finished spraying all the wheat at Lickham with Dicurane pre-emergence spray.

October 23: Von, Mother and I went to Avoncroft Cattle Breeders at Bromsgrove, Worcestershire, to collect the Pinpur bull, from which they had been collecting semen over the last six months. They collected 7,000 straws in total for home and overseas distribution, but for the overseas collection he had to be on the station for six months before the semen could be qualified for Australia, New Zealand, etc. On our way back we called to see Von's ex headmistress from the Bridlington Convent, Sister Mary Mildred, at the convent at Erdington where she lived. It caused quite a stir in the convent having a bull on the front doorstep. The following day Von took Mother to see Aunty Ethel at Scarborough. They then went on to Bridlington to see cousin Madge Whitfield and then Grandad and Aunty Lil, who was in bed with a bad chest (too much smoking). They then brought Aunty Ethel home to stay for the weekend. Helen took her back to Scarborough on the Monday as Von was taking her cookery class.

October 27: Fiona Rose (nee Jamieson, daughter of Graham Jamieson, the NFU county secretary), died in a car accident in Scotland. She was only married in June in the USA: her parents had asked us to take some English tea over when we were there the previous year, as she didn't like the American tea.

October 29: I met Bob Leonard and Mark Caley at Vicarage Farm in the morning: they wanted to value Vicarage Farm for Andrew Marr, as his sister, Caroline Brown, possibly wanted to sell it due to her divorce settlement.

Chris and I finished putting all the chipboard sheeting on the stable to pigeon cote box block, from the old eaves to the new purlins on the new shed to seal the new shed from the fold yard. We received a cheque for £3,900 from FMC for the last lot of steers and one for £4,962 from Mortimer's for the malting barley that had gone a month previously. I paid Oaklands another £962 for the clay drain pots for draining at Lickham.

November 1: the five of us plus Dorothy Hunter went to Torremolinos for a week's holiday as it was Angus's half-term week. This was when I went down in the family folklore for wearing shorts on a freezing cold day up in the mountains. Don't think I have worn them since. After we returned from our holiday, it was a matter of setting to on preparations for winter, sorting out all the cattle into various lots and getting them in from the fields to the fold yards. We took 79 bulls and steers into the fold yard at Vicarage Farm, and all the cows and younger calves into the yard at Wold. I took four fat steers and two heifers to FMC at Seamer and received a cheque for £765 from MAFF for suckler cow subsidy. I put it into the bank and saw Mr Ringrose, the manager, re the possible purchase of Vicarage Farm. I paid £627 to YEB for the three farms' electricity for the previous three months, also Humberside County Council £30 for the petrol licence for three years. This was after we had got a certificate from the electricity board saying that the pump was correctly wired. Later in the month Rotherham and Northern roller shutter door people came and fitted a roller door on the new shed at the top of the drive. This made the farmstead much more secure as everything was enclosed. Fred Lancaster was back wiring up the motor. It stopped automatically when it reached the top and could be stopped manually at any stage. I paid Mr Tutty £2,010 for September fuel, mainly for tractor and drier fuel. Wages and drawings were running at £600 a week.

Von and I went to the MLC testing station at York to see a young bull we had on test there—Woldsman Roseman. He was being tested on growth rate and food conversion rate, etc. He looked very small in comparison to the continentals, which were the same age and similar weight. It made life much easier that both Andrew and Helen could share our trips to Cundall at the weekends and run Mother about visiting.

Nick, Geoffrey and Lynn Ullyott, Grandad and Aunty Lil came for Sunday lunch, and Margaret and David Maltas came up for the evening.

We received a cheque for £23,232 from Feedex for the wheat they took in October; Helen put this into the bank in Beverley. I paid Steve Stephenson (AIS) £7,800 for the sprayer and chemicals and Sissons of Beswick £2,227 for painting and repairs.

November 24: all of us, in our spare time, were halter training the nine steers which we were taking to Smithfield. Andrew was making a sliding door for the end of the new shed going into the shelter belt up to the end of the new drier shed. He also took a load of wheat into Pauls' in Beverley and brought a load of 13 per cent beef nuts back. I paid Ruston Parva Lime Co £2,069 for lime and spreading, also Garry Hyde, of Sancton, £721 for the annual hedge trimming. He made an excellent job and everyone knew where he had been working. Chris started a week's holiday after a busy four months of working six or seven days a week. Malcolm Harrison, from ADAS, came to see the winter barley at Vicarage Farm, which was scorched with Chandor. He took samples of the affected roots. Andrew and Mike Lazenby were down at Lickham cleaning out the middle dyke with Lambs' digger. Andrew was driving the tractor whilst Mike was operating the digger. These dykes have to be cleaned out periodically as they get clogged up with weeds and silt and the outlets of the drains need to be kept open and above the water level in the beck, which forms the northern boundary of the farm.

Received a cheque from FMC for £2,196 for the four steers and two heifers. I took two more bulls, two heifers and one steer to Seamer; also paid various bills—£2,000 in total.

For our Sunday treat Von and I went over to Gordon Davidson at Chester for seven calves, for which I paid him £510. Some of these were Blonde d'Aquitaine and Charolais crosses, which were more expensive than the Red Polls. We called at Cheethams at Hyde on the way back, had our lunch with them and collected seven more Red Poll calves. These calves were for putting onto newly-calved cows with their own calf and two or three foster calves. Since we stopped milking the cows for milk production, the older cows had well-developed udders and were giving on average 900 to 1,000 gallons of milk per lactation. It would have been cruel to the cow to leave her with so much potential milk production, so we put two to three more calves to each cow. As the calves got big enough we would wean off the biggest foster calves one at a time until the cow was left to dry off with her own calf. This avoided having any udder problems. The only problem with this system was the number of animals on the farm as there were approximately 60 cows, each rearing, on average, three calves.

I took the books into the accountant, Chas A Wood and Co in Bridlington, and paid them £1,848 for the previous year's audit. Rix's rep, Duncan Lambert, came and I gave him an order for Derv at 28p per litre, gas oil (tractor diesel) at 17p per litre, burning oil at 19p per litre and petrol at 30.25p per litre. Received a cheque from Feedex for £13,000 and one from

MAFF, via John Binnington, for the 60 per cent drainage grant for the drainage work at Lickham.

December 1: Andrew took 26.5 tonnes of Hunter's peas, which we had dried, into Dawsons at Market Weighton. A couple of days later we were all very interested to see that Peter Blacker, our pea group treasurer, had bought Burn Butts Farm at Hutton Cranswick for £910,000 for 501 acres - £1,816 per acre. A record price at the time. This farm had been farmed by the late Sam Brumfield and was sold with vacant possession. This was a very good farm on good deep-bodied land at the foot of the Yorkshire Wolds.

December 4—today was the day: Chris Waite came and took the nine steers plus Eddie Jowsey and son Wayne, to Smithfield Show at Earls Court in London, to get settled in and ready for the show on Monday. Quite an undertaking to have nine animals to look after in such different surroundings. It was a massive building. The sleeping accommodation for stockmen was in a section just away from the cattle: it was a little bit like sleeping in a massive dormitory with very little privacy, if any, and not much room space. They were woken up at dawn by a cockerel from the poultry section. Some stockmen even slept with their animals – don't know whether it was to keep warm or to prevent their animals being nobbled by other stockmen.

The following day I dropped Von, Mother and Helen in York to go shopping. I went on to Cundall to collect Angus from school and then returned to York and we all had lunch together. The next day we had our retired vicar, Arthur Lawes and Auntie Farnaby to lunch.

On the Monday I took Alec Snowden and William and Charles Lamb to Smithfield in the car and Andrew took Grandad and Angus in the van. We left the van at Earls Court for Eddie and Wayne to come back in at the end of the show. We parked the car in Earls Court car park at 9am and proceeded in to help Eddie get the cattle ready, washing and grooming them, then to lead them in the show ring. We did very well in the show with the steers, getting first, second and third places in the over 21-month class; first, second and third in 16–21 month class and first, second and fourth in the baby or under 16-month class, achieving champion and reserve champion in the Red Poll classes. All the animals showed themselves very well and did us and the breed a lot of good. Everyone was involved and thoroughly enjoyed themselves, the only problem being this was the last time Red Polls were exhibited at Smithfield, as no-one else entered after that. Seven of us—Alec, Andrew, William, Charles, Grandad, Angus and me—left the show at 6pm and I drove. We had a hilarious drive home with so many back-seat drivers directing me through London. Angus was not at all pleased at having to come home: he had been granted a special day off to go to the show but had to be back at school first thing on Tuesday (as did Charles) when he really wanted to stay with Eddie and Wayne at the show. Von and Chris had to stay at home holding the fort.

Helen took Angus back to school early doors on Tuesday as we had to go to a Public Inquiry at Lairgate Hall in Beverley regarding the public footpath at Lickham Hall at Scorborough. The Ramblers Association wanted to keep open the public footpath and bridleway at Lickham, which the council had tried to get closed (with which we were fully in agreement). As the footpath and bridleway were not linked it seemed pointless to keep them open. Von, Mother, Grandad, Andrew, Helen and I all attended the Inquiry, supported by John Sleight, Frank Taylor and George Money, who all knew the footpaths. George had worked on the farm most of his life. Dr Geoffrey Eastwood, of the Ramblers Association, objected to this, and put up a very poor case, with no-one else there to support him. We all went to lunch at the Tiger Inn. At the end of the two-day Inquiry the inspector who was in charge decided to make no decision and leave it until the next definitive review. We all felt this was a total waste of our time and public money. The situation was the footpath went from the road at the corner of Scorborough Lane, to the bottom of the garden at the farm, and the bridleway went from the farm entrance to the front gate of the buildings, where the cattle grid is now. There was approximately 100 yards where the bridle path and the footpath did not connect. The footpath was originally meant for men walking to the farm from the village and the bridleway was for the Royal Mail.

I had sold all the steers at the show to Playles Meats, a London butcher, for £1 per kg liveweight—4.788kgs. All the details of the animals were displayed, including their weight, on the headboards above the cattle standings, so when the show was over Eddie only had to collect up our very heavy show box and his forks and brushes, etc. The show box was very heavy when it was packed up with all the show necessities. They left the show at 5.30pm and the travelling conditions up the M1 were terrible, as it had started to snow and was freezing. They eventually got home at 1.30am on the

Saturday after an experience Eddie never forgot.

December 13: we received a cheque for £1,796 from the FMC for the last five that went to Seamer and put this and the Playles cheque for £4,788 into the bank. Winter was now really setting in; it was freezing keen at night and snowing off and on all day. Peter and Stella Harvey came up for a meal that night, to tell us about their trip to New Zealand. I kept looking out of the window and said it was snowing hard; I said this a couple of times, but they seemed oblivious to my comments and went on chatting At about 11pm they decided that they should go home, got as far as the top of the drive and became stuck fast in a snowdrift. Stella could not believe that they could not get out but they ended up staying the night. The following morning Andrew was out at first light with the forklift clearing the road to the village.

December 16: Chris and I started taking up the post-and-rail fence round the pond at West End in Lund village, so that the elm trees round the pond could be felled because of Dutch elm disease. However, they were still good timber and were able to be sold for the benefit of the parish council. Von and I fetched Angus from school for the end of term; the roads were very bad with slush and snow. Andrew went to meet Molly Course, Mother's friend, from the train in York. She was coming as usual to stay for Christmas. It was the end of term for the students living at Lickham; they rang to say they had no water and the heating was off, so we had to get Bob Rodgers to see to the pump and the heating system.

December 19—Von's birthday: She had done a party for Helms, Hardys, Walkers Morfords and Snowdens. Tony Morford and Von share the same birthday, so we usually went out together or had a meal. There were about 20 of us altogether. After this we were into the usual round of carol services at Lund and Scorborough, the chapel service and the schools, etc.

Then the carol singers would arrive a couple of nights before Christmas-Will Woodall with his little handbag, into which people put their donations. He brought the same handbag round for donkey's years, all a part of the church singers. They all had supper before they left. Another night we had the chapel singers - again supper - followed by the members of Bainton Young Farmers Club, who were not perhaps as melodious as the previous two, but still much appreciated. It was a big part of Christmas and people staying for the first time were amazed that groups of people would get swathed up in overcoats and boots and trudge round the countryside in the depth of winter to stand outside houses to sing carols and freeze to death, all for a few pounds to donate to the church or a charity. This is all part of the rural way of life and what makes the village what it is.

January 5: Von had to take Molly into Hull to catch the train back to Bournemouth, as York was beneath 16 feet of floodwater. This was mainly because of all the snow that had melted and come down the rivers into York from the Dales, etc. The students were back at Lickham ready for the new term at Bishop Burton Agricultural College. Craig Norwood came up to apologise for leaving the house in such a mess before Christmas: these were really a decent set of students.

January 15: the diesel in Chris's tractor froze up as it was minus 10 degrees C, so we took advantage of the cold frosty weather to get the muck out of the loose boxes and the yards, taking it down to Wood Flat to spread on the stubble down there.

Now that the milking parlour was completely redundant and not used for anything, we filled in the central pit with Garton gravel and Andrew made a cattle crush with access gates from the old collecting yard. This building had seen changes from being loose boxes to tie-up milking stalls, then milking parlour, then handling area for weighing cattle and treating, tuberculin testing, brucellosis blood testing, freeze branding, etc. Eventually, in the year 2000, it became the farm office.

January 17: Angus rang from school, very proud to tell us he has been given the rank of senior leader in his last year at Cundall. The following day Andrew went off to Germany with Martin Barrett and Chris Byass and company to the Fendt tractor factory at Bielefeld.

Von went into Hull to Sir Henry Cooper High School, where Margaret Snowden was teaching, to give a microwave demonstration. She then went back to take her own classes at Gallows Lane in Beverley.

Our landlord at Vicarage Farm, Caroline Brown, came bringing her daughter Suzy, a very nice girl who wanted to go to Bishop Burton College in the autumn and was hoping for some work experience. We agreed to have her: she would start working for us on March 1.

Sissons were working at 39 and 41 South Street, Middleton, stripping off the tiles on the roof over the utility rooms and bathrooms and re-felting them. Chris and I took tiles from the old wagon shed roof to replace them.

January 21: after we had spread foldyard manure from the yards down at Wood Flat, Chris went to try and plough, but the ground was so hard with the frost he was unable to get into the land with his plough. We were all back to work under cover after that. We put the old urea tank in the cake house at the end of the parlour and collecting yard block, into the roof area above the handling area as a header tank to supply the water tanks and the yards with water. We also moved the large water storage tank from the cakehouse into the stable passage for a quick fill to the sprayer with a two inch outlet to the sprayer. This was a 1,000 gallon tank with loose metal covers. We received a cheque from MAFF, via John Binnington, for £3,291 for the 60 per cent drainage grant for Lickham.

January 23: Andrew and co got back from Germany at 3.30am after having a very educational and interesting visit. Then he was off to Manchester at 10am to meet Dorothy for her gran's birthday party. All that side of the family seemed to work in the prison service, even Aunty Mary. They had been round all the big prisons in the country at different times.

A couple of days later Chris finally got a start to plough in Wood Flat after the frost had given sufficiently. Andrew and I went up to High Mowthorpe to see the ammonia treatment of straw, as we were thinking of getting an oven to treat straw with ammonia. William Lamb and I went to Henley's Nurseries at Market Weighton to get a quote for 200 trees and shrubs, etc for planting round the newly-cleared West End pond area in Lund, and various other places round the village. This was all via the parish council, of which he and I are current chairman and vice-chairman. Von and Ernie Teal had arranged a quiz in the village hall against a team from Walkington, which was all great fun and in the spirit of competitive rivalry.

We received a cheque for £2,342 from MAFF—a 10 per cent investment grant on new machinery—which was for the Sanderson forklift, Massey Ferguson corn drill and the power harrow. This grant was to stimulate investment in the machinery industry.

Helen and Andrew were very good at collecting and returning Angus to school at exeats. It was a 100-mile round trip, but it was a good school and both the boys had been happy there. In the meantime I could get on drying wheat for Mortimer's and Halder's. Received a cheque from FMC for £9,700 for 20 steers, two heifers and one cow, as well as £161 for bonus on animals supplied last year.

February 3: Straw Feed Services delivered the oven for treating straw with ammonia, also the vessel to hold the ammonia, which they filled with two tonnes of anhydrous ammonia. Brian and Fred Lancaster ran a new electricity supply to this from the old drier via the Dutch barn roof to the stanchion at the end of the Dutch barn where the oven is situated. This oven has two nine foot high doors and will accommodate two of the eight by four by four foot bales. The straw feed services rep came the following week to show us how to operate the oven, which was for treating the straw by breaking down the cellulose in it to make it more nutritious. We gave the suckler cows two bales of barley straw daily. They were not very keen on it for a start but, as there was no choice, they had to get on with it. They were only getting a small amount of concentrate in addition to this during the winter months when they were suckling their calves. We used this method for feeding for several years, but as the cost of ammonia and electricity rose it proved too expensive.

Von was parked in the Market Place in Beverley with the Mercedes and left the front wheels in lock. A traffic warden had drawn the attention of a policeman to the fact that one of the front tyres was not up to legal requirements. She was reprimanded and told she was liable for a £50 fine. I went into Hull the next day to the National Tyre Service to get two new tyres on the front. Meanwhile I was drying corn at midnight for Halder's ready for them to collect the following day. Eddie went to collect the young Red Poll bull, Woldsman Roseman, from the MLC testing station at York. He was in the top six of the test for food conversion rate, but mid-way for growth rate. I ordered 1,100 litres of burning oil at 17.25p per litre, and 2,200 litres of tractor diesel at 16.25p per litre, from Hardaker's fuel in Hull.

February 15: Von and I were judging the Brains Trust eliminator at Bishop Burton for the YFC Northern Area.

Andrew and Helen were third in the same eliminator at Brandesburton. The following day Chris started spreading 100kgs per acre of Nitram, 34.5 per cent nitrogen which Allison's, of Pocklington, were delivering for ACT

(Agricultural Central Trading). He spread this on the two fields in front of Vicarage Farm and then started on the winter wheat at 75kgs per acre.

February 26: Andrew, Angus and I went to the Burn Butts farm sale at Hutton Cranswick for the executors of the late Mr Sam Brumfield, which was conducted by Brian Swan, of Hornsey's, the Market Weighton auctioneers. The following day the five of us went to Ivor Innes to have a photograph taken to celebrate Helen's 18th birthday. We had Geoffrey and Lynn Ullyott to show us their photographs of their trip to Australia. They had been to see his parents, Peter and Betty Ullyott, who lived at Kojonup, 100 miles east of Perth, Western Australia.

March 1: Michael Jackson from Newport came to see some of the tractors and we sold him the 1968 Massey Ferguson 135 (MFW 451F), the 1969 Ford 5000 (SBT 954H) and the 1966 Ford 5000 (HWF 251D) with the McConnell tail slave forklift on for £3,000 plus VAT. We were at the point of having far more tractors than people to drive them and the export market for second-hand tractors was quite good.

The next day was a sad day; Von, Mother and I went to Mrs Horace Marshall's funeral. For a long time during the war and after she used to help Mrs Wharram in the fish and chip shop. I always remember going into there for a penn'orth of chips. In those days fish and chips cost 6d (two and half pence) and people would come from all the surrounding villages on Wednesday and Saturday nights for their weekly treat. There was always a queue waiting to be served. Horace Marshall was shepherd for the Lambs at Clematis Farm for as long as I could remember. Added to all this, Joan Helm's mother, Mrs Mitchell, who lived in Bridlington, died the same day aged 57.

That evening Von and I went to St Peter's School at York to meet the new headmaster, Mr Hughes: Angus was going there in September.

March 3: Chris started spreading fertilizer, 22.11.11 on all the grasses at 150 kgs per acre. I had to go into Beverley in a hurry as I got a court summons to appear at Brough Magistrates court for non-payment of rates arrears. However, when I got there I found out that they actually owed us £57. I went to Henley's at Market Weighton and collected 200 shrubs and trees on behalf of the parish council for planting round West End pond, Queen's Mead and various other places in the village. The next day Chris and Bernard Calvert and I planted all of these: quite a lot of shrubs round the West

End pond on the bank, some trees on Queen's Mead and various other places round the village. Grandad and I collected nine more semi-mature trees from Wykeham estate, near Scarborough, to plant down the side of the paddock and as replacements in Watergarth.

Received a cheque for £3,300 from FMC for the last lot of fat bulls and steers and Von put it into the bank.

March 8: I did a deal with Reynard's of Tadcaster for a new Ford Fiesta for Helen's 18th birthday. We traded in the old BVY 295R Maxi in part exchange and I paid £3,200 net. The Fiesta was a 1.1 litre sunburst red, with a three year warranty. They allowed us £755 for the Maxi. The following day I collected Helen from the further education college in Beverley and we went off to Tadcaster in the Maxi, kidding her all the way that it was a second-hand banger and that it was all we could get. Her face was a picture when she saw it. It was nearly as red as the car.

Peter Brown came and I signed the grazing agreement for the two grasses we were taking at Watton for summer grazing; £1,150 payable on April 1, second half on July 1.

March 11: the vet arrived first thing to see a young bull, Woldsman International, and signed a veterinary certificate to say that he was healthy and correct. Eddie then took him off to York to the MLC testing station to be tested for food conversion ratio, growth rate, temperament, etc: he was to be on the station for approximately six months. Chris and I started to re-set the post-and-rail fence round West End pond, which we had to remove so that all the old elms could be felled. We had replanted the trees and shrubs on the bank. We also fenced round the corner of Mr Middleton's paddock at the crossroads at Lund.

March 13: Von was judging at the county public speaking competition at Market Weighton School—Billy Pinkney was county president and treated the judges royally. Von chauffeured him quite a bit: he was our solicitor and excellent company.

March 15: Suzy Brown, Peter and Caroline's daughter from Fountain Farm, Kilnwick, started working for us for a six-month period prior to her going to Bishop Burton. She had to have a day off every week for day release at the college. I had the morning in the office paying lots of small bills, 23 in all, totalling £3,311. Then all of us weighed the fattening bulls and steers at Vicarage Farm. We marked 14 that were ready to go.

The following day Betty Bentley died. She had had a long and debilitating illness. Betty had been president of the Lund WI for many years and was a very enthusiastic member, full of life and humour. Von had lost a good friend. Pat would struggle with Bruce and Alice being so young.

Von and I went to the Beverley Pea Growers' dinner at the Ferguson Fawsitt at Walkington. It was always a good evening when all the members and their families got together.

March 19: took a cheque for £1,001.50 from the parish council to Henley's at Market Weighton to pay for the trees, shrubs, stakes, guards and ties. Then I took the receipted bill into Humberside County Council at County Hall in Beverley to claim the grant. This was a project sponsored by the county council.

The next day I took all the family, plus Mother, to Market Rasen to the wedding of my cousin Sheila's daughter. Julie Veitch was marrying Andrew Dodson and the reception was at Market Rasen racecourse, which was all very nice.

Mothering Sunday—a three-line whip: all the family went and the traditional posies were given by each child to their mother. In the evening Von and I took Angus back to school and we attended an evangelical service in Cundall Manor. A bit happy-clappy.

March 22: Andrew and I put the fall-pipe drains from the new shed into the cistern at the end of the bull pen and connected the fall-pipes into these whilst Chris, Eddie and Suzy were stripping the tiles off the old wagon shed roof. In the afternoon Von, Mother, Andrew, Helen and I went to Betty Bentley's funeral. The church was absolutely packed and there were people who could not get into church, proving she was a very popular person. It's always sad when children are left without a mother.

The weather was beginning to take up and become a bit more spring-like. Chris started spreading 34.5 per cent nitrogen on the wheats at 125kgs per acre. Eddie, Suzy and I turned out 16 dry cows and in-calf heifers into Hut Field. Andrew ploughed the pit and the kale land which had been grazed. Then he went to roll wheat at Lickham. Land work was beginning to progress, Suzy was rolling winter wheats with a tractor and gang rollers. Chris started spreading 34.5 per cent nitrogen at 100kgs per acre on the wheats, second time round. Von took her end of term gentlemen's evening class for cookery at Gallows Lane; I don't think they did much work: it sounded to me as if they had a great party, much enjoyed by all.

March 27: Von and Helen took Mother to Scarborough to stay with Aunty Ethel for a week at the Prince of Wales Hotel for Aunty Ethel to see if she would like to move there permanently. They had one floor totally for residents: it was on the sea front and had many advantages.

The next day Von and I were invited to Roger and Joyce Parkin's home at Wansford to help their nephew Robin Ullyott celebrate his 21st birthday, as his father and mother were out in Australia. Joyce was Peter Ullyott's sister. The following day Suzy and I were taking cattle out to grasses to Watton and Lickham: it was a relief to be getting cattle turned out from the yards at Wold House and Vicarage Farm, as they were very full with stock and the manure was building up.

March 31: Jim Cox, who had been foreman for us for many years before he retired, died. When I was a young lad he taught me a lot, and was a very good friend to me. In the 1940s he used to take me to see Hull City play at Boothferry Park. Once, in 1949, we went on Boxing Day when Hull City was playing Brentford at home. We were on the railway side of the ground in a total crowd of just over 49,000—all standing. The ground had its own passenger rail service from Paragon Station in those days. Raich Carter was the player manager at that time. The team was very near the top of the then Second Division. Hull City had a record attendance just after Christmas, when the team played Manchester United in the sixth round of the FA Cup. Again it was a home game and it was an all ticket match. There was a crowd of 55,000, but we were not in it as we could not get tickets from our usual source. Unfortunately, Hull City lost, 1-0. Jim, who was also a keen cricketer, did jobs such as felling overgrown hedges for us long after he retired. He was even mowing thistles and nettles in the grass in Water Garth in 1981. He never drove a tractor in his life, just like his brother, Billy, who was our cowman. They lived in two cottages at West End, Lund.

April 1: All of us were digging footings out between the stanchions of the new shed in the shelter belt behind the wagon shed and putting up shuttering ready for Ready Mix Concrete to put into the foundations. I paid RMC £192 for eight cubic yards of concrete and the same again two days later to finish the footings. We received a £2,754 cheque from FMC for seven bulls.

April 2: Von and I went to Jim Cox's funeral: I had lost a good friend.

Andrew started spraying all the winter cereal crops with spring herbicide. Paid £2,327.50 for half year's rent at Dalton Estate office for 172 acres. Also paid Todd and Thorpe £2,200 for half year's rent for Vicarage Farm—145 acres.

April 10: Von, Mother and I went to the wedding of Eddie Jowsey's son, Darren, to Julie McKee at Middleton Church, and afterwards at the Bell Hotel in Driffield for the reception. It was a very pretty wedding, with several young bridesmaids. Sadly the marriage didn't last and they split up within six months. In the evening Von and I went to Debbie Brumfield's 21st birthday party. In the morning before the wedding I took Harold Cox a big forkful of manure down to the village with the forklift, and put it straight into Bumble Bee Park, and did the same thing for Bernard Clark into his garden at the corner of Queen's Mead.

The following day it was Easter Sunday, so again there was a three line whip and we all went to church. It was a very cold day and snowed a bit. There were 11 of us in total for lunch that day.

April 14: we had the dreaded end-of-year Barrett's bill—that is up to the end of September. Miss Moat, a school friend of Aunty Ethel, who was secretary to Charlie Barrett, only sent the bills out annually. I paid them with a cheque for £1,240.

Von took Mother to Alan and Dorothy Duggleby's at Pinder Hill farm at Beeford. It was Ethel Hobson's 101st birthday party. She was one of my great-grandfather's sisters. There was quite a family gathering with all the Charters and Kirkwoods, who are all relatives.

The following day Aunty Joan Brumfield, of Cherry Burton, came to tea—she was David, Tim and Gill's mother. John Jenkinson from Ulrome was here to see about building the new wall in the shelter belt between the stanchions of the new shed and making good various gable ends, doorways, etc. He would use new rustic bricks on the outside and second-hand bricks from the old wagon shed and collecting yard walls on the inside.

April 18: Gill Slack and Paul Walker came to tea and then they held a YFC committee meeting in the kitchen. Mother, Von and I went to Aike to see High Grange Farm, which Joe Huxtable had bought and where Anne and Peter Clayton were going to live. We then went round by Wilfholme and saw the Three Jolly Tars pub. Andrew had taken Dorothy to York to catch the train to Liverpool, where she was on a dressmaking course.

April 21: Von booked, at Curtis's travel agents, nine flights to go to Canada for the third world Red Poll congress on July 17, returning on August 2. We could not do the American part of the tour, as we were going to be into harvest. Von took her class for adult cookery—the class was mainly for retired or single men.

The next night it was Bainton YFC's annual dinner dance at Luigi's in Hornsea. We took Helen and Andrew took Dorothy. The next day Von paid Curtis's £1,500 for four flights for herself, Helen, Angus and I from Heathrow to Vancouver and then across to Calgary, where we would join the congress tour, returning to Heathrow from Toronto. Helen had been for several job interviews without much success; she really wanted to go into a bank.

Paul Byass arrived and told us that he and Kate had adopted a baby boy, George. Paul had been on dialysis for a number of years and they were unable to have a family. Paul had developed kidney failure when he was in New Zealand in the early 1960s.

The following day I was at Bishop Burton all day on a wheat yield efficiency group seminar. Andrew took Angus to the implement sale on the Driffield Showfield, and then Von and I took Angus, plus trunk and bicycle, back for his last term at Cundall Manor prep school. His headmaster, Jeremy Valentine and his wife, Sue, were also leaving at the end of term. He was going to New Earswick as vicar. He started at Cundall just before Andrew did and was to finish as Angus did. We liked them both very much. It was announced in Lund Church that they had appointed a new vicar for our benefice, the Rev David Hoskin, who was a curate at Bridlington Priory. He and his wife, Jan, and children, Stephanie and Christopher, would be moving into the rectory at Lockington.

April 28: we received a cheque from MAFF for £950, this being the 10 per cent investment grant on the straw oven and sprayer. I paid Brian Lancaster £1,350 for wiring all the lights in the new shed, stable block, roller door motors and straw oven. Sam Walton was here sowing five acres with cabbages in the field next to the Park for grazing for the cows in the coming winter. Alan and Sue Jones—Alan worked for Central TV—came and bought two Red Poll cows to milk for making Red Poll cheese and paid £900 for the pair. Von went to a village hall meeting at night. Helen biked to Bainton to bring back the Land Rover; it had had a new half shaft fitted.

May 2: I took Von and Mother to Scarborough to see Aunty Ethel and Von and I went to see Doug and Jean Creaser at their flat near the harbour. We had a shock in the morning as Dick Byass had died suddenly. They had Springfield House built in Lund before they retired from Manor Farm, North Dalton.

Freemans erecting the new shed, 1982.

May 4: Von and I went down to London to the Red Poll Society annual meeting; this was held at the Farmers Club in Whitehall Court. In those days you could park on the road right outside the Ministry of Defence. Von would feed the parking meter whilst I was at the meeting and then she would go and do a little shopping or see an exhibition. On our way home we called at St Albans to see Adrian Sherriff and stayed for tea with him and Penny. Angus was most disappointed as we had to return the cup for the cow with the best udder, which we had won at the Royal Show the previous year.

Graham Gardham sent 8,500 rustic bricks for the wall of the new shed, and John Jenkinson started to build the new wall between the stanchions the next day. Chris was fetching and carrying and mixing mortar for him. He also had to tidy up the gable ends of the old buildings, join in the cross walls into the new walls, as well as the doorways into the front paddock and the stackyard. The same evening we had 45 Bainton YFC members here for a mock auction and valuation. The next day all of us were cleaning all the good, old bricks from the collecting yard and the old wagon shed wall. Andrew and I knocked in the top of the old cistern in what was the old cake-house floor, which is now in the middle of the fold yard, and then we pushed all the old brick rubble and concrete into this now redundant cistern, which was 20 feet deep and 15 feet in diameter.

After all this was done and the walls and drains re-aligned, Andrew made feed barrier gates for the full length of the yard, 100 feet in total, from the front door into the paddock to the back door into the stackyard. He left a good wide feed passage and access to the three yards we had made by putting cross gates to the garage wall, now making all the three yards accessible to the feedway. This could also be split into two separate yards and was accessible to the old stable block, which is now a handling area. All the gate hanging posts were in sleeves set into the concrete and could be taken out and made into one big area or yard. After all these sleeves were set the whole yard was concreted over level.

As we were going on the Red Poll congress in July we wanted some mementos to give to our hosts, so it was decided to have some unique mugs to take with us (not a good idea as they were so heavy to carry). Von, Mother and I went to Piggery Potteries at Epworth to see about same and we ordered 100 mugs, at £1.05 each, with Great Britain Red Poll Cattle Society on them. Margaret and David Maltas came for tea.

May 10: it was Richard Byass's funeral: Von, Mother and I went. The church was absolutely packed. It was Mrs Bulmer senior's funeral at South Dalton the following day. My cousin, Diana Warry, from Devon, came to stay. Helen met her at York Station after she had her car serviced. Von spent the next couple of days taking Mother and Diana round all the local sights and the North Yorkshire Moors.

May 14: Bainton YFC came for poultry trussing practice, ready for the rally. I kept out of the way, as it was the parish council annual meeting. The following day Andrew and Dorothy were out for most of the day and Helen went to York with the new boyfriend Robin, Roger Jagger's son. Emma Holtby and Mark Richardson brought their Jack Russell bitch, Florence, to see our Jack Russell, Robin, and left it overnight. The following day Chris drilled the 50 acre across the road with Waverax peas and Andrew rolled it down after him. Eddie and Suzy started to halter train heifers and cows for the Royal Show. Angus rang in the evening: he had been to stay with Sandy Smith at Whitby for the weekend and on the way back to school saw two of their young school mates hitching a lift. They had run away from school. He and Sandy jumped out of the pickup, thrust them into the back and took them back to school. The police were furious with the two boys and told them that invariably if boys were missing for more than four hours, they usually turned up dead. That frightened both of them to death.

The journey into Hull had now been made much easier by the opening of the new western bypass, which went from Killingwoldgraves roundabout on the A1079 to the new roundabout on the old A1174, just beyond Dunswell on the Beverley to Hull road.

May 20: Von had organised a WI trip to visit the mills in Bradford. They went to five mills in all and stopped on the way back at Harry Ramsden's for a fish and chip tea. The bus cost £2 each.

Helen was very excited; she had received a letter from the National Westminster Bank offering her a job. She wrote back immediately accepting the offer; she would start work in early August immediately we returned from Canada. A couple of days later Von, Mother and I went to the wedding of Susan Tock and Marcus Hodgson at Amotherby Church. Tom Helm did the annual valuation for Dee and Atkinson for the end of year tax valuation. Suzy was off poorly—actually I think the dust had been getting to her. Von went to Bishop Burton for an advisory meeting. Andrew, Eddie and I started stripping all the tiles from the garage and saddle room roofs, and then put one of the front eave beams from the wagon shed roof over the middle garage and the saddle room, to make a third garage at the front. Afterwards Andrew and John Sissons (Bridlington) felted and re-lathed all three garages and then re tiled them.

May 29: we all went to the YFC Rally at Alvesby at South Humberside— quite a hike. Humberside didn't go down very well with the old East Yorkshire. Not the Young Farmers, the area. AIS were here, they sprayed all the wheats with Corbel and Bravo for mildew and rust. Alan Jones rang; he would like 10 more cows or in-calf heifers. Quite a nice order.

June 6: Von and I were invited to the Valentines at Cundall for dinner with the Manfields; a nice gesture as they had been good friends as well as headmaster and matron. It has been an excellent prep school for the boys: there were 40 boys at the school when Andrew started in 1973 and 160 when Angus left in 1982.

June 9: had a nice surprise: Viv Williams from Feedex came up and gave us £1 a tonne bonus on the 506 tonnes of wheat they had bought from us the previous November. I sold him the last 40 or so tonnes of wheat for £121 per tonne. Von had 17 Burton Agnes WI members for a cookery demonstration in the kitchen. It seemed to go OK.

We wanted to concrete the entire new shed floor where the wagon shed had been; we broke all the bricks that were left, levelled them about and then blinded them with concrete so that we could put a damp proof membrane over before finally concreting.

June 14: received a cheque from Alan Jones for £5,150 for the 10 cows and in-calf heifers and also one from MAFF, via John Binnington, for drainage grant for £1,160. Andrew baled 87 bales of hay with the Howard baler for Frank Taylor at Park Farm, Scorborough. He then took the forklift and two trailers there and led and stacked it all under cover for them. Beverley Pea Growers was hiring the Mercedes van for the duration of the pea harvest at £10 a day and John Dearing came to collect it. They were to use it for ferrying parts and men about on and off shift.

It was the WI group rally—Lund tied with Lockington, who were always arch rivals.

It was half-term leave for Angus: Jeremy Valentine had gone into the mobile phone business. He had got one for us and it was very useful, working from our landline with an aerial from the house roof, and had a range of about half a mile. It was very new technology and would save a lot of running about, especially in harvest.

I got two gallons of emulsion paint at Lindsey's in Hull, and Alec Snowden and I painted the church porch, inside the south wall, all the window cavities and part of the vestry. Von and I had supper at Margaret and Alec's. The following day we had a houseful—church first thing, all six of us plus Molly Course who was staying with us, Aunty Farnaby and Arthur Lawes (our ex-vicar) and Grandad and Aunty Lil to lunch. Talk about open house!

The next day I finished painting the vestry, whilst Von and Molly cleaned all the sanctuary, chancel and half the pews.

June 22: it was Ivan and Bronny Marshall's silver wedding anniversary. Ken Grantham from Barrett's started servicing the combines in the new shed on the newly concreted floor—it was cleaner than their workshops! Chris was helping him. It then started with three days of solid rain. It was so wet underfoot that we had to fetch the cows and calves in from the front paddock and Hut Field. One evening, when it eventually faired up, Molly and Von had been up the road with the dogs and when they got back into the kitchen Angus was there in floods of tears. When Von asked him what the matter was, he said: 'I've passed!' Jeremy Valentine had just telephoned to tell him that he had passed his entrance exam to St Peter's in York. I don't know if he was crying with relief that he had passed or whether it was the prospect of changing schools and having another three years of learning—school and he never agreed.

A couple of days later I collected a marquee from Shiptonthorpe garage. Andrew and I put it up in Miss Stephenson's paddock, ready for the Friday evening preview of the flower festival, which we were having in the village that weekend. It poured with rain. Edward and Margaret Duggleby (my cousin from Frodingham) came up to the farm afterwards. The flower festival was mainly in church with refreshments in the village hall. Elizabeth Stephenson opened her house to show the china and glassware she had been collecting since a child. Entry fee for the festival was £3 a head, coffee and tea and scones for Saturday and Sunday was 30p. Afternoon tea was 40p. We had a service in church on the Sunday evening, with 27 in the choir. The vicar took the service and the archdeacon was the preacher. A total of £1,600 was taken over the weekend but there was about £400 in expenses to take off this. In the midst of all this, Johanne and Grizelle from Germany came to Wold. They asked Von if they could share a double bed—Von: 'No, not under our roof.' They were on a YFC exchange and Helen was hosting them at our house. The YFC had a barbecue at Bracken for its golden jubilee and had fireworks and a bonfire, which would not burn as it was too wet.

Cawood's collected six heifers and a steer to go to FMC at Seamer. FMC also paid £3,131 for the last seven bulls that went. We got the cows back out again after two nights in.

Molly took Mother back home to Bournemouth with her for a couple of weeks' holiday, and to give Von a break. Eddie was washing bulls, cows and heifers ready for the Royal Show. It was at the same time that Barry Prudom, the murderer, was shot dead in a bunker on the Malton cricket ground, Helen was in Malton taking the Germans round at the same time. Sam Walton's bitch had six pups to our Robin and Von ordered a bitch pup.

July 1: Von and I went to Epworth to Piggery Potteries and we bought 50 second quality mugs for £32. It was Angus's last sports day at Cundall: he got first in the four by 400 relay, second in the javelin and fourth in the discus. Then he came home for a long weekend.

July 4: Eddie and Angus took three heifers and one cow with the Land Rover and trailer to the Royal Show. Sam Walton took two bulls and a cow with their mare and foal in their horsebox, followed by Ellen in the car. Von and I took Grandad and his friend, Jack Gregory, in the car with the caravan behind. We got them all bedded down in the cattle lines with the caravan in situ, which Eddie, Angus, Grandad and Jack were sharing for the duration of the show. Von and I stayed with Miss Mary Cas-

Capps Duke at the 1982 Royal Show.

ling at Stratford-upon-Avon for two nights. The next day all of us were at the show and Andrew and Dorothy came down for the day.

July 6—Show Day: We went to the showground to help them all get the cattle ready for the show. We had two bulls, Eddie taking one and me the other. I got first with the bull, Capps Duke. Eddie got third with Woldsman Apex. We got first and fourth with dry cows and fourth, fifth and sixth with the three heifers-in-calf. We got reserve championship with the cow, Woldsman Primrose: competition was very strong. After judging Von and I came home, bringing a reluctant Angus, who had been thoroughly enjoying himself but had to be back to school. While we were at the show, Andrew and Chris baled and cleared 20 acres of hay, got 130 bales and stacked it in the Dutch barn. On the Thursday, the last day of the show, Grandad and Jack Gregory left the showground after breakfast with the Land Rover and caravan. They got home about 3.30pm, whilst Eddie had to wait until the show was over before Chris Waite could get in to collect the seven animals. They got home at 11pm.

July 8: Our junior member of the partnership, Andrew, had been very enthusiastic to buy a new Fendt tractor so we had ordered a new Fendt 614 Favorit from Barrett's, £22,846 net for delivery the second week in August. Suzy was back to work, but went home early—she thought she had glandular fever. Von and I went to the Huxtables at Kilnwick Percy for supper.

July 10: Von and co had organised the second village show in the village hall. We had all been busy previously, getting tables out in preparation for the entries. We were down to the village hall by 8am. Andrew said he was going into Beverley, so I said to him: 'For goodness' sake get your hair cut whilst you are there.' His hair was very long and bushy in those days. Later that morning, when entries were closing, Alec and I were standing at the far end of the village hall and I said to Alec: 'Who is that youth that has just come in?' He replied: 'You ought to know, he's your son!' Andrew had had a short back and sides.

Richard Morford started working for us for the harvest period, during his vacation from university. Ian Praine visited: he was a friend of Brian Maltas and lived in Lockerbie. He went to work for Lord Hotham for the harvest period. The next day Andrew, Helen and Dorothy went to the Yorkshire Show and then on to Cundall and brought Angus home. That was the end of term, and end of prep school for Angus. In the meantime we were struggling to make hay in the Park bottom and in the 12 acre bog field at Lickham.

July 14: Von and I had a day off at the Red Poll cattle society field day at Mrs Walmsley's farm at Gedding, Bury St Edmunds in Suffolk. She was almost 100 years old and had one of the oldest herds in the country. The following day I did a deal with Martin Barrett for a six furrow Dowdeswell reversible plough, £3,918. I paid about 20 small bills all up to the end of June, as we were going on the third world congress and tour in Canada.

July 16: Von, Helen, Angus and I drove down to St Albans and picked Adrian Sherriff up to go to Heathrow. He would take the car home and meet us on our return. I had all the tickets for the flight to Toronto; we met the Huxtables and John Plumb at the Air Canada desk and gave them their tickets. The Cheethams, who were coming down from Cheshire, had not arrived when our final call for the flight came over the tannoy, so I could do no more than leave their tickets with the Air Canada desk, and hope Bert would read my mind. Fortunately he did: they fell onto the plane, flight staff closed the door behind them and we took off. They were both very flushed and flustered—there was a rail strike so they had to come by coach and were an hour late arriving. We landed in Vancouver in early evening and stayed two nights at the Grosvenor Hotel. We did a tour of Vancouver, a lovely city, and then flew to Calgary for the world-famous stampede.

Monday July 19: we all gathered together for the official tour to commence. There were 11 Americans, 24 Australians, 16 Canadians, seven New Zealanders, nine of us and two Brazilians. We were joined every few days by different Canadians as we passed through their areas.

We were up early and heading south from Calgary to Cream Creek, to visit the Helmrast's herd, nearly at the USA border. From there we visited Fort Mcleod. It was blazing hot. We went on to Writing-On-Stone Provincial Park, where it was supposedly ancient writing on the natural stone wall. I was dubious. That day we travelled 600 miles—that was to prove to be the norm for many of our days to come.

The following day, Tuesday, saw us back on the coach for a tour of the Banff National Park—a beautiful area. We also visited Lake Louise, which was an amazing blue, so high in the mountains. That evening we reached Red Deer, which was to be our base for four nights for the conference.

Little did we know that this was the one time that we were to have more than one night sleeping in the same bed.

On the Wednesday we went north to Edmonton; where we visited the McRories, of Java. He was president of the Alberta club. We were fed like fighting cocks, as we were wherever we visited. From there we went to the Blach's herd and saw some excellent stock and some huge machinery. The paintwork on all the machinery was far better than ours, but of course they are so far inland and away from the salt atmosphere of the sea it does not corrode the paintwork. The stock was kept outside the year round too, in minus 20 degrees in the winter. No wonder their ears were much shorter, as they lost a quarter of an inch of ear each year to frostbite.

Whilst coming back through Edmonton, the coach had to stop by the kerbside, as there was a tremendous hail storm. The hailstones were so big it was frightening: in the coach it was like being shot at by a machine gun.

The following day, Thursday, was an optional free day, or we could visit the state exposition and the weather modification centre, where they were trying to moderate or disperse the hailstones before they did too much damage. Here we saw samples of hailstones that had been collected from the heart of the hailstorm the previous evening; they were bigger than golf balls and nearly as big as tennis balls.

Friday saw the start of the conference. I was first up to give the report for the British Red Poll Cattle Society, which I illustrated with slides from round the shows and herds the previous year. We were treated in the evening to a state banquet, sponsored by the Government of Alberta. The Minister of Agriculture, Nigel Pengelly, and Mrs Austerman, Member of Parliament and state representative for the state of Alberta, were present.

The following day, Saturday, was taken up by reports from representatives from other countries—members always enjoy these reports as they can identify with most of the problems. The conference closed with the best speaker: he was Frank Jacobs, co-ordinator for the Stockmen's Memorial Foundation. He gave a very amusing talk on his life's experience amongst cattle breeders, and summarised all the speakers, chairmen, etc, with remarkable accuracy and conciseness, creating great entertainment with his excellent recall. No-one could have possibly followed him so the conference closed on a high note. Great credit must go to the Marshall and Howe families for organising this part of the conference so very well.

The following day the tour recommenced with a visit to the Marshall herd at Innisfail, to enjoy their warm hospitality—and, in turn, the mosquitoes enjoyed us. We then visited the Hillary's hog lot and the Gisler's dairy unit before ending the day at a Hereford stud at Kilmorlie Farms, Bowden.

Sunday started off with a pancake breakfast and a short church service, and then off up the long flat prairie roads to Three Hills and the Howe farmstead. Beautiful weather, good company, wonderful hospitality and excellent cattle: what more could we ask? Then across the flatlands to Howard and Laverna Francis's where we saw their stock and his quarter horse, which he demonstrated. We finished off with a wonderful barbecue, hosted by the local Lions club. Monday saw us visit the Gardiner Dam. By now we were all getting to know each other—with much laughter and banter. After this we went to Alice Pocock's old homestead, where there was a building, erected in 1918, to house 44 working horses. It was built totally from wood and still in excellent condition. Unfortunately, the following year the whole farmstead was destroyed in a huge fire. The day continued with a call at the Sod House at Elbow, which was built entirely of sods of earth. We ended the day with a banquet at Moose Jaw.

Being four of us, we were fortunate to be called first for our room for the night at the Crossroads Motel. We fell into bed but Angus would keep looking out of the window and saying: 'So-and-so still hasn't got their room.' We kept telling him to get to sleep and then Helen said: 'I've been bitten.' She too was told get to sleep, then it was my turn: I got bitten round the back of my neck—by bedbugs—and I still have the marks today.

The following day, Tuesday, we visited the Hunt's farm at Moose Jaw, where they were crossing Red Polls with Main Anjou and Herefords. Then we made the long trip across the very flat prairie to Regina, the capital of Saskatchewan. We visited the natural history museum—very interesting—and watched the Canadian Mounted Police carry out their sunset ceremony at their headquarters: they all looked very young. In the evening we all joined together to celebrate the silver wedding of Marilyn and Kevin Graham, from Australia, which fell on that day.

We were up at 7am for breakfast at the Brandon wheat pool, where we enjoyed pancakes, bacon, eggs, and maple syrup. We then saw their most modern computerised sale unit and had a walk above the cattle yards. The whole floor of the sale ring was a weighbridge, where even the attendant's weight was recorded. This visit was followed by a tour of the experimental station of Manitoba. The Minister of Agriculture, Bill Erusky, was guest speaker at the banquet that night. We then had a tour of the new sports complex, which housed three ice rinks, a rodeo stadium, and dozens of other superb amenities. The beds at the experimental station were as hard as rocks, but we were all too tired to care.

July 29: we went to the Threshermen's Reunion at Austin, where we saw cattle and old machinery, which we felt was not too well maintained, but, of course, it was never under cover. This was all very different and interesting to us. That was just another 1,000 miles covered since leaving Red Deer in Alberta. We saw more of Canada in two weeks than most Canadians ever will. We stayed at the University of Manitoba that night—well, not the Brazilians as they had a hotel in town. The rest of us managed with much laughter, as we were all in single rooms. We were roused at 3.45am by Ken Elliott, of New Zealand, and his confounded bagpipes. Until heads started to appear through doors we had not realised that there were others staying there also—people were not amused! We were off on the coach at 5am to the airport for our flight from Winnipeg to Toronto, where we had a champagne breakfast. My word, they did look after us well.

Isobel Vaughan-Morgan joined us there: she and John Wass were doing the second half of the tour in America. On arrival at Toronto we went up the CN tower and admired the panoramic views of the area, and then, with no time to change, we were off to the Rae's herd in Ontario.

Bed at 11.30pm—long days.

Saturday saw us at Mr and Mrs Morton's farm at Pontypool, Peterborough, where we saw, as well as his stock, trees being tapped for maple syrup. It takes 40 gallons of raw syrup to make one gallon of refined syrup. Then on to Neil and Jean Moncrief's herd at Cavan, where we saw some excellent stock. We visited the very sophisticated hydraulic lift lock system for boats at Peterborough, where water and boats were lifted 65 feet. Then on to the Holmes at Barrie where we saw their cattle before leaving for Mount Forest to inspect Mr and Mrs Fenner's stock. The Fenners wintered in Florida and their neighbour kept an eye on their cattle—a very different system to ours. Had another wonderful banquet at Moor Forest church hall, and then on to Kitchener.

Sunday was the last day of the tour for us: we all went to Niagara and saw the falls, which were absolutely amazing. There were tears when we parted company. What grand folk Red Poll breeders are worldwide, and what a wonderful opportunity a tour like that offered to get to know what happens in other parts of the world.

Everyone mixed so well together—from David Crenshaw, from Alabama with his southern drawl, to Robbie Watson's totally different NZ tones and the Ozzy twang, all interspersed with the Canadian speech, which is something on its own. What great hosts they made, particularly Pearl and Joe Marshall and Grace and Harold Howe. Who's for New Zealand in 1986?

August 3: we had an overnight flight from Toronto to Heathrow, where our good friend Adrian Sherriff met us with our car. Our cases and bags were even fuller than when we embarked, when we had the presentation

249

mugs for our hosts. We took Adrian back to St Albans before making our way home along the A1 during what was one of the hottest days of the summer. Angus and Helen were asleep in the back of the car and Von was asleep in the passenger seat. I had the utmost difficulty keeping awake as it was so hot. Fortunately the traffic was reasonably light and we were home safely by 3pm.

While we had been away, Andrew had been busy combining the winter barley in the fields in front of Vicarage Farm: they were cut, cleared and the corn dried when we got home.

August 5: pea viners started vining the Waverex peas, in the 50 acre across the road. They took the headlands off and then went next door to Frank Etherington's and did the same there. They returned to finish ours by midnight the following day. They yielded 4.5 tonnes per hectare. I paid the water bills for all the meters, £328; Beverley Borough Council first half year's rates for the three farms, £339; and RMC for concrete for the fold yard and the new shed, £1,343. Next day Chris and Richard borrowed two Superflow drags from William Lamb and started to drag the 50 acre pea land, along with Nick, who was using our drag. Afterwards Chris started to combine the wheat in the 52 acre across the road and went round four times by night.

August 7—Saturday: Von, Mother and I went to Gordon Davidson's at Chester, and bought eight bull calves from him for £700. These were Charolais and Blonde d'Aquitaine crosses. On the way back we called at Cheethams at Hyde, Cheshire, and paid him £60 for one bull calf. Whilst we were away Angus backed the old Land Rover into Eddie's car and smashed in the front wing, so he was not the flavour of the month.

Andrew and Chris started to combine about 5pm and had about 50 tonnes by night. The following day Chris and Nick finished the Virtue wheat in the 52 acre, and it yielded about 180 tonnes, or 3.5 tonnes per acre. They then did Short Lands in the village and it did about three tonnes per acre. I sold Feedex 200 tonnes of wheat for £110 per tonne, to go immediately; they, in turn, sold it to a merchant in North Yorkshire, who sold it on to Marshalls in Edinburgh.

The next day two lorries that had been delivering loads of coal to Drax power station, collected two big loads of wheat to take back to Scotland: this was to be the norm for the next couple of weeks. The drivers of the first four loads of wheat that were collected came back for subsequent loads. I had made a note of the weights that they had collected on their first loads and this proved most useful as when we got paid a month later for these first four loads, around 100 tonnes, we were paid two tonnes short on each of three loads, and one tonne short on the fourth. I contacted Feedex, who told me to contact the North Yorkshire merchant, who admitted the error, and said we had been paid for loads of barley instead of wheat. It was not until more than a year later that I found out that this merchant had ended up in jail after incidents of a similar nature. This was not the only instance of that kind.

That was when we decided to make use of our FHD scheme plan to install a 50 tonne weighbridge. This was designed and planned by Avery's and had an 18 inch fall from the top to the bottom of the weighbridge, which was 50 feet long with a 50 tonne capacity. The groundwork was done by Simpsons, of Cranswick, and the reinforcements by Forgale, of Leeds. All the groundworks and concrete were eligible for a 30 per cent grant. However, the actual load cells and terminal points only got 10 per cent grant, as they were considered machinery. We really thought at the time that this was rather more than the farm warranted but, in actual fact, it proved to be one of the best investments we ever made. When we were buying we had to buy in a retail market and pay what we were asked, but when we were selling in a wholesale market we had to accept buyers' weights and take what we were given. The weighbridge proved most useful during the harvest period, when we weighed every trailer load of corn that came in from the combine and could get an immediate and accurate assessment of the field's yield.

One Sunday evening, when Von and I had gone to bed the gate alarm went off; I jumped out of bed and looked down the road and thought I was hallucinating. Von asked: 'What is it?' I replied: 'There is a boat coming up the drive.' A friend, who was taking part in a yacht race the following day, had to have the weight of his yacht verified so the only place to get it weighed at short notice was with us. When I went down in my dressing gown and wellington boots he was very embarrassed. Many friends and neighbours used our weighbridge for checking their trailer loads of corn when delivering either to other farms or to mills. The weighbridge was checked annually by weights and measures, along with all other weighbridges in the area. It once got struck by lightning and we had to have new load cells fitted.

Whilst Chris and Nick were busy combining wheat, Aunty Ethel from Scarborough decided to move from Green Gables Hotel, on the west bank in Scarborough, to the Prince of Wales Hotel on the sea front. Von, Andrew and Richard Morford took the van, and had an hilarious day moving her furniture via the lifts in both premises. They were the entertainment for the morning for the residents of both establishments. The family saying—'has it got Shepherd's castors?'—dates back to that day because Aunty Ethel kept telling them the furniture would move easily as it was fitted with Shepherd's castors.

August 10: it appeared that dry wheat was at a premium as Feedex bought another 200 tonnes of wheat, some of which was bound for Scotland and some for their own mill.

August 14: Mother's 87th birthday. In the middle of a busy harvest day one of the dry cows in the grass behind the church at Watton Abbey had got into the dyke and, with just her head and shoulders above water, was marooned. Andrew, Eddie and I had to go down with the forklift and haul her out. We took her home in the trailer behind the Land Rover, washed her down, gave her a large antibiotic injection and kept her in the yard for a couple of days. Three weeks later she calved a heifer calf by our imported bull Pinpur Intercontinental, so the calf was registered as Woldsman Interdyke.

August 16: Joan Helm was over the moon as Lund had come first equal in the Britain in Bloom competition and we were now representing England in the UK competition.

August 19: Andrew got his new Fendt Favorit 614 tractor (ERH 840Y). Dorothy came to see it, but I think the tractor took priority that day. Martin Barrett came and explained all the tractor's different functions—more like a Rolls Royce than the previous tractors we had had. John Dearing returned the Merc van from the pea group—4,000 miles completed during the harvesting season.

The next day I sold Cranswick Mill 200 tonnes of wheat for £110 per tonne delivered. The following evening Von and I went to David and Angela Harrold's in the village for a meal and get-together. They live in the house which had been, 100 years previously, great-great-grandfather's third butcher's shop in Lund. Little did we know then that their son, Christian, who was only a wee child in those days, would become our agronomist some 30 years later. It is a small world. Von went to York and met Sister Mary Mildred from the train. She was coming to stay for her annual holiday.

August 22: Von took Sister to the Catholic Church in Beverley for the 10.30am mass. Then Von and I went to a luncheon party at John Ringrose's home. We returned home and took Mother and Sister to the Holtbys at North Ferriby to see Robin's latest litter of six puppies, which were all nicely marked. The following day Andrew and Chris both took loads of wheat into Cranswick Mill, in total approximately 25 tonnes. I sold Feedex 100 tonnes of barley to go into intervention for £107 per tonne ex-farm, also another 20 tonnes to Mortimer's for same. It was proving to be a very catchy harvest and our neighbours, the Bulmer brothers across the road, were combining until nearly 1am. The weather forecast was bad, and it was right. Various hauliers continued collecting various load of corn. Andrew loaded one for Hunters with the forklift, and then took a load of our wheat to Cranswick Mill himself. Martin Barrett came and I paid him £27,038, which included VAT, for the new tractor. At the same time we received a cheque from Beverley Pea Group for this year's harvest for £15,758, which helped a lot.

August 25: got a start combining wheat again at Lickham and got approximately 90 tonnes from 28 acres in Moat Field. Von and Mother had Freda Downes, Stella and Peter Harvey, Mrs Byass, Margaret White and Aunty Farnaby up for coffee. Aunty Farnaby stayed for tea and then Margaret Shipley, Jean Thompson and four children arrived in the midst of this, plus Mary Casling, head of home economics at Bishop Burton College. Talk about open house. The next day Halder's came for three loads of barley to go for intervention. Chris, Nick and Richard each took loads of wheat to Cranswick Mill. Then all were combining wheat at Lickham, with the wagon train bringing it all home to dry. Then, at 4pm, we were rained off. I paid AIS £5,738 for spraying and chemicals. Mark Cheetham brought three bull calves and stayed for lunch.

August 28: I sold Maurice Robson the produce of 12 acres of Triumph spring barley, approximately 20 odd tonnes at £120 per tonne. Barkers from Dunswell were bringing barley to dry and store. Frank Taylor baled about 700 small bales of wheat straw for us, for use in the straw boiler at Lickham, which we stacked in the fold yard at Lickham. That same evening Von, Mother, Sister and I went to the flower festival at Sledmere House— could we put any more into a day? This was after we had been rained off again from combining.

Garry Hyde started trimming and cutting the hedges at Lund for us: he really made an excellent job. We got a load of peas from Steve Wright at North Dalton to dry. We put them into the old dryer to dry in the ventilated bins. We finished combining at Lickham, after Angus had bogged the corncart. We had to transfer the corn into another trailer with buckets—all 10 tonnes of it! I then pulled it out with the Fendt, and then did the same for our neighbours, the Bulmers, as they had done the same thing across the beck. It was a very wet harvest. The whole farm at Lickham, approximately 150 acres yielded just over 500 tonnes of wheat.

August 29: got the combines back up to Wold and started in the two fields behind Vicarage Farm, it was much easier on Wold land and nearer to base, with no road work for the corncarts. Andrew and Richard burned the remainder of the straw at Lickham, after Frank Taylor had what they wanted for themselves. John and Alan Barker were bringing barley in to dry and store and Steve Wright sent the last loads of his peas, about 45 tonnes, which we stored in the old drier.

August 30: Chris and Nick finished combining all the wheat behind Vicarage Farm just before the heavens opened again. This was the end of harvest for the year, in what had been a difficult and catchy time. On a brighter note, Eddie and Angus had to fetch home a cow that had had a heifer calf from Bridge's paddock in Lund. The next week was taken up with cleaning up odds and ends after harvest, delivering corn and drying corn for various people.

We had to have the vet to do a caesarean operation on a heifer that had a very big heifer calf to the Pinpur bull. I went into the house to get buckets of warm, clean water, towels, etc. Sister was already dressed in her clean cream habit ready for Von to take her to catch the train back to the convent in Stone, Staffordshire. I said to her: 'We are just going to do a caesarean operation on a cow, would you like to come and watch?' With that Sister hitched up her habit and was off across the fold yard at a trot. She got to the door of the box when Angus Mitchell, the vet, looked up in amazement, and said: 'Good God, what's this, the last rites!' Sister was most interested and was right up to the front. Obviously Angus had a bit of blood on his hands, which he would occasionally shake off. Sister's nice clean habit was a very good absorbent for this! After the operation was successfully completed Sister had to change back into her working habit to return to the convent. She might have been arrested for a bloody crime otherwise! Both mother and calf very quickly recovered to full health and both went on to have many more calves. In fact we registered the calf as Woldsman Intercaesar's Mildred: she went on to win first prize as a heifer-in-calf at the Royal Show and produced another 11 calves after that. The whole operation took Angus just over one hour to complete, with our help passing scalpels, etc—and heavenly guidance!

September 1: Mrs Ellis and her sister, Mrs Hesletine, were at Lickham cleaning up and moving beds, etc. Von took Sister and Mary Casling, who had come to tea, to see the church being decorated for Angela Teal's wedding (Arthur Lawes was to take the ceremony) and then they all came back to tea. The next day Grandad, Angus and I went down to Lickham to pull plums. We filled two washing baskets, a large box and several smaller ones. The Victoria plum trees there are really good fruiters. When we got back it was to find that Mother's friends, Ethel Hodgkinson and Nurse Ingleby had come to tea, together with Miss Simpson, Helen's old housemistress. They all went home laden with plums.

September 3: Mother, Angus, Von and I went to New Earswick to Jeremy Valentine's licensing ceremony.

September 6: it was now the time to be getting ready to prepare for the following year's harvest—ploughing, cultivating, fertilizing and sowing winter wheat and barley before the winter weather set in. After Mrs Allison had retired, the Dalton Estate had decided to sell Gomery Hall Farm at Scorborough, some 300 odd acres. Andrew and I met Paul Butler and Chris Tate to have a walk round the farm and to decide on our strategy. We asked Paul if he would bid for us at the auction, at which Tom Helm of Dee and Atkinson was selling. We gave him a limit to go to but it made £1,000 more than our limit. The rest is history.

Brian and Margaret Prescott, my cousin and Helen's godparents, were here for the night. We had decided to put central heating into 41 South Street, Middleton, and Bob Rodgers of Driffield started doing the work: this was the cottage we let out as a holiday cottage. Phil Mallett, from Driffield, was knocking out the old fireplace where we were going to put the boiler and putting an oil tank into the outhouse. Von and I went to Gordon Davidson's at Chester and bought a cow with two calves on her and a heifer calf from him. He had bought six Hereford cross bull calves for us in Chester market the day previously. I paid him a total of £1,362. Then we picked up one calf at Bert Cheetham's and paid him £250 for this and three calves bought previously. People were still bringing corn in to dry.

Chris Atkinson brought his mobile seed dresser and dressed 20 tonnes of our own seed with Agrosan, some of it with Draza slug pellets mixed in. Andrew got the new Dowdeswell plough from Barrett's and had his tractor in for its first 100-hour service.

September 12: Angus started at St Peter's—a new start for him. We took him to school with his trunk and tuck box, etc, and looked round the boarding house, School House—the same one that Andrew was in. It certainly had had a makeover since Andrew was there. We hoped he would be happy there: Angus and school didn't really agree.

September 14: Phil Mallett and Bob Rodgers both finished installing the central heating and plastering out where the oil tank went at 41 South Street in Middleton. The vet came to cleanse a cow which had recently calved; he also saw the heifer that had the caesarean operation. He was pleased with the result. That was after I had removed the external stitches some three or four days previously.

September 18: Eddie started a week's holiday after working nearly seven days a week for the previous two months. Helen and I were putting desks together at 41 South Street and moving furniture in and about ready for the students coming in. Andrew, Helen, Von and I went to Ian Snowden's 21st birthday party at Luigi's in Hornsea: a very good evening. The next day, Paul Hodson and Richard Banks moved into 41 South Street.

September 20: after Chris had finished all the drilling at Wold he moved to Lickham to start on Railway Side after Andrew had ploughed it. Richard rolled it and Chris sowed fertilizer. Nick was power harrowing in front of Chris drilling Virtue wheat.

Yorkshire Water Authority workers were here weeding and dredging the beck. We have to pay land drainage rates annually to Beverley and North Holderness Internal Drainage Board, which is based at Crockey Hill, near York. They do a good job keeping the beck, which is our northern boundary at Lickham, silt and weed free.

We had a very pleasant afternoon in the village when I was presented with a rose bowl on behalf of the village as winner of the best kept village competition. Afterwards we all went up to the village hall for tea, provided by the ladies of the village. Eddie was not having very good weather for his holiday as it had been very wet and the rest of us were confined to doing inside jobs.

September 23: we resumed land work at Lickham—Andrew finished ploughing the headlands on Railway Side with Richard rolling down after him. This was after he had collected six tonnes of Virtue seed wheat from Mortimer's in Driffield. Chris and Andrew were then power-harrowing and sowing fertilizer before starting to sow winter wheat. We received a cheque for £13,034 from Feedex for the 100 or so tonnes of wheat and one for £8,000 from Mortimer's for barley. In the meantime I had been kept very busy drying corn for various people: having a number of individual bins helps to keep the different lots separate. It helped being able to sell quite early a lot of our own dried corn at a reasonably good price as the quality was better than a lot of the later corn, which had been spoilt by the wet weather.

At the end of the week we lost Nick Snowden and Richard Morford from the labour force as they were to return to university in Newcastle the following week. They had been a good help in what was the busiest time of the year. We invited them, along with about 20 other people, to a party which Von put on mainly for the young ones, plus Alec and Margaret Snowden and Peter and Rosalind Walker.

September 26: it was too wet for any land work, so Chris did the daily routine amongst stock, and there was a three line whip for all six of us to go to Scorborough church harvest festival. We took Angus back to school at St Peter's after his first exeat since starting there. He seemed to have settled reasonably well.

The next day Eddie was back to work, so we were back to our normal four man labour force. The straw central heating boiler at Lickham was not efficient enough for the students there: they would come back from college after 4pm, put a bale of straw in the boiler and expect to have hot water in five minutes. So instead, they put some old tyres into the boiler to get the water hot more quickly. Consequently the water boiled and melted the solder on the joints of the pipes. There was water everywhere and they had no hot water at all for a few days. We dispensed with the straw boiler and our plumber installed an oil-fired boiler. The straw boiler worked perfectly well when John and Margaret Sleight were at Lickham when John would stoke it regularly. Bob Rodgers, our plumber who was based in Driffield, was doing work at the Pegasus Club, where they were pulling out a diesel tank, two thirds full of oil. We took the low loader and forklift into Driffield and paid them £230 by cheque for the tank and oil. We took it down to Lickham as our oil tank for the new boiler.

At Watton Abbey, Peter Brown had a large cattle corral with a crush, gates, etc. As he no longer required the equipment we bought it from him and took it all to Vicarage Farm to use as a holding area in the stack yard, for a new open yard outside with access to the newly erected lean-to on the Dutch barn. That evening, Andrew and Von were picking damsons and Bramley apples from the forklift bucket.

September 28: Joe and Audrey Huxtable came for supper and to see the Canadian slides from the conference tour in July. We reminisced about the 32oz steak the chap on the next table to us half consumed at the Victoria Station, Vancouver, in July. He took the remainder home for his evening meal the next day. No wonder he was a large gentleman!

September 29: it was too wet for any outside work Von and Andrew continued picking damsons with the aid of the Sanderson bucket over the newly-planted beech hedge and then picking good apples from the Bramley trees. They really were good fruiters. Later Andrew and I went to Lickham and dug up five bags of potatoes, which were in the peat soil near the dyke in the bog field. Von and Mother went down to the WI produce show in Lockington.

The following day Andrew and Chris were ploughing and working the land opposite Frank Taylor's Park Farm at Scorborough, and got about 20 acres done. I paid various bills amounting to almost £4,000.

October 4: Von had been suffering for quite a while with her varicose veins. I had to go to London with the parish council, so Andrew took her into the Nuffield Hospital to have an operation on her leg. She was in hospital for four days. It was our 21st wedding anniversary the day before she came out, so I asked the florist to deliver 21 red roses, but they must have been in bunches of 10 as they only delivered 20.

William and Gill Lamb, Bernard and Heather Calvert, Alwyn Middleton, Joan Helm, Len Teal, Mike Lazenby and I all went to London for the Britain in Bloom presentation. Kenneth Baker MP, the then Minister for Information Technology, presented me with the plaque which is on the outside wall of the old forge, now used as a village shelter. Unfortunately, in our great hilarity on the train coming home, the plaque managed to get left on the luggage rack. We contacted the British Rail lost luggage department and a few days later we received the plaque.

October 9: I collected Von from the hospital in Westbourne Avenue; I was full of cold at the time. Von had Sister Raper to check her leg and replace the dressing. During the next few days we had a constant stream of people coming sick visiting, including churchwarden Alwyn Middleton and the vicar, David Hoskin. Von was told that she had to exercise her leg and walk up to two miles a day.

October 11: normal service was resumed after the previous week's excitement of visiting London, regaining the plaque and Von's operation. Phil Mallet was rendering the new walls in the new shed with Chris helping him. Garry Hyde was doing the annual trimming of hedges and Andrew, Eddie and I concreted the northern entrance to the fold yard at Vicarage Farm with nine cubic meters of concrete. This was after we had set two RSJs at the ends of the wall on which to hang the new door. The Northern Roller Shutter men were finishing fitting the second door at the northern end of the new shed going into the stackyard and Fred Lancaster and his man were wiring the motor for the door and the lights. This made this building completely secure and weatherproof. Bernard Sissons was working at Lickham, doing the five-yearly maintenance and paint up of the house and buildings.

October 12: we had students from Hull University doing a geographical survey at Wold. I have always thought that the big dale behind the farm would make an ideal landfill site if and when the council run out of sites to use. Andrew and Chris were working the last field to be sown at Lickham near the village. Andrew ploughed about 20 acres with Chris following sowing fertilizer after which Andrew power-harrowed in front of Chris drilling; they got about half of it sown with Virtue winter wheat. In the evening Von,

Andrew, Helen and I went to Bainton YFC annual general meeting and Helen came home with the cup for the intermediate member gaining the most number of points in all competitions and for attendance.

October 13: The vet arrived first thing to see some calves and gave Gemma the dog her annual vaccination. Garry Hyde finished cutting all hedges. I took Von into hospital in Hull to see the surgeon and have her stitches removed—keep walking! Mr Todd came to see the central heating installation at Vicarage Farm, and agreed to give us a 20-year tenant right on the cost. Andrew and Eddie were hanging the new fold yard door at Vicarage Farm, and piping up the water troughs ready for the cattle coming in for the winter. Chris fitted a door and jamb to the feeding passage of the bull pen in the new shed at Wold, and Andrew and Eddie piped up a water bowl for it from the new header tank.

William and Gill Lamb came for a meal that evening and brought twin sister, Jenny, with them.

The following day all of us were sorting cattle most of the day, getting them into appropriate batches for winter housing. Von had the doctor to see her, also Alwyn Middleton (again) and Mrs Reffold.

October 15: it was a nice, fine day so, after several wet days of doing inside jobs, Andrew and Chris finished ploughing and working Moat Field at Lickham and had it all drilled by night. This completed all the autumn cultivations and plantings of winter cereals for the year. Von was still having a constant stream of visitors with Lance Wardell and four members of the Bridge family during the course of the day.

The following day I met Angus in Market Weighton from the bus. It was Andrew's 20th birthday the day after and Angus's 14th on the Monday but Von was still on light duties so these were celebrated at home. Mother helped as best she could and was in her element being in charge.

October 18: Chris started two weeks' holiday after three months of virtually continuous work.

October 27: I sold Maurice Robson (Mortimer's) 500 tonnes of wheat at £114 per tonne, ex farm, to go immediately. The following day Chris Waite collected eight loads of wheat (approximately 180 tonnes) for Mortimer's. Eddie, Angus and I started bringing the heifers home from the grass at Watton Abbey. I paid Charlie Barrett £4,500 for the six furrow reversible Dowdeswell plough. We finished collecting all the heifers from the abbey the following day. David Cornwell (Pauls' rep) came and I paid him £11,277 for autumn fertilizer and Steve Stephenson (AIS rep) £4,000 for pre-emergence herbicide, both for the winter wheat and barley. Chris Waite collected five more loads of wheat and also two more loads on the Saturday morning.

November 1: Andrew was ploughing Air Station field. Eddie and I were sorting cattle out, getting all the weaned calves away from their mothers and the cows into the foldyard at Wold. This was the twice yearly sort out of cattle, at spring and autumn, when the cattle are sorted, and ear numbers are all checked and recorded. There are approximately 250 head of cattle on the farms at any one time and so they have to be closely monitored using the tag numbers of every animal in each yard. Chris Waite was continuing to move wheat.

November 3: Chris Waite got the last loads of wheat for Mortimer's—500 tonne lot.

November 5—my 46th birthday: Mother and I went to Cheethams, from whom I bought nine store bull calves and paid him £2,030 for these nine plus three calves that Bert had brought over the previous week. Bernard Sissons was decorating the sitting room.

November 6: Saturday—Alec Snowden and I set two posts at the pit on Beverley Road to hang a gate to lock it up, as we were getting so many fly tippers dumping on the top of the pit that rubbish was blowing about all over Lambs' and our fields, dependant on which way the wind was blowing. Also the rat population was increasing with the amount of organic waste being dumped.

November 8: Chris was back at work and helping Andrew move the workshop out of the big implement shed with the inspection pit into the old combine shed next door. Malcolm Harrison from the Agricultural Development and Advisory Service (ADAS) came to look at the winter wheat at Lickham, which was being affected by the autumn pre-emergence herbicide.

November 9: Joe Huxtable and I went to the Red Poll Council meeting in London, picking up Charlie Kidson at Wakefield on the way. It poured with rain the whole way home—not a very nice journey.

The next day, Von, Andrew and I went to Reynard's of Tadcaster to collect his new Ford Capri Cabaret (ENW 969Y) in cardinal red, which cost

£4,700 with no trade in. He really did fancy himself in it.

November 11: Grandad and I took two heifers and a young bull to a Red Poll show and sale at Sennybridge, South Wales, which Diana Thomas had organised. We sold the bull for £600 less commission, but sold the two heifers privately after the sale for £350 and £330 respectively. I was the judge at this show so did not enter our animals into it.

Sam Walton was bringing wheat up to dry—latterly it had been a very catchy, wet harvest. Both Andrew and Chris were ploughing but, as it had been a very wet week, they were unable to finish ploughing the headlands.

November 16: Phil Mallett was back to render the walls at the back of the new shed, with Chris helping him. Fred Lancaster was wiring new power sockets and three-phase plugs in the old combine shed, which Andrew was going to use as his workshop, as it is smaller and can be kept warmer in the winter. The vet came in the afternoon to pregnancy diagnose the in-calf heifers which had been at Watton Abbey in the summer. All were in calf. Eddie and I injected them with Ivormec as well as all the young heifers and bulls in Wold foldyard. The Ivormec injection kills all the gut and lung worms and all internal and external parasites as well as ringworm and lice. This not only prevents the animals from scratching and losing their hair in the winter but also all the unsightly scabby rings caused by ringworm.

The following day, Grandad and I took two in-calf heifers to Gordon Davidson's at Chester for which he paid me £1,000 plus two bull calves back. He had bought us eight bull calves the day before in Chester Market and I paid him £760 for these.

November 18: Grandad and I were on the road again: we took three in-calf heifers to Mr D R Hills at Whitley Grange, South Ottrington, Northallerton. He paid me £1,590 for these. They were a present for his wife for when she and a friend returned from a holiday in South Africa.

November 20: I was tidying up in the new shed and drying wheat for Sam Walton, and in the evening Von and I went for supper to Sam and Ellen's at Village Farm, Lockington.

On the Monday morning Andrew and I went into Graham Gratrix in Driffield for 40 sheets of Styrofoam insulation for the inside of the workshop roof so that it would make it a little bit warmer and also deaden the sound. Mother and Von went to Freda Downes for a committee meeting to discuss the closing down of the Lund WI. National, in its wisdom, had decided to split Yorkshire up. It was too strong and had too much influence, so they would 'break' Yorkshire. That was like a red rag to a bull and many WIs closed down. Mother and Mrs Captain Middleton had formed the Lund branch of the WI in 1932, when Mrs Middleton became the first president.

Mother then took over and was president for 32 years until Betty Bentley took up office. It was a sad time for them as they enjoyed the WI but, added to everything else, the costs which had to be paid to National were exorbitant. So they decided to form a new organisation called the Yorkshire Countrywomen's Association—and it replaced the WI in many villages in the county.

Andrew, Eddie and I were weighing all the young bulls and sorting out the newly-weaned calves at Vicarage Farm, and again injecting them all with Ivormec. I sold Pauls' 100 tonnes of wheat at £120 per tonne, which would be delivered to Beverley the following week.

Because of our winning the Britain in Bloom competition, the parish council had John Rowson take a picture of the centre of the village with the Wellington Inn, the forge and the church in the background and put it into a Christmas card. I collected these from John and delivered them to Joan Helm, who would sell them for a very modest profit for parish council funds. Needless to say, we still had some left for the following year.

November 24: Cawood's transport collected seven fat bulls to take to FMC at Seamer. Andrew started making the first door for the new workshop—steel frame to be clad in galvanized sheeting. We had a nice surprise that evening as Ron Downes, of Mortimer's, brought a cheque from them for £56,130 for the 519 tonnes lot of wheat—that was after they had deducted their account for seed barley and wheat of £3,036. Von went to the Bishop Burton College Countrywomen's for the first time: they had a meal and a speaker and she enjoyed it. Chris, Eddie and I made a yard in the new shed for 15 maiden heifers; we vaccinated them and put them in. I took two cull cows that were not in calf to Driffield Market.

November 26: went to Scots in Hull for sliding door double track gear to hang the new doors for the workshop, which was the old combine shed. Paul Byass, who was now rep for Cranswick Mill, arrived and I sold him 100 tonnes of wheat at £120 per tonne for us to deliver next week. Von had arranged a village quiz in the village hall and we had Paul Butler as quizmaster and chairman. Many villagers attended and quite an interesting evening was had by all.

November 27: I finished drying Sam Walton's wheat, which was closely followed by Frank Etherington bringing about 60 tonnes of his to be dried: I got it all done by night. Von and Helen went Christmas shopping in York and brought Angus home for the night. In the evening we both went to Morris and Sue Clarkson's at Kiplingcotes with friends. Andrew went to Manchester, met Dorothy and stayed with her grandparents for the weekend. The following day, Sunday, Chris Waite collected three loads of Frank Etherington's wheat. We sold Andrew's old green Ford Capri car to a Mr and Mrs McFarland, of Beverley, for £650.

November 29: We received a cheque for £1,042 from Driffield Market Auctions for the two fat cows that I had taken the previous week (this was a very good price as they had finished their breeding life) and another from Jack Duck for £927 for drying corn. I did a deal with Chris Thompson from Bainton Station (it was their horse that fell down the cesspit a few years earlier) for his three year old Mercedes 809 seven and a half tonne gross, flat lorry for £1,400, which he delivered in the evening. I paid several month end bills totalling £3,000. Mortimer's sent a load of wheat in to dry and Chris Waite collected it the next morning, December 1.

December 2: Von and Margaret Snowden did a cookery demonstration in our kitchen, for the 50th centenary of the WI. Rosalind Walker followed that with a flower demonstration. It was a very successful evening and the last meeting before the boundaries break-up.

December 4: our international Red Poll breeder friends were catching up with us. Mandy Richardson from Western Australia, daughter of a Red Poll breeder, was coming for the weekend. Helen met her off the train at York before collecting Angus from school. We had various folk in for Sunday lunch after Von and I had been to chapel, and then in the evening we took Angus back to St Peter's.

December 6: Andrew and Dorothy left at 5am for the Smithfield Show in London. Von, Helen, William Lamb and I left a bit later to follow them down the M1. Von and Helen went round the shops whilst William and I went to the show. Andrew then took Dorothy back to Liverpool, arriving home by 1am. We had stopped on the way down at Leicester Forest East for a pit stop, and who should be coming out as we went in but Robin Ullyott. He told us that he was going for an interview at Richardson's at Driffield the following day.

December 7: Chris and Andrew stripped down the Mercedes lorry, took the body off and cleaned all down. They removed the old home-made sleeper compartment: it had been accessed via an entrance through the hole where the back window was. We took off the tank—which was the sleeper compartment—and replaced it with the window before taking it to Mick Boddy's in Driffield to get the cab re-sprayed.

The Christmas season was now upon us: we were gearing up for the carol concert and Christmas singers but before all these events started, Von, Mother, Aunty Farnaby and I went to see the Beverley Operatic Society performance of Oliver! It was a very good show—Oliver was played by a nine-year-old boy chosen from the 100 children who applied. We usually went to that show via John Wilson our bank manager at the Midland Bank in Beverley. They had an excellent cast, which included Sylvia Ferguson, who had an excellent voice and was always the lead singer. She was the wife of Dr Ferguson, Chief Medical Officer of Health.

Andrew and I were in very hot water from Von, we had 'borrowed' her filleting knife from the kitchen to cut the Styrofoam insulation when we were fitting it into the roof. She was not amused so we had to replace it with a new one. We had to go shopping in Hull to replace it and get some Brownie points. I was enrolled into the Lund Mothers' Union as projectionist to show slides of Elizabeth Stephenson's recent visit to Russia: I seemed to attend quite a few Mothers' Union events. Chris was taking wheat into Cranswick Mill. He completed their 100 tonne lot and then started taking Pauls' lot into Beverley.

December 10—big day: We held a party to celebrate the winning of the Britain in Bloom competition. Mike Lazenby and I collected the trestles from the chapel and Gill Lamb collected the MU pots, the WI pots and the copper and took it all to the village hall. Von was in the hall directing operations and getting everything ready. All the trestle tables were put up and Gill's sheets put on the tables, which Rosalind decorated with garlands. They blew up balloons and we men fetched Billy Thompson's organ, to be played by his wife, Audrey, and two drums from Middleton as well as the wine. As there was no liquor licence allowed for the village hall at that time, the wine had to be given away. There were paper plates and napkins and trifle dishes, etc. Then we came home and Von finished off preparing all the food she was taking. We went back and picked up Mrs Sever and Joan Helm and they were into the fray! All went swimmingly, plenty of food and drink, a marvellous raffle with 14 bottles, braces of pheasants, a hare, chickens (all with feathers on), chocolates and lots of other goodies.

Dancing was to Billy Thompson's band, followed by games with George Walker as MC. One game was passing a ruler round; when the music stopped the person with the ruler had to have—and put on—a garment from a bag that George had. Miss Stephenson ended up in directoire knickers and Beryl Fenton in a black corselet. All great fun, which ended about midnight, with everyone leaving tired but happy. An excellent village in which to live.

The following morning it was a matter of clearing up after the Lord Mayor's show, Von and I were there most of the morning.

The same day, Robin Jagger and Helen were driving to York and had a car crash at the bend at the top of the hill coming out of Goodmanham. Someone coming from the other direction took the corner too fast. Robin's tyre marks were well off the road. All the side of Robin's Fiesta was stoved in and it was a real mess. He was not a happy bunny.

December 12: Sunday—Von and I went to David and Barbara Brumfield's for their Christmas party, joining all the great and the good. A very good do. Andrew took Mother to Aunty Marjorie Andrew's for tea and then he and Dorothy took Angus back to school.

The following day Mary Casling came to stay for a few days. She had taught Von for several years when she was head of domestic science at Bishop Burton and became a friend. She had retired to Stratford-upon-Avon but was taking her doctorate at Hull University and, periodically, had to see her professor.

Chris finished taking Pauls' lot of wheat into Beverley clearing all our wheat from the 1982 harvest. We had sold a total of 1,369.50 tonnes of wheat from 407 acres, which equated to 3.36 tonnes per acre. This was quite an improvement on 20 years earlier, when the approximate average yield was less than 1.5 tonnes per acre.

December 16: I took Andrew into Mick Boddy's in Driffield to collect the Mercedes lorry after its respray. I got new u-bolts from Jennison's for anchoring the body to the chassis, also some floor boards from Naylor's to repair the body. Von and Mother went to Scarborough to deliver cards and presents to Aunty Ethel, and then on to Bridlington to see Mr Thompson, Margaret Shipley's father. He had just had a plastic tube fitted in his chest, but looked well. Then they went on to see Grandad and Aunty Lil and Uncle Sun and Aunty Nelly, who was suffering terribly with Parkinson's.

Mrs Purdy, from MAFF, came to do a head count of cattle for the non-marketing of milk (golden handshake final payment). Von, Mother and I met Molly Course from the train in York before going on to St Peter's to collect Angus, plus trunk and tuck box as it was end of term. Then all five of us attended the York Minster end-of-term carol service before retiring to nearby Le Girondin for supper.

December 19: Von's birthday. She and I went to John and Marjorie Spencer's in Driffield for drinks at lunch time, and then to the carol service at Lund Church where Helen was reading a lesson. As it was Von's birthday we invited Tony and Val Morford and Richard for supper: Tony and Von share the same birthday. I had bought Von a hostess trolley for her birthday/Christmas present: it came in handy as Dorothy and Robin and all the family were there too.

The following day Andrew and Chris took the Mercedes lorry into Humberside Motors at North Cave to be serviced and ready for the MoT. Then Andrew and I finished putting up all the Styrofoam insulation and Chris took the spare fibreglass insulation—about eight rolls in all—to put in the attic at Vicarage Farm. Paid various month end bills.

The following night we had the YFC carol singers singing for their supper. There were about 25 of them in all—one or two leading, the others following. Paid yet more month end bills: trying to start the New Year with a clean sheet.

December 23: the last wages day for this year. Had the church carol singers in that evening—15 of them in all. They all seemed to enjoy themselves going round the village and then the outer farms—ours last—so they could come in, get warm, have their supper and relax. It was a standard joke that Willie Woodall collected the money in one of his wife's handbags: he'd been using the same one since Adam was a lad!

Everyone making all the stock comfortable before Christmas, getting them well bedded up with straw so that there was the bare minimum of work to do over the long weekend (it was a four-day Christmas break as Christmas Day fell on a Saturday that year). Grandad and Aunty Lil came to stay for the festive season—Christmas could now start!

The following night we had the chapel singers—George Walker and his sister Elizabeth led the singers very well. The Lund Chapel members—excellent singers with plenty of volume—always went carol singing round several villages, again leaving us until the last: they also stopped for supper.

Christmas Eve: midnight service and communion, starting at 11.30pm and then it was back home where Santa Claus had to get pillow cases filled—even at their ages!

Christmas Day: all out first thing to get stock fed first off. There were 12 of us for Christmas lunch, after which we had the traditional opening of presents before watching the Queen. Then it was a walk with the dogs before Christmas tea.

December 29: Wednesday and everyone back to work, bedding up the yards, getting food in, etc. for the following New Year's Eve long weekend. In the evening we went for drinks to John and Margaret Wilson's, our friendly bank manager and his wife, in York road.

December 30: to the Bridges in Lund for celebrations in the evening. They were new to the village but were quickly adapting to village life.

New Year's Eve: to Lambs for New Year's Eve celebrations. Another busy year was drawing to a close, leaving us looking forward to the next chapter in our lives...

Footnote:

Having just celebrated my 80th birthday, Yvonne and I appreciate that we are not going to live long enough to complete this family history in the diary format so we are taking Helen's advice and finishing Volume One in 1982.

Volume Two will consist of most of the Christmas letters, which went out annually from this time on. It was Helen's idea that we should do all this, and now we think she is getting cold feet...

Weights, measures, money and wages

Some of the weights and measures in this book are the ones used by contemporaries of the times in question. They are summarised in the table below.

Money:

4 farthings	=	1d (penny)			
12d (pence)	=	1s (shilling)	1s	=	5p
20s (shillings)	=	£1 (pound)			
21s (shillings)	=	1 guinea			

Weight:

16oz (ounces)	=	1lb (pound)	1lb	=	0.45 kilograms
14lb (pounds)	=	1 stone	1 stone	=	6.35 kilograms
2 stones	=	1qr (quarter)	1qr	=	12.70 kilograms
4qr (quarters)	=	1cwt (hundredweight)	1cwt	=	50.80 kilograms
20cwt	=	1 ton	1 ton	=	1.02 tonnes

Weight of grain:

1qr of wheat	=	36 stones	=	4.44 to the ton
1qr of barley	=	32 stones	=	5.00 to the ton
1qr oats	=	24 stones	=	6.66 to the ton

Volume:

2 pints	=	1 quart	1 quart	=	1.14 litres
4 quarts	=	1 gallon	1 gallon	=	4.55 litres
2 gallons	=	1 peck	1 peck	=	9.09 litres
4 pecks	=	1 bushel	1 bushel	=	36.40 litres
8 bushels	=	1qr (quarter)	1 quarter	=	2.91 hectolitres

Distance:

12in (inches)	=	1ft (foot)	1ft	=	0.305 metres
3ft (feet)	=	1yd (yard)	1yd	=	0.91 metres
22yds (yards)	=	1 chain	1 chain	=	20.12 metres
10 chains	=	1 furlong	1 furlong	=	201.17 metres
8 furlongs	=	1 mile	1 mile	=	1.61 kilometres

Area:

30¼sq yds	=	1 perch		1 perch	=	25.29sq metres
40 perches	=	1 rood	=	1210sq yds	=	1011.56sq metres
4 roods	=	1 acre	=	4840sq yds	=	0.405 hectares
2.471 acres	=	1 hectare				

Average wages, hours and prescribed wages of male farm workers aged 20 and over, 1976-2000 are in the table below.
Data supplied by NFU, Beverley branch.

Wages at year ending December:	Full-time male workers aged 20 and over			General farm workers: full-time males aged 20 and over		
	Average weekly wage (£)	Average Hours	Prescribed wages (£)	Average weekly wage (£)	Average Hours	Prescribed wages (£)
1976	50.50	46.0	44.90	47.36	45.3	43.13
1977	54.84	46.6	48.40	51.16	45.4	45.99
1978	61.80	46.3	54.28	57.62	45.2	51.69
1979	72.04	46.8	63.44	66.57	45.6	59.83
1980	86.48	46.2	76.09	80.58	45.5	72.09
1981	97.07	46.8	85.59	89.82	45.9	80.71
1982	106.65	46.6	94.67	98.49	45.5	88.09